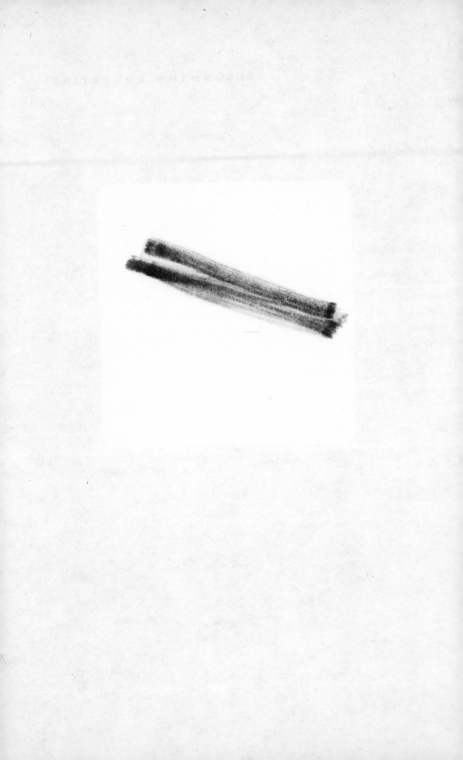

SECONDARY EDUCATION:
Origins and Directions

Robert O. Hahn

CALIFORNIA STATE COLLEGE AT LOS ANGELES

David B. Bidna

SAN FERNANDO VALLEY STATE COLLEGE

The Macmillan Company, NEW YORK

Collier-Macmillan Limited, LONDON

Third Printing, 1966

Library of Congress catalog card number: 65-10326

THE MACMILLAN COMPANY, NEW YORK
COLLIER-MACMILLAN CANADA, LTD., TORONTO, ONTARIO

Printed in the United States of America

Designed by N. Sylvester

PREFACE

Secondary education has come of age. Where the elementary
school stood thirty years ago there stands today the American junior and senior high school, with the junior college
moving into focus. Population pressures are projecting the
high schools of the nation into public view.

Throughout the past thirty years, from the day the Eight-
Year Study began, the secondary schools have been developing much of their own discipline, a history, a philosophy, a
methodology, and a curriculum.

It is the purpose of this volume to present to the student
preparing to teach in that junior high school or this senior
high school a compilation of origins and direction. From
what sources has the modern American secondary school
developed, what crises has it faced, and where is it going?
It is not to answer any of these questions that these readings
were collected, for in the truly democratic sense, all any
volume can do is raise the questions with the hope that each

new recruit to the teaching profession will assist in the development of a more effective educative process for adolescent youth.

We have chosen both liberal and conservative writings in order that the reader may place the present educative system in its proper perspective with the forces that would at once besiege and assist it.

The challenge of our historical legacy and future fulfillment is hereby presented to those men and women preparing to take their place in the ranks of the teaching profession.

We would like to gratefully acknowledge the services of Miss Saundra H. Hurwitz for her persevering efforts in the preparation of the manuscript.

Robert O. Hahn
David B. Bidna

CONTENTS

SECONDARY EDUCATION

Critics and Defenders

~~~~~~

Education is news. Weekly news magazines regularly carry sections devoted exclusively to education. Major metropolitan newspapers employ special editors to cover extensively the field of education. Feature articles dealing with educational issues are considered circulation boosters in nationally distributed periodicals. Since World War II educational problems have become the concern not only of professional educators but also of the general public. In the following section the reader will find selections on education written by scholars, educators, prominent lay people, professional writers, and outright enemies of public education. Although the opinions presented may appear to the student of secondary education as attractive, outrageous, appealing, or vicious, he must remember that in a democratic society each man has the right to present his opinion as he perceives it, and this opinion cannot be ignored.

Historian Arthur Bestor and free-lance writer Mortimer Smith present the academician's point of view; they have identified themselves with the Council for Basic Education, which states as its purpose that intellectual training must be restored in the public schools.

Defending public education are professional educators, Harold Shane and Sidney Hook, who contend that the American educational system has made a remarkable contribution toward the expansion of our democratic ideals. They challenge those who believe that the schools of the nineteenth century were superior to the schools of today with facts and figures to support their arguments. Professional educators are aware of the criticisms of the public in regard to the quality of the modern secondary school, and in some respects agree with this criticism. Accordingly they have expressed their views in professional journals. Unfortunately the popular press has not generally granted "equal time" or comparable space to their appeals. Thus the public has been exposed, for the most part, to only one point of view.

Highly publicized and articulate, Admiral Hyman Rickover is representative of the public lay group, particularly the scientist who has deplored the inadequate preparation of our secondary students for the space age. Contrasting American high schools with their allegedly superior counterparts in Europe, especially those in the Soviet Union, is a favorite pastime of this group, and to them the press has been most generous. The motives of these critics appear to be genuine, prompted by a serious concern for improving the American education system.

Spokesmen for the professional writers group include Fred Hechinger, author and education editor of *The New York Times*. Many in this group have written best-selling books which in some cases have performed a real service for education. On the other hand, because of their lack of insight about educational problems, they have often confused the reading public.

Most hostile toward public schools is the group that has used a number of emotionally charged issues as weapons to further their cause: subversion in the schools, Federal aid to education, reduction of taxes for public schools, curtailment of the power of the National Education Association, and support of the United Nations, each of which they feel poses a threat to their view of American life.

The ability of the teacher to identify basic issues will become a valuable asset to him if he learns to recognize the emotional impact of such words or phrases as *life adjustment, needs, intellectual training, and standards.* Further, a careful examination of the facts quoted in these readings will disclose that some of the authors may be using statistics in a misleading fashion or by comparing unequated symbols.

The selections included in this section suggest the vast variety of opinions that will confront the secondary schoolteacher; he must be aware of these criticisms and actions; he must learn how to respond to them.

STATEMENT OF PURPOSE

Council for Basic Education

~~~~~~

The Council for Basic Education was established in the belief that the purpose of education is the harmonious development of the mind, the will, and the conscience of each individual so that he may use to the full his intrinsic powers and shoulder the responsibilities of good citizenship. The Council believes in the principle of universal education and in the tax-supported public-school system. It insists that only by the maintenance of high academic standards can the ideal of democratic education be realized—the ideal of offering to all the children of all the people of the United States not merely an opportunity to attend school, but the privilege of receiving there the soundest education that is afforded any place in the world.

SOURCE: Council for Basic Education, "Statement of Purpose" (Washington, D.C., 1956), pp. 2, 3. Reprinted by permission.

Because the security and well-being of the nation call for constant vigilance to preserve the best in the present educational system, to develop new methods and procedures, and to eliminate weaknesses, the Council proposes to initiate and support measures to ensure:

1. That all students without exception receive adequate instruction in the basic intellectual disciplines, especially English, mathematics, science, history, and foreign languages;

2. That the fullest possible opportunity is afforded to students of high ability to reach mature levels of achievement without waste of time;

3. That clear standards of actual accomplishment are used to measure each student's progress and to govern promotion to higher levels of the educational system;

4. That teachers are thoroughly educated in the subjects they teach and in current developments therein;

5. That vocational training is offered in due subordination to the school's fundamental purpose of intellectual discipline, and that standards of achievement are maintained as rigorously in vocational as in academic fields;

6. That school administrators are encouraged and supported in resisting pressures to divert school time to activities of minor educational significance, to curricula overemphasizing social adjustment at the expense of intellectual discipline, and to programs that call upon the school to assume responsibilities properly belonging to the home, to religious bodies, and to other agencies.

FOUNDING GROUP OF COUNCIL FOR BASIC EDUCATION

Arthur Bestor, Professor of History, University of Illinois, and author of "Educational Wastelands" and "The Restoration of Learning."

Paxton Blair, Ex-Justice, New York Supreme Court, New York City.

Maynard M. Boring, Manager, Technical Personnel Division, General Electric Company, and Past President, American Society for Engineering Education.

Harold L. Clapp, Professor of Romance Languages, Grinnell College.

Sereck H. Fox, R. P. Scherer Corporation, Detroit, Michigan.

Harry J. Fuller, Professor of Botany, University of Illinois.

Howard A. Meyerhoff, Executive Director, Scientific Manpower Commission, Washington, D.C.

Mortimer Smith, author of "And Madly Teach" and "The Diminished Mind" and editor of "The Public Schools in Crisis."

Sydney Steele, Industrial Assistant to the Vice-President, Atlas Powder Company.

Howard Whitman, journalist and author of articles on educational topics in *Colliers, Readers' Digest*, etc.

AN INTERVIEW WITH THE COUNCIL

FOR BASIC EDUCATION

The Council for Basic Education (CBE) opposes "progressive education"?   T F

CBE opposes federal aid to education?   T F

CBE wants to return to the good old days, "when schools taught the three R's and taught them properly"?   T F

CBE is opposed to such "educational frills" as the use of audio-visual aids, field trips, and courses in typing?   T F

CBE is opposed to having driver training taught by the schools?   T F

CBE feels that college courses in "how to teach" are useless?   T F

The Council for Basic Education—with headquarters in Washington—is one of the most talked about (and cursed) organizations in the educational field. But a close look at the statements

SOURCE: "An Interview with the Council for Basic Education," *School Management* (1959), pp. 26–65. Reprinted by permission.

of CBE's friends and enemies indicates that perhaps neither really knows what the organization is all about. . . .

. . . Where does CBE really stand? . . . Recently, a School Management editor went to Washington to interview three of CBE's top leaders.

In interviewing these men, no attempt was made by our editors to argue CBE's position. The sole intent was to gain information, to find out where it stood on major issues in education.

Thomas Bledsoe, executive secretary of CBE, is a former professor at Illinois University and until recently was in the publishing business.

Mortimer Smith, editor of CBE's monthly bulletin and chief propagandist for the organization, is a former free-lance writer who became interested in education and decided to devote his life to trying to reform it.

Samuel Withers, associate secretary of CBE, is on leave from his job as a high school English teacher in Scarsdale, N.Y.

The following questions and answers are taken from the transcript of a tape-recorded interview with these three men.

Q. Gentlemen, as you see it, is there anything good about education in the public schools of today?

BLEDSOE: Certainly. There's a lot that's good. But there's a lot that's bad, too. The Council for Basic Education is not in business to attack the schools—we're in business to improve them. We feel that anybody who says "Everything is all right in the schools today" is just blind. And yet, an awful lot of people in education seem to think that way. When we point out some of the bad things in education, it is not just for the purpose of pointing a finger. It is for the purpose of getting them improved.

Q. What are some of these bad things that you see? Where would you start?

BLEDSOE: I think the best place to start is right in the first grade —with the reading program. This is perhaps the best example of what is wrong with the schools today. During the last 30 years, there has been a shift from the old phonic method of teaching reading to the "look-say" method. The result has been that many,

many people graduate from elementary school—and even high school—without knowing how to read.

Q. Many educators say that this is a fake controversy that you have thought up. They say that the phonic method is being used in the schools and that it is being combined with the newer and more progressive look-say method. Would you agree with this?

SMITH: I would say that many of these educators of whom you speak don't always know what is going on in the field of reading instruction. The standard position of the official reading experts is that phonic instruction is something that must be delayed. . . .

WITHERS: Actually, it's impossible to get systematic phonic instruction widely practiced in America's schools today, because there's no reading series generally available that is based on anything but the look-say method. To teach phonics a teacher must either construct her own system or persuade the administration to buy one of the many successful supplementary phonics systems. . . .

SMITH: More emphasis is placed today on "reading readiness" than on teaching. This is part of the life adjustment business—not forcing a student to read until some tests show he's ready.

Q. You think, then, that all children should be expected to read at exactly the same time—presumably in the first grade?

BLEDSOE: Not at all. But the reading readiness idea has been carried to such an extreme that there are schools where children do not start reading until they're in the third, fourth or fifth grades. But when a child enters school, the one thing he wants to learn more than anything else is how to read. . . .

Q. *In 1959, Dr. James B. Conant published a report on the American high school. He called for a tightening of standards in the secondary schools. Do you, in the main, agree with his report?*

BLEDSOE: We agree with some of the things he says, but in general we don't think he went far enough. . . .

Q. Could we take some of his recommendations and see how

you feel about them? For example, on the question of counseling he says there should be one full-time counselor for every 250 or 300 high school pupils. Do you agree with that?

BLEDSOE: Conant tends to use quantitative rather than qualitative standards. Therefore, frequently he doesn't make it clear exactly what he's talking about. It seems to us that the fundamental issue in counseling is the *kind* of counseling—what you are counseling about and what kind of people are doing it. We feel that counseling in schools should basically be academic counseling. At present, the organized counseling and guidance programs tend to be vocationally and psychologically oriented.

SMITH: Counseling should not be primarily to solve a student's personal and psychological problems or his problems of social adjustment. I think there has been a tendency, too, in counseling to direct an individual toward a vocational career at too early a date. When a sixth grade student is told that he can't go to college because he doesn't have the ability, he is being deprived of this opportunity at an awfully early date.

BLEDSOE: Another thing that Conant doesn't talk much about is who should do the counseling. He does say the counselor should have some teaching experience, but he doesn't say what kind. There are an awful lot of people who have never taught anything but physical education who end up in the guidance department.

Q. Conant calls for individualized programs for each student. He says that there should be no labeling of vocational, commercial or college preparatory programs. And he calls for flexibility so students can shift from one emphasis to another. Does this fit in with your program?

SMITH: We are not supporters of vocational education in the public schools except at a very minimum level. We favor a track system because it offers an opportunity for at least a significant part of the student body to get a solid academic program. But we deplore, in most tracks, the over-heavy emphasis on vocationalism.

BLEDSOE: We believe that all students should be trained in the academic subjects—in history, mathematics and English.

Q. Conant would agree with you there. He says the requirements for graduation for all students should include four years of English, three or four years of social studies, two years of history and a senior course in American problems or American government. He also includes a year of mathematics and at least one year of science. Would you differ with him on this minimum program?

BLEDSOE: Yes, we think it's too minimum. Also, again he is giving only quantitative measurements. We'd like to know what is included in those four years of English. Conant has never very specifically defined that. Four years of sitting in a classroom labeled "English" is not necessarily good education. A good English program sets up some definite standards and requirements.

Q. Conant does say the time devoted to English composition during the four years should occupy about half the total time. Each student, he says, should be required to write an average of one theme a week.

BLEDSOE: This is one of Conant's best recommendations.

Q. Do you disagree with his minimum program of three years of social studies?

BLEDSOE: I must admit the phrase *social studies* gives us the creeps. Beyond that, we don't know any valid reason why every year a student is in high school he should not have at least one course in this field. If we were presenting a curriculum, we would talk about four years rather than three, and we would talk about specific subjects rather than social studies in general.

Q. How about the minimum of one year of math in the ninth grade which he recommends?

BLEDSOE: That is awfully inadequate.

Q. What would be your minimum mathematics program for all students?

WITHERS: If you really try to set out to teach all students, except those who are really mentally retarded, we would like to see mathematics a regular part of the curriculum throughout high school. Now the kind of mathematics that can be taught throughout is not going to be the same. You can't teach a child with an IQ of 80 the kind of mathematics that you can teach to a child with an IQ of 160.

BLEDSOE: The students who are slow are the last ones who ought to have to be giving up on mathematics at the end of the ninth grade. You can be sure that at the end of the ninth grade they haven't learned much mathematics. Maybe at the end of four years you can give your slowest children a reasonable grasp of arithmetic and a small working knowledge of algebra. I think you can show these students, if you set out to, that certain things in algebra are really useful in the normal conduct of existence.

Q. Would you want to eliminate such things as clerical programs in the high schools—typing, stenography, home economics, and things like that?

SMITH: My feeling is that these are useful skills, although homemaking, for example, tends to get tremendously out of hand. I don't think they are proper subjects for academic credit. I do not think they should be taught *instead of* academic subjects. If they can be taught in addition to, or in off hours, then they can be useful. But the general tendency in high schools today is to make a course in home economics, for example, equal in credit, and therefore academically equivalent, to a course in English. This doesn't make any sense to us. I think it has become a way of nibbling at and drastically cutting down the academic content of the curriculum.

WITHERS: I wouldn't go quote so far as you've gone. I would give perhaps a half credit to courses like this—assume that they are secondary. I think we ought to make a distinction, too, on tracks. If you have a school large enough to have a four-track system, these courses could have more weight in the fourth track than in the other three.

Q. These courses that we've been discussing really fall somewhere between the academic and the truly vocational courses. Where does vocational education fit in the schools?

BLEDSOE: It really doesn't. Vocational education is very expensive education. When you start equipping machine shops you're getting into money. Furthermore, we doubt the real value of vocational education. A student who learns how to run a tractor, because his school is in an agricultural area, is not going to find much use for this skill if he moves to the big city. On the other hand, if he learns to read and to write and to reason, he can use these skills no matter what part of the country he lives in.

SMITH: Another objection to vocational education is that a lot of it, of necessity, tends to be out of date. If you equip shops in a society that changes technologically as rapidly as we do, it's hard to keep up with the times.

Q. A great number of these vocational programs are used to hold on to students who otherwise would leave the schools. Isn't this important?

BLEDSOE: This is an awfully pessimistic attitude. I don't think there are so many students who are not salvageable so far as education is concerned.

Q. This is an attempt to salvage them, is it not?

BLEDSOE: Not educationally. This is an attempt to interest them in something that has no real relation to education. I'm not sure that we can afford to give up so easily, especially at the present time. I think the Council for Basic Education would certainly feel as strongly as any organization in the country that we ought to make the attempt to really educate, genuinely educate, far more than we are attempting to do now.

SMITH: The boys that you shuffle off to machine shop, because you decide you've got to keep them in school and you can't teach them anything, are our future voters and citizens. If we give up on them at this stage in their learning, we've also given up on them implicitly in the second stage.

Q. *Dr. Conant recommended a minimum program for academically talented students. It included four years of mathematics, four years of one foreign language, three years of science, in addition to the required four years of English and three years of social studies. This would be for the top 15 percent of most classes. How does this sit with you?*

BLEDSOE: Until you begin to talk about these things in qualitative, as well as quantitative, terms you really haven't stated what you're talking about. You really haven't set up anything except the framework, which may or may not mean something. Now, if this is a qualitatively demanding and rigorous program, then this is what we're talking about. But this is a mighty big *if*. It's awfully easy for a school system that does a thoroughly mediocre job to say, "Sure we meet the standards of the Conant report," and a lot of them are doing just this.

WITHERS: I'd like to challenge Conant on another point. He calls this his program for the academically talented, the top 15 percent. We say that this is the program 80 percent of the student body can—and should—undertake. The notion, for example, that foreign languages are the exclusive province of the academically talented student is wildly irrational. Any objective observer who was in a foreign country during the war saw little kids running along the side of the road speaking to them in irreverent —but fluent—English. We believe that 80 percent of the student body, at least, should be taking six periods of academic work every single day.

Q. You're suggesting that 80 percent of the students could take the program Conant has reserved for the academically talented?

WITHERS: I'm pretty fresh out of the classroom. I know that there are a lot of pupils who just seem not to be able to get it. You have to make a distinction between them and the others. There are students, maybe 15 or 20 percent, who, no matter how hard they try, from kindergarten on up, could not get any form of an academic program. I think 20 percent is high.

There are also a lot of malingerers, who are capable of doing the work but who don't. I've seen plenty of those in the last 14 years of teaching high school. Now, we've gotten into the habit of passing them automatically. "Oh well, they're not interested." And very often, they're called not capable because they are not interested. This, I think is the fault of our system of education. We don't bring students into school any more and say this is work. We don't tell them that this is something that is going to benefit them in the future but they've got to work hard in order to get the benefits. Instead, we try to sugar coat everything; we worry about life adjustment, so that in the end we give the students the idea that school is not work but is a lark. This starts in the very early grades, and by the time a student is in high school it's pretty hard to get him to sit down and really go to work.

Q. *Did the type of education you favor ever exist in the United States?*

SMITH: Not for the whole population.

Q. Did it ever exist at all?

SMITH: I would be hard put to substantiate this, but I suspect there was some period, perhaps about 1915, when the public schools in this country more nearly approximated what we are after. There existed then a combination of traditional education with the best of the early progressive. Certainly the whole life adjustment movement hadn't arisen at that period. The public schools were, I think, more committed in those days to the intellectual training that we're talking about.

BLEDSOE: True. But, on the other hand, if overnight you could introduce the schools of 1915 in 1960 you would have no solution to the educational problems of our present time.

SMITH: If you could take some of the point of view of the administrator—the professional educator—of that era, and transfer it to 1960, with appropriate changes in the curriculum, then I think you would be approaching our goal.

I think, for what it's worth, it could probably be shown that in 1915 many of the superintendents were scholarly men in the sense of having a classical background. They were not the businessmen and factory managers that they've become today.

Q. Aren't the very same people who were brought up in these schools of 1915 the ones who are leading today's schools? Isn't the product of this education of 1915 providing the leadership that you oppose today?

BLEDSOE: Basic education, thank God, is no guarantee that people are going to come out thinking the same thing. But really, I deplore this comparison with 1915 because I think it is irrelevant. This is especially so because one of the stock criticisms of what we're trying to say is "They want to go back to the good old days."

There never were any good old days in the terms that we're talking about. What we need is a good new day in which we will try to really give adequate intellectual training to 80 or 85 percent of the students. This demands a lot of work and experimentation. And it means teaching things that we ought to be really working on and that most schools aren't.

MEDIOCRITY IN OUR SCHOOLS

Arthur E. Bestor

The time has certainly come for a fresh and disinterested appraisal by the public at large of American educational policy. During the past quarter century the schools have experienced the effects of depressions, conscription, inflation, and cold war. They have faced rapidly expanding enrollment and major shifts of population. They have had to feel their way through a storm of conflicting ideologies: individualism vs. collectivism, pragmatism vs. neo-Thomism, isolation vs. internationalism, and the rest. American educators have dealt with these problems and issues in a frankly empirical spirit. The American people have been

SOURCE: Arthur E. Bestor, "Mediocrity in Our Schools," *The Saturday Review,* June 25, 1955. Reprinted by permission.

willing that they should and have postponed the embarrassing questions about ultimate purposes and long-term consequences.

These questions, however, cannot permanently remain unasked. There is no such thing as experimentation unless there is some final evaluation of results. And evaluation is impossible unless we know clearly what our purposes are and ought to be. To define the purposes of public education is a public responsibility. It cannot be delegated to professional "experts" if the public schools are to remain under effective public control.

Mr. Smith is asking no return to the past, but he is demanding a school system that will face the intellectual problems of modern life instead of retreating from them into the infantilism of "Life Adjustment Education." He rejects such programs as the latter not because they are "practical," but because they are the opposite. As he shrewdly observes, "A school program which teaches little beyond how to fix a fuse, drive a car, set the dinner table, and enhance your personal appearance *isn't useful enough* if your aim is the development of maturity and citizenship." (*Italics mine.*)

In his sober and thoughtful book, Mortimer Smith recognizes, of course, that modifications of the curriculum must be made for the slow learner, but he insists "the revision needs to be in the direction of discovering new and better methods and techniques for reaching the group with the values of the cultural heritage." Any alternative plan, Mr. Smith points out, is at bottom antidemocratic. To shove the slow learner "into a variety of non-academic courses devoid of real content" is to treat him "as a second-class citizen of the educational world," doomed for the rest of his life "to intellectual and cultural subservience." He reminds us that the safety of society as a whole is involved: "If we expect the boy with an IQ of 90 to become a citizen and make the judgments required of a citizen we ought to be busy devising ways of making him understand the ideas which have shaped his country and world and we ought to be teaching him how to 'communicate' intelligibly."

That Mr. Smith is almost certain to be venomously denounced as as "enemy" of the public schools by certain professional educationists is sad, but true. The concluding chapters of his book discuss the obstacles that lie in the path of educational reform.

Greatest of these, in Mr. Smith's opinion—an opinion with which I concur—is the virtually uncontrolled power that professors of education exercise, in direct and indirect ways, over the nominally public educational system. That the inertia of such a great vested interest should stand in the way of education improvement is natural enough. A sinister development of recent years is the ruthless use of this power to stifle criticism, to vilify critics, and to discredit any citizens' group that might take an independent position on school matters. The evidence of this is marshaled by Mr. Smith in a chapter entitled "Putting Parents in Their Place." It is one of the most impressive as well as one of the most frightening sections of the book.

EUROPEAN VS. AMERICAN SECONDARY SCHOOLS

H. G. Rickover, USN

. . . Since the *above-average* pupil is two to three years ahead of the *average* pupil in mental age, he can complete the curriculum in a shorter period, or he can absorb more academic subjects or study them more deeply. But the same type of mental food which the above-average pupil needs is needed also by the less gifted. Even the *below-average* child who may be two to three years behind the average in mental age and whose maximum capacity may be limited to the sixth grade—even he ought to be taught the same basic course of study given in the first six elementary years, though at a much slower rate. It may take him

SOURCE: H. G. Rickover, "European vs. American Secondary Schools," *Phi Delta Kappan*, November, 1958. Reprinted by permission.

until age 15 or 16 to complete the sixth grade. But if he can be motivated to want to, he can at least be taught the three R's.

For all children, the educational process must be one of collecting factual knowledge to the limit of their absorptive capacity. Recreation, manual or clerical training, etiquette, and similar know-how have little effect on the mind itself, and it is with the mind that the school must solely concern itself. The poorer a child's natural endowments, the more does he need to have his mind trained.

We should not have to support schools if we want no more than "adjustment" of children to life as it *is*. Children learn this in simpler societies just by "living" and by the incidental training they receive from the grown-ups around them. A child is being properly educated only when he is learning to become independent of his parents. We have schools because we know that in today's world everyone is daily called upon to make decisions for which he needs a background of general knowledge, not obtainable merely by "learning through living." To acquire such knowledge, fact upon fact, takes time and effort. Nothing can really make it "fun." If we try to spare our children mental effort and to protect them against disappointments or personal failures through flunking exams, we send them ill prepared into a competitive world. This is most dangerous in a democracy, for, as Jefferson warned us: "If a nation expects to be ignorant and free, in a state of civilization, it expects what never was and never will be." Note the qualification, "in a state of civilization." Formal school education was not as vitally needed in American pioneer society as it is in twentieth-century America. The degree of ignorance which a democracy can tolerate varies in inverse ratio to the advance of the nation toward higher cultural and scientific levels.

Our elementary and secondary education must thus provide first, for the average and below-average student, a sufficiently broad terminal education to fit him into a modern technological society; and second, for the talented student, a solid underpinning for subsequent professional education. Neither of these two objectives is achieved in the majority of American public school systems. Unlike all other Western countries of similar civilization, we lack a national standard for curricula, for school-leaving examinations, for diplomas, or for teacher qualifications. There is a wide variety in the school systems of different states, even for different cities in the same state. We have some excellent school systems, but many more are poor ones.

Why do most of our public schools fail in the objectives I have mentioned? Basically, I think, because today these two purposes are *not* the objectives of our schools. We are reaping the consequences of the destruction of traditional education by the Dewey-Kilpatrick experimentalist philosophy. While we have fortunately been spared wide application of progressive teaching methods in the schools themselves—thanks primarily to the heroic resistance and good judgment of our teachers—the spirit of Dewey permeates our teacher colleges and our state boards of education. It makes its pernicious influence felt in the steady deterioration of secondary school curricula, the overlong prolongation of elementary schooling, and the denial to teachers of professional status.

DEWEY'S CONTRIBUTIONS—AND FAILURES

We must give credit to Dewey and his followers for having improved what once was altogether too autocratic a relationship between teacher and pupil, and for bringing a relaxed and friendly atmosphere into our classrooms. But we must also, on his own pragmatic terms, reject Dewey's claim that experimentalist education "adjusts" the child to life in a changing society such as ours and that it does this better than traditional education.

Dewey's desire to alter curricula so as to teach subjects which will be of use to the child in life can be accepted only *if* we interpret the term *use* in its broadest sense. Unfortunately, his ideas have led to elimination of many academic subjects on the grounds that they would not be "useful" in life, and to substitution of trivial, recreational, and vocational subjects alleged to be of more practical value. The student thus receives neither intellectual training nor the factual knowledge which will help him to understand the world he lives in, or to make well-reasoned decisions in his private life or as a responsible citizen in a modern democracy. He is instead handed a bag of "know-how tricks": he is helped to become a pleasant, nicely mannered young person, able to get along with whatever group he joins. Even for the average pupil, these subjects are not mentally stimulating—they barely touch his mind.

Our schools once had the important task of Americanizing large numbers of children whose first need was to "adjust" themselves to a new country. This the schools have done magnificently. But today ours is a pretty homogeneous country, a country where the majority no longer live in poverty, where most families consider themselves middle class and enjoy a material standard of living much higher than that of the middle classes of the past. Traditionally, training of children in manners, appearance, poise, and consideration for others has been a distinctive function of the middle-class family. Nowhere have the schools to which middle-class children go been expected to take over this function which belongs to the home. Formal school education has always and everywhere been concerned solely with development of mental powers, with due attention also being given to physical exercise for purposes of safeguarding the pupil's health.

TIME ONLY FOR INTELLECTUAL TRAINING

Intellectual training can be combined with home training only when schools are residential—as are the famed English "public" schools. In a short school day there is not enough time to do both. I suggest we turn back to the home what is properly the function of the home and permit the public schools to concentrate on what is properly their function—the education of young minds.

To that end, we must break the experimentalist hold on curricula and teacher certification. Pedagogy is an important skill in a teacher's professional equipment, but it is less important than thorough and deep knowledge of subject matter. Teacher colleges are now almost totally given over to pedagogy, school administration, and psychology. Teaching cannot become a true profession until, like all professions, it demands of its practitioners that they pursue a lengthy course of study in the special field of their choice. You cannot make of "pedagogy" as such or of "school administration" as such a field of academic study comparable to

law or medicine. They are in a sense the minors in a professional
course of study; the major must always be the specific subject to
be taught later—a teacher must be a true scholar in his own field.
His scholarship will, of course, differ depending on whether he
teaches history, let us say, in elementary or secondary school, or
in college. Different degrees of depth and breadth of knowledge
will be required; also different methods of presenting the subject
to the pupil.

TEACHERS DENIED CHANCE TO BE SCHOLARS

Today, our teachers are, in effect, denied the opportunity to
make themselves such scholars, because their right to teach and
their professional advancement are tied to required courses in
pedagogy which few of them would choose if they were given the
freedom to plan their own course of study. Teachers do not have
unlimited time to complete their professional training. If they
are forced to waste much of it on pedagogical trivia, they have
that much less time for serious study, and the losers are our
children, of course.

Dewey's denial of absolute values; his insistence that learning
leading to growth must be based on the experience of the child;
and that the aims of education must be to modify behavior rather
than to impart knowledge—all this gives American education a
transitory flavor, ties it closely to the society into which the child
is to be fitted. It also provides an effective smokescreen preventing comparison of American education with that of countries having similar ways of life. Indeed, we have long lived in educational
isolation, and it is time we look around and see what is being
done in other countries. . . .

William K. Medlin, Clarence B. Lindquist, and Marshall L. Schmitt

Many evidences of American interest in Russia's schools have appeared since that nation's first sputnik was launched and America increased its efforts in the race for outer space. Among other groups that have intensified the study of Russian education, the U.S. Office of Education in 1959 sent a mission to Russia for this purpose. Its three specialists spent a month studying certain significant aspects of schooling in Russia. A summary of their findings is presented here.

"Our study is not a comparative one of the Soviet and American systems of education, nor is it an attempt to evaluate the schooling and teacher education provided in the U.S.S.R. . . .

We have aimed here to provide the interested readers with a document based on our own studies of, and experiences in, the Soviet Union's educational domain. We have also drawn upon those of others. Our efforts are buttressed by official Soviet views, educational materials in daily use, and Government statements. With special attention to the sciences and polytechnic training, we have presented factual materials which carefully describe these curriculum areas. This approach has enabled us to become further acquainted with Soviet educational practices, and to point out what appear to us to be some of their strengths and weaknesses. While we tend naturally to be influenced by our own cultural experiences in making these observations, we attempt to

---

SOURCE: William K. Medlin, Clarence B. Lindquist, and Marshall L. Schmitt, *Soviet Education Programs* (Washington, D.C.: U.S. Department of Health, Education, and Welfare, 1959), pp. 201–210. Reprinted by permission.

place them within the Soviet context. The reader is invited to consider these observations.

THE SCHOOL SYSTEM

Building on modest but strong foundations, educators in the Soviet Union have erected, in a little more than one generation, a system of mass education. Soviet general education is a vigorous and dynamic institution, embracing, until the 1958–59 reforms, the traditional curriculum patterns characteristic of various European schools. It is in form a 4 plus 3 plus 3 (or 7 plus 3) system, with differentiation of pupils at the end of grade 7. The system seems to be designed mainly to provide higher institutions and technical schools with students well grounded in basic mathematics, science, and the mother tongue. Students admitted to higher education include the best ones, determined on a merit (subject-matter achievement) basis. Perhaps the outstanding feature of the system is its trend in recent years toward offering complete secondary education on a mass basis and with a dual purpose—academic and polytechnic. Partly to improve on the opportunities available to all Soviet children aspiring to complete secondary education, and partly to respond to State needs and weaknesses in the old curriculum, Soviet educators are adjusting their school structures to render them more practical for their society and more accessible to all children. Thus two major aspects of the system stand out: mass education on a scale hitherto not practiced in Europe and Asia (for the U.S.S.R. is a Eurasian country); and advancement by children through a unified school establishment or "ladder" system in accordance with their individual capacities and, within State-specified limits, their preferences. The changes now underway are considered later in this chapter.

THE TEACHING

Until recently, the major emphasis in schools has been on formal methods of learning and teaching. Teachers have aimed primarily to give children measurable quantities of fact-learning. A unified curriculum was designed for the academic preparation of pupils going toward higher institutes. Classroom methods of long-established use, like the textbook and recitation, have occupied the center of pedagogical work. Controlled by centralized forms of political authority, this formalism has functioned as an instrument of the authoritarian philosophy of education practiced in the Soviet Union. Coupled with a program of ideological indoctrination, this situation has apparently tended to hinder creative and self-conscious activities among children, activities which might emerge from practicing other pedagogical ideas. Teachers are, on the whole, skilled in the use of their methods and knowledgeable in their respective subject areas. Consistency appears to reign and to produce satisfactory results for the purpose of Soviet education. . . .

THE CURRICULUM

The curriculum is unified, the same for all schools in the country. Slight variations occur in non-Russian nationality areas in literature, history, and geography. Subjects are taught in parallel sequences over a period of years, rather than in concentrations at different levels of the educational ladder. While the parallel method of instruction may allow for more flexible treatment of subjects and interrelationships with other subjects than do some other methods, there are potential disadvantages of limiting the level of maturity achieved in a given branch and of making impossible a flexible program of electives for serving varied interests and specialities. Some evidence of limited maturity was seen in the social studies work carried on in Soviet schools. The question is, however, admittedly open to more extensive research.

We found that Soviet schools offer strong, basic education in mathematics and sciences. The mathematics curriculum in particular is designed to prepare youth for specialization in engineering and scientific work. According to our observations, their programs in mathematics, physics, chemistry and biology are roughly comparable to those given in American high schools, where students take a mathematics-science-oriented curriculum in the college preparatory program, but the main difference lies in two areas: First, in the U.S.S.R., all graduates of the Soviet 10-year school receive the same amount of mathematics and science instruction, whereas in the United States some of the same subjects which are *required* of Soviet youngsters are *elective*. Secondly, the Soviet curriculum advances the pupil, especially after grade 5, at a faster rate in mathematics and science concepts than do the usual American high school curriculums. From these standpoints Soviet high school pupils may appear to have on the average a better grounding in fundamentals of science and mathematics than do their American counterparts on completing secondary education; but we see these differences primarily as differences in *emphasis,* not necessarily as a difference in the adequacy of mathematics and science preparation for the respective societies. . . .

As a kind of diversification from the unified curriculum, Soviet educators encourage pupil participation in the Pioneer circle activities, which in their subject and cultural-centered programs provide opportunity for development of talents. We wish to emphasize particularly this aspect of their program, its facilities, organization, and apparent successes. In addition to offering this creative and formative *foyer,* Soviet educators are beginning to provide other afterschool classes for curriculum enrichment, especially in the sciences.

Trends in Soviet curriculum development are definitely toward introducing vastly increased practical and life-related experiences for children and youth during their entire educational career. The aim appears to be twofold: to facilitate mastery of the mathematics and sciences subjects; and to inculcate in pupils an interest in, and respect for, labor. In regard to the practical applications of theory, the Soviet trend contrasts with that in the United States. Some leading American science educators are advocating that teachers pay less attention to application and give greater emphasis to understanding basic scientific principles. There is considerable ferment concerning the American mathematics curriculum, and work is going on with the objective of introducing curricular reforms consonant with modern trends in mathematics problems and thinking. We did not detect this particular trend in Soviet education, although their educators do speak about the need to modernize instruction in mathematics and sciences.

Physics curriculum offers another example. For several years the Physical Science Study Committee, with headquarters at the Massachusetts Institute of Technology and supported by a grant from the National Science Foundation, has been working on a revision of the physics curriculum in the high school. A number of physicists working in collaboration with high school teachers have produced curriculum materials which are designed to develop understanding of basic concepts and principles. In this material, technology, which is the application of science, receives secondary emphasis. It is the belief of the Committee that once the basic understanding of physical notions has been achieved by the pupil, it will be easier for him to comprehend the specific applications later in life as he encounters them. The Committee has felt that in past years too much attention has been given to specific applications, such as the way a refrigerator operates. Numerous similar examples could be cited.

The Soviet school's curriculum in mathematics-science seems comparatively stronger than its social-studies-humanities curriculum, with the probable exception of Russian language education and training in the arts. While our mission did not aim to cover the social sciences or arts, opportunities for some observations did occur. Coupled with knowledge of Soviet syllabus and textbook material in this area,[1] these visits left us with an impression that there are shortcomings here, especially in regard to scientifically derived information about other peoples and their cultures. At the same time, ambitious programs are well under way in the teaching of foreign languages.

TEACHER TRAINING

Soviet education is moving steadily toward a 4-year program of elementary teacher training and has a 5-year program in secondary teacher education, both at the higher (college) level.

---

[1] For example, see W. E. Medlin *et al., Sciences and Humanities in Soviet Schools* (Washington, D.C.: U.S. Department of Health, Education, and Welfare, Office of Education, 1959), 49 pp.

The 2-year pedagogical school is disappearing, and the universities, as well as the 5-year pedagogical institute, are preparing important segments of secondary school teaching personnel. Soviet secondary teachers (i.e., from grade 5 up), and increasing numbers of elementary teachers, are therefore now receiving preparation similar in time period (but not in total hours) to that now received by corresponding American teachers. While the secondary teacher in the U.S.S.R. receives more instruction in subject matter areas than does his average American counterpart, we noted certain deficiencies in the general education taken by the Soviet student. Professional training and practice in pedagogy are provided by Soviet programs in considerable measure, but we did not have opportunities to observe student teachers in action. According to criticism by some Soviet educators facilities for, and the carrying out of, student practice need improvement.

All graduates of the 3-year programs must write a thesis and pass a State examination in addition to passing regular course tests. Considering the entire teacher education program, our opinion is that, except in the field of general education (liberal arts), the Soviet secondary teacher graduating today has a level of preparation about equivalent to that achieved by a graduate from a 5-year program in an accredited American university or college. Up until the present time, the Soviet student has required 15 years to complete his program; the American, 17 years. We note, however, that Soviet schools are increasing their primary-secondary program to 11 years. It should also be remembered that the school work in the U.S.S.R. goes on 6 days, compared to 5 days in the United States.

THE FATE OF PEDAGOGUESE

Fred M. Hechinger

~~~~~~

Albert Lynd, author of "Quackery in the Public Schools," one of the three major works published this fall, used to teach history in college. He is now a businessman. He is a member of the school board in Sharon, Mass., believes in the public schools, thinks public education ought to have much better financial support, and is sure that teachers' colleges and professors of education are ruining the schools. . . .

Arthur E. Bestor, who is professor of history at the University of Illinois, shares Mr. Lynd's alarm. Like Mr. Lynd, he is against the domination by pedagogy over education. Pedagogy, he writes in "Educational Wastelands: The Retreat From Learning In Our Public Schools," "tells *how* something can be taught most effectively, but it provides no basis whatever for deciding *what* should be taught." He objects to specialists in pedagogy making the decisions on what is to be the content of public school instruction.

Finally, there is Paul Woodring, who taught in many places, including high schools, and [was] professor of psychology at Western Washington College of Education. In "Let's Talk Sense About Our Schools" . . . he might even say something about talking sense about our schools. . . .

Where is the problem and the real disagreement? Messrs. Lynd and Bestor tried to pinpoint the blame for everything that seems wrong with public education today, and in pinpointing they picked the teachers colleges as their target. There is a measure of truth in Mr. Lynd's amusing, sharp satire of the superadministrators, the group of dynamicians (if I may coin a new word that is only slightly more obscure than many of the ones

SOURCE: Fred M. Hechinger, "The Fate of Pedagoguese," *The Saturday Review*, December 12, 1953. Reprinted by permission.

now in use), and the miserable jargon. He is justly scornful of a teachers college course on "urban cities." He detests, with good reason, the bargain basement collection of courses and sub-courses in methodology. There is probably no good excuse for a Master's thesis on "The Effects of Coaching on the Acquisition of Skill in Baseball Free Throw," though I am sure that a pretty devastating list of topics could be assembled from the files of the academic departments of the universities, too. (In all fairness, furthermore, it should be added that this gem of an example originated not at a teachers college, but at the University of Wisconsin. . . .)

There is also just cause for the complaint, contained in all three books, that too much stress on methods and the omission of real knowledge of subject matter are both an indication of shallowness and a boost to the trend of anti-intellectualism. It is quite right to say—as do our authors—that pragmatism, the philosophy made noted and notable by John Dewey, is a dangerous idea in education because it sticks too closely to "what is" and threatens to ignore "what should or might be." (Dewey himself would not have accepted pragmatism as the philosophy of things as they are. He was too deeply interested in social reform—so deeply that Mr. Lynd, who emphatically clears him of any Communist charges, still considers him a Socialist. But he would have insisted that theories are not much good unless they can be made to work, and this is a point of view not entirely alien to the American industrialist and businessman.) It is certainly fair to say that our schools and our colleges—teachers colleges as well as liberal arts institutions and, especially, the great universities—have offered too varied, too scattered, too confusing a diet. Since many teachers have grown up on that diet, their intellectual constitution may be found wanting. The worst of them may actually suffer from malnutrition.

But the real error of these critical views is their insinuation that pragmatism was foisted on the American people by the educationists. This is historically nonsense. America was a pragmatic, anti-intellectual country by virtue of its pioneering, frontier background—long before the first teachers college exerted its influence. When the public high schools began to drop the "academic subjects"—Latin, foreign languages, etc.—the pressure to do so had usually been exerted by the "practical" men on the school boards,

not by educators. Those were the days when businessmen at-
tacked as "frills" not the modern subjects which are today associated with progressive education, but rather "all that useless
stuff" which is generally known as the humanities. This does not
clear the educators of all blame. But the most serious charge that
can be brought against them is that, instead of exerting educational leadership, they followed too closely the climate of public
opinion. . . . What will eventually save the day, I believe, is the
increasing "infiltration" by the liberal arts into the teachers college
curriculum and of good and essential education courses into the
liberal arts colleges. This has been happening for a number of
years, and though it may not have been a sufficiently rapid and
thorough trend, it is not wise to overlook it. It is always useful
to set up a straw man and knock him down if you want to make
a very complete and radical point; but it is not a very constructive
procedure. That it was the procedure often adopted by the lesser
"progressives" (their straw man being the "traditional" school)
does not make it either wise or helpful for the leaders of the
counter-movement to be equally misguided and misleading.

But, even at the risk of being accused of the straw-man technique myself, it seems necessary to recall that the "old" school
was much worse than most critics of the new school are willing
to admit or are capable of remembering. Curriculum and methods were not even very suitable for the selected group of pupils
who went to high school; they would have been disastrous had
they been applied to the great mass of pupils (who did not then
go to high school at all). There were, of course, good teachers
who were immune to the absurdities of the "old" school, just as
there are today good teachers who have benefited from the lib-
eralization without succumbing to the follies of the "new" school.

One of the errors of the critics—and it should be said that
Mr. Bestor recognized that error and writes very effectively about
this problem—is that they often overlook the difference between
elementary and secondary school. It is absurd to argue that the
application of a wealth of new psychological knowledge to the
teaching of the elementary grades has not been beneficial. It has
been without question the most startling step forward that education has taken in this century. Contrary to Mr. Lynd's observation,
this has been a development which has profoundly influenced

teaching far beyond the borders of the United States. It is today a world trend, not an American experiment, and it is not considered nearly as controversial in other countries as it is here.

The real problem is to realize that the purposes of elementary school and of high school are quite different. "The procedures that will kindle interest in the elementary school will not do so in the high school," Mr. Bestor writes quite rightly. "They may even destroy interest, for nothing is more repellent to the youthful mind than something he considers childish. . . . Experts in pedagogy, however, seem blithely unaware of their ignorance concerning the higher stages of the learning process." This is a valid charge, and the sooner corrections are made the better. But improvement is not going to come from a blanket attack on new methods and on the new school. . . .

Mr. Bestor writes some very important words: "Genuine liberal education is not a course in first aid. It is a serious effort to train men to recognize symptoms, to trace them to fundamental causes, and to deal intelligently with the latter." This is an excellent definition (though its author does not always trace the schools' shortcomings to their fundamental causes). When Mr. Bestor looks for a remedy he asks for the establishment of a permanent "federation of the learned society" and a "Permanent Scientific and Scholarly Commission on Secondary Education" which would deliberately exclude from membership the education associations and the "professional educationists." Then there would, in addition, be a third group of organized laymen.

The danger of this kind of "remedy" is obvious. I admit that the exclusiveness of some of the educationist groups is harmful to education; but I also recognize that their present exclusiveness is the result of past exclusion—of being snubbed by the academic world and of not being accepted by the universities. If there is educationist isolation today, it is not voluntary but enforced by the events of yesterday. Moreover, in many important places across the country the isolation has begun to wear thin. Many teachers colleges have accepted more and more liberal arts content as part of their curriculum. . . .

There are no final solutions in sight—in education as little as elsewhere. There can only be good trends and harmful currents. There can be no absolute, monolithic answer to "what is needed."

To say that *only* the liberal arts, *only* the humanities, *only* the teaching of the academicians can offer salvation is as misleading as to claim that *only* vocational training or *only* the catering to "present needs" can lead us ahead. That there should be argument—heated, sometimes angry and shrill argument—between the many "schools" of education is inevitable, welcome and essential. The clashes will lead to compromise. Compromise will show the way to better, more reasonable ways of teachings.

THE DECLINE OF EDUCATIONAL PHILOSOPHY

Paul Woodring

In saying that we ought to be more sophisticated about educational problems, I do not at all mean to say that we must agree. In our pluralistic culture, full agreement on philosophical issues is neither possible nor necessary. But tolerance of diversity does not mean that any individual who aspires to leadership can be excused from the responsibility for having some firm convictions of his own, based upon evidence, clear thinking, and value judgments.

I have before me the answers to a questionnaire in which each of a group of teachers, all of whom hold master's degrees, was asked to state in his own words his philosophy of education. The answers of more than half are truly appalling. "We learn by doing," said one. "Education is life," said another. "We learn what we live," said a third, while a fourth opined that "education is

SOURCE: Paul Woodring, "The Decline of Educational Philosophy," *Phi Delta Kappan*, October, 1958. Reprinted by permission.

growth." None seemed to be able to explain what he meant by these venerable cliches and none seemed to understand that a cliche, however ancient, is not a philosophy. I assume that if one of these teachers is later asked by a citizen whether driver education is consistent with his educational philosophy, he will reply, "Education is life," and leave the questioner with his mouth hanging open. I wonder what he will reply if asked his views on racial segregation.

I hope I am making it clear that my criticism of these teachers is not that their philosophy was faulty, but that they gave no real evidence of having any philosophy. Happily, a much smaller number of those questioned were able to state their philosophy with varying degrees of clarity.

No one of us has the right to say what is the "proper" educational philosophy for American teachers; all we have a right to do is express our own views for their acceptance or rejection, using the most forceful arguments at our command. But while we cannot say what is the best philosophy, we can certainly say that some points of view are not philosophical at all. A refusal to make decisions or to organize our ideas in such a way as to reveal internal inconsistencies is not a philosophy. . . .

How much of our failure in educational philosophy can reasonably be attributed to the impact of progressive education? Many people have assumed that progressivism was a philosophy and some of the critics who have accepted this assumption have attributed all the ills of our schools to this philosophy. This, I think, is mistaken on two counts. First, because the great majority of American teachers have never accepted more than randomly selected portions of progressive education and second, because it was not, properly speaking, a philosophy at all.

WHY CAN'T WE DEAL WITH THE CRITICS?

Our failure to grapple with the philosophical problems has made us much less effective than we ought to be in dealing with the critics of the public schools, for much of recent criticism is philosophical in its import. In answering the criticisms of Bestor, Hutchins, Adler, and Mortimer Smith it is futile to content ourselves with pointing out the over-generalizations, the exaggerations, and the occasional misstatements of fact, for the intelligent reading public regards these as but minor details, even as legitimate literary devices. The important issues are philosophical, and so long as the literate public believes that the critics have a firmer philosophical base than that of the educators they will continue to lend their support to the critics.

If you wish to reply to Mortimer Adler, it will do no good to point out that Adler ignores the measurable facts of individual differences in learning capacity—though it is true that he does. It will do no good because Adler holds to a philosophical position that is prone to reject empirical evidence or at least to subordinate it to rational thought. If you wish to reply to Adler you must do it by a direct attack upon his view of the ultimate nature of man, which he holds to be everywhere and at all times the same. If you wish to undertake such a task you would be wise to make sure that your own logic is impeccable, for Adler is skilled in forensics.

If you wish to take on Bestor, a somewhat simpler but still not an easy task, you will find it futile to point out the sweeping generalizations in some of his earlier publications, for it is not these that have won him a wide following. Nor will it do much good to point out that he is biased against educators or, as he prefers to call them, "educationists," because too many of your readers share his bias. Bestor's popularity grows, in large part, from his concept that the proper role of the schools is intellectual development and that all other aims must be held in due subordination to this fundamental purpose. He holds, too, that the most effective way to develop intellectual excellence is through the academic disciplines taught as separate subjects. Of these two issues the first is clearly philosophical and the second has important philosophical overtones.

A great many intellectuals, in and out of universities, share Bestor's views on both these issues. Any educator hoping to make a successful counter-attack must come squarely to grips with them. Merely demonstrating that other goals—social, recreational, or vocational—are desirable *social* aims will not weaken the position of Bestor and other critics of recent educational trends; any effective reply must include convincing evidence that these are the proper aims of the public school and that no other agency can achieve them as well. And any effective attack on the position that intellectual development is best achieved through the separate academic disciplines must include evidence that it is best achieved in some other way with the teachers available or likely soon to become available.

The literate public is not greatly interested in the conflicts between professional educators and academic groups within the universities, but it is very much interested in the question of what is the primary purpose of institutionalized education and the question of how this purpose may best be accomplished. At the present moment in history it is prone to agree with the critics that the schools have tried to do too much, have accepted too many of the responsibilities best retained by the home, and that as a result they have neglected their fundamental responsibility.

LET'S ASK THE RIGHT QUESTIONS

Educators and their critics alike have been too much concerned with the question of whether the schools of fifty years ago achieved their academic aims better than do the schools of today. Critics are fond of trying to prove that the schools of grandfather's day had admirable aims and achieved them. The evidence does not support them, but neither does it support the view of many educators that the older schools were iniquitous institutions fit only for scorn and ridicule. Let us learn what we can from the past while resolutely facing the future. The real and important question is not whether the schools of 1900 were better or worse than those of today but whether the schools of 1958 are as good as they might be, ought to be, and can become. Children entering the first grade this fall will not yet be fifty when the year 2000 rolls around; the question is whether we are adequately preparing them for the age in which they will live.

EVERY TEACHER A PHILOSOPHER

To fill the philosophical vacuum in the schools will require that every teacher and every administrator take a more sophisticated view of the fundamental problems of education. Each teacher should have a clear idea of what he is trying to accomplish and of how his aims are related to the basic problems of reality, of truth, and of value. The secondary teacher should understand how his subject fits into the scheme of things and should understand its limitations and its relation to other subjects and other activities. Any teacher should have a clear view of the role of the school in its relation to other social institutions in order not to preempt the responsibilities of the home and the community. The administrator, even more than the teacher, should be able to interpret the role of the school to the community and to work with community leaders in re-defining that role. If he is to do this effectively he must be at least as well oriented philosophically as the most intelligent adults in the community, for his job is not that of "selling" a program but that of participating in intellectual discourse at the highest levels. . . .

The long-range solution to our problems will require that teachers on all levels, including the academic scholars in our universities, take a more knowledgeable and sophisticated view of the philosophic issues in education. Classicists, scientists, and historians, particularly those who plan to devote a large part of their time to college teaching, need the same broad orientation in fundamental educational issues as do the elementary and secondary teachers, and eventually this orientation will become a part of the preparation of college teachers. When this occurs, the tensions between professional educators and scholars in other fields will be greatly lessened, but this happy day seems a long way off because of the sad state of confusion in educational philosophy. First, we must put our own house in order.

THE POISON IN THE WELL

Rosalie Gordon

〰〰〰〰〰〰〰〰〰〰〰〰〰〰〰〰〰〰〰〰〰〰〰〰〰〰〰

. . . The largest teacher organization in America is the National Education Association. It has innumerable committees, sub-committees, state and local branches which reach into every phase of educational activity. It claims a tremendous membership among the nation's teachers and its monthly publication, the *NEA Journal,* goes regularly to each of these members. But like all mass organizations which the majority of the membership has neither the time nor the inclination to watch too closely, the NEA is pretty tightly controlled at the center by a group of officials who, if not outright leftists, could hardly be described as pro-Americans. And this has been true for many years. As early as 1934, one of these proliferating committees of the NEA made a report to the 72nd annual meeting of the NEA. It was presented by the man who subsequently became executive secretary of the NEA. This report said:

> A dying laissez-faire must be completely destroyed and all of us, including the "owners," must be subjected to a large degree of social control.

So as to leave no doubt what they meant by "social control" here is what these revolutionary souls in the National Education Association were feeding to their teacher members:

> . . . the credit agencies, the basic industries and utilities cannot be centrally planned and operated under private ownership.

What then? They would join "in creating a swift nation-wide campaign of adult education which will support President Roosevelt in taking these over and operating them at full capacity as a

---

SOURCE: Rosalie Gordon, *What's Happened to Our Schools?* (New Rochelle, N.Y.: America's Future, 1956). Reprinted by permission.

unified national system in the interest of the people." There was almost the complete blueprint for a socialist society in America, as promulgated by the National Education Association!

From that time to the present day, one after another of the revolutionary "thinkers" of Teachers College, Columbia, and their disciples appeared before the National Education Association and its sub-groups, wrote for the *NEA Journal* and other educational publications, constantly pressing on the teachers of America the need for their "new social order"—to be brought about through the public schools. This led the National Education Association into some pretty strange fields. In 1937, for instance, one of NEA's yearbooks described Earl Browder, then head of the Communist Party here, as "an able and restrained radical." The *NEA Journal* in 1945 plugged heavily a book by Henry Wallace containing his plan for government control of our lives—and declared it should be made "part of the required study of every high school and college student." In many schools it was.

Before long, teachers were getting almost no other philosophy from their professional journals and their associations than this degraded European one all dressed up in the bright tinsel of the "new social order." And as new and younger teachers appeared on the scene, coming out of many schools of education like Teachers College, where the same poisonous philosophy was fed to them, they became less and less resistant to the spreading disease.

Along with all this went the poisoning of the textbooks—not only for the students but for the teachers themselves. One of Dr. Counts' collaborators in Teachers College was Dr. Harold O. Rugg. First Dr. Rugg wrote a book for professional educators— for teachers—called "The Great Technology." In it he set forth the philosophy we have been examining above—the philosophy of the "new social order" under which a central government equipped with all-pervading powers would completely regulate our lives, taking over entirely parts of the economic system and controlling and managing the rest. Dr. Rugg told the teachers it was up to them to condition "a new public mind" to bring this about. And this conditioning must be done in the schools. The teachers must disabuse their pupils' minds of any archaic ideas they might have about our history. They must be told that the

American Revolution was not a revolt of men who wanted to be free against an all-powerful, tyrannical and tax-eating government. It was just a brawl between American "landlords" and the British nobility, and the men who led the Revolution were merely interested in their own property. The students must be taught that our free-enterprise system is a failure—it breeds poverty and inequality and the only fair system is a planned one run by the government.

But Dr. Rugg did not stop with the teachers. He wrote 14 textbooks, 14 student workbooks and 14 teacher guides and he himself boasted that this service was studied by some *5,000,000 young Americans.* Dr. Rugg, perhaps overcome by his astounding success, went a little too far. He decided to re-educate the entire population for the "new social order" and began to advocate adult education groups which would get their indoctrination from the teachers along with their children. Dr. Rugg was a bit too brash with some of his statements and thus brought himself to the attention of various patriotic citizens and groups who began to look into what he had been doing with his textbooks in the schools. So shocked were they with what they found that they succeeded in stopping the use of the Rugg textbooks in many schools.

But Dr. Counts, Dr. Rugg, Dr. William H. Kilpatrick, Dr. George W. Hartmann, Dr. Boyd H. Bode, Dr. John L. Childs—to name a few of this handful of revolutionary souls—had laid a solid groundwork for putting over their baleful system on the youth of America. The textbooks simply became more subtle— and therefore more dangerous. And as soon as a group of irate citizens here and there objected to one which praised Communist Russia too blatantly, it was replaced with another that omitted the praise of Communist Russia but plugged for all its socialist ingredients without calling them socialist.

It is possible in this limited space to give just a few examples of the type of textbooks from which more than a generation of American children have been, and are being, taught. . . .

Here's one textbook for seventh graders called *Democracy at Work.* It gets over its unnamed socialist indoctrination through simple little stories. One is called "Safeguarding Against Misfortune: Social Security." Then there are some very sad little tales about people out of work, followed by this heading: "Government to the Rescue." Another story called "Sharing the National Income" has a mythical visitor from Mars asking: "Have you Americans made any attempt to reduce poverty by redistributing your national income?" And there's even a reference list for further reading, including Harry Hopkins' "Spending to Save: The Complete Story of Relief" and Maxwell Stewart's "Social Security." Harry Hopkins, of course, was the cynical alter-ego of Franklin D. Roosevelt, who expounded the theory of "tax and tax, spend and spend, elect and elect." Maxwell Stewart is a long-time Communist-fronter who was named under oath before a Senate Committee as a Communist.

In a textbook for high school students called *Democracy and Social Policy* appears the following: "It is clear that the great majority of Americans expect the government to play a bigger role in economic affairs in the future than at any time in the past. Some persons think the efforts of government agencies should be restricted to aiding and supervising private industry, trade and finance. Others think it desirable for the government to become a partner in various kinds of economic enterprise. These differences are important. They are far less important, though, than the fact that there is a large measure of agreement that the government cannot avoid increased economic responsibility of some kind, perhaps of many kinds."

The above examples could be multiplied endlessly from textbooks on every conceivable subject in every grade from first through high school. The social revolutionaries, you must agree, have done their work well. Is it any wonder then, that a recent survey of 5,000 high school seniors throughout the United States produced the following startling results among the youngsters who expect to be the future leaders of our constitutional, free-enterprise system:

Over 60 percent believe the profit motive can be killed off without hurting the American system.

Fifty-six percent think the best way to improve our standard of living is not by workers producing more but by giving workers more wages.

Sixty percent think employees get too little and owners too much of the profits of a company.

Seventy-five percent believe that when an industry puts in new machinery, the owners get most of the gains resulting from modernization.

More than 60 percent think manufacturers can raise wages by 10 cents an hour without raising the prices of the products they make.

Is it any wonder that Dr. Oliver Carlson reported with shock overhearing a conversation among a group of high school juniors discussing their future. It went like this: "I'll get mine in two thousand three." A younger boy, with envy: "I've got to wait till two thousand and five." An older girl: "I'm the lucky one—I get mine in the year two thousand." With at least another year, and maybe five, of education ahead of them and almost a lifetime in the work-a-day world, they were avidly looking forward to the time when they could start to draw their Federal Old-Age Pensions!

WE CAN BE PROUD OF THE FACTS

Harold G. Shane

〜〜〜〜〜〜〜〜〜〜〜〜〜〜〜〜〜〜〜〜〜〜〜〜〜〜〜〜〜〜〜〜〜〜

Would you like to have some ammunition, and not be caught with that frustrated feeling, when next you hear that our children aren't learning the fundamentals? Are you interested in some evidence to explode the charge that the schools are breeding a nation of dim-wits and are brain wasting by neglecting our gifted children? Or that instead of teaching history and geography the schools teach children how to act when they go

SOURCE: Harold G. Shane, "We Can Be Proud of the Facts," *The Nation's Schools,* September, 1957. Reprinted by permission.

out on a date and call it social studies? If your answer is Yes, let's apply the rules of evidence to some of the recent derogatory statements directed at our elementary and secondary schools. Let us look at the record and substitute information for mis-information the next time a school patron says that he has read or heard that elementary schools are "too easy" on children or that our high schools have deteriorated.

Have our high school programs deteriorated? Since factual information supports a proud 50-year record in elementary educa-tion, what about the record of the American high school? It was stated recently that "the schools have retreated from modern life" because of the way they have de-emphasized science and mathematics. The speaker, an articulate and ardent proponent of a return to "basic education," contended that the percentage of high school students taking science and mathematics had declined from approximately 85 percent to about 55 percent since 1900.[1] These figures are a beautiful illustration of how information, taken out of context, can be used to support a faulty argument.

As I write, I have before me recent official records from the U.S. Department of Health, Education, and Welfare.[2] These reports show, in round numbers, that 400,000 children were taking science and mathematics courses at the turn of the cen-tury out of a total population of 75,603,000. Fifty years later, while our population increased by some 100 percent, the number of high school students enrolled in science had increased by 600 percent and mathematics class enrollments had grown by 900 percent.

Bear in mind that this tremendous gain was registered during a period nearly all our children had an opportunity to go into

[1] Mary Stewart, "The Leisure Activities of Grammar School Pupils," *British Journal of Educational Psychology*, Vol. 20, February, 1950, pp. 11–34.

[2] A. R. Williams, "The Magazine Reading of Secondary School Children," *British Journal of Educational Psychology*, Vol. 21, November, 1951, pp. 186–198; Arthur Bestor, "We Are Less Educated Than 50 Years Ago," *U.S. News and World Report*, Vol. 41, November 30, 1956, pp. 68–82; U.S. Department of Health, Education, and Welfare, "Offerings and Enrollments in Science and Mathematics in Public High Schools," (Washington, D.C.: Government Printing Office, 1956), pp. 24. Supplementary population figures cited are from the Biennial Survey of Education (1950–52) also issued by the Government Printing Office.

high school, not merely the children of the socially or economically privileged. The schools certainly have not "retreated" when
today from six to nine times as many of our intellectually competent boys and girls are taking science and mathematics courses
as were taking these courses at the century's turn.

Are languages being ignored? The status of foreign language
teaching also has been viewed with alarm by the proponents of
"fundamental" education. Here, again, the story is an interesting
one. According to the careful records of the Modern Language
Association, there was a 400-percent increase at the elementary
level in the teaching of a second language in Grade 6 and below
in a recent three-year (1951–54) period.[3] By 1957 the total number of young children engaged in foreign language study hovered
near the 400,000 mark. At the high school level the number of
pupils studying one of the four major languages most commonly
offered (Spanish, Latin, French, and German) had increased
threefold while the U.S. population has merely doubled.[4] The
number of children taking high school Spanish, for instance, was
too small to be recorded by the Office of Education in 1900;
about a half million students are now enrolled.

Latin class enrollments have proportionately kept pace with
the national population increase, and 10 children take French
today for every one who studied it in 1900.[5] Only German language teaching has shown a net decline, and this is traceable
in part to an antipathy to all things Germanic during two World
Wars. During these periods some schools dropped the language
in response to public demand. . . .

Does public education cost too much? One of the proudest
achievements of our public schools is the way they have given
the public its increasingly high level of pupil achievement *at
increasingly lower cost!* A typical misrepresentation of the cost
of education appeared in a recent article, circulated among businessmen. The writer pointed out that ". . . we are now spending
three times as large a part of our national income, *after war*

---

[3] K. W. Mildenberger, *The Status of Foreign Language Teaching in
American Elementary Schools* (Washington, D.C., U.S. Department of
Health, Education, and Welfare, 1955).

[4] U.S. Office of Education: *Biennial Survey of Education* (1948–50).

[5] *Ibid.*

costs, on education than [sic] we did in 1900." [6] The catch is the phrase *after war costs.*

Actually, the proportion of our national income spent on education has averaged approximately 3 percent for many years and has shown little significant variation for decades. Yet the proportionate number of students has greatly increased. In 1900, there were 699,403 students in our high schools. In 1956 there were 8,472,478! We now educate 12 or 13 children at the high school level for every one enrolled in 1900, yet the percentage of income invested in their education remains identical.

What do report cards report? The charge has often been made by critics that schools have disregarded parental opinion by dropping the ABC type of marking system on report cards. This point is cited as an example to prove that the public isn't getting what it wants from the schools. Let's explode this myth!

In the first place, most high schools and virtually all universities and colleges continue to use grades of the ABC type, a fact many critics ignore. Even at the elementary school level traditional report cards are the rule. A student in one of my classes polled the 15 largest cities in his midwestern state and found that all but one of these school systems still used ABC grades, even at the elementary level. As a further check I polled 35 suburban school systems noted for their distinguished educational programs. In Grade 6 and below a substantial majority of my replies stated that ABC grades (which are sometimes coupled with parent conferences) were currently in use!

In the second place, there is reason seriously to doubt that parents really want ABC type grades. Recently I asked 700 Chicago area parents what they most wanted to know about their child in elementary school. Most of them wanted to be assured that he is an effective human being and that he is getting along well with other children. Only about one parent in three was primarily interested in grades. In short, the hubbub raised about marks in school not only conceals the fact that most schools still have ABC grading systems, but ignores the fact that many parents probably want to know more about their children than a grade of "C" or "A" reveals. . . .

[6] Roger A. Freeman, "Dollars and Sense in Education," The Civic Federation, Bulletin 498, November, 1956, p. 3.

Does education lack purpose? It sees fitting to close this review of the reassuring achievements of our public schools with a passing glance at the fuzziest of the critcisms they have received. "The schools have lost their purpose," it has been alleged, because "unessential activities are squeezing out the basic subjects."

Enrollment trends and test scores, previously mentioned, clearly show that relatively more children are taking basic subjects today than in the past, and that the individual child (despite the one year decrease in his age in a given grade) is learning more subject matter than ever before. Obviously, the schools have not defaulted on their academic goals. But are the schools doing more than merely passing along the best in our cultural heritage? Are they preserving and extending moral values? The answer is a resounding Yes, and the evidence is abundant.

The products of our educational system are, with each passing decade, demonstrating our growing maturity as a nation. They are making real the American dream that human beings can live together with dignity and self-respect.

In 50 years the integrity of our country has stood firm through many harsh tests. In depression and war the graduates of our schools and colleges have proved that, while a few of us may be petty or mean, the average American is someone to be proud of. He has shown vision that lifts him above himself. He is friendly and basically respectful to others, but he has proved he can and will fight in every quarter of the globe for the things in which he believes. The typical product of our educational system may occasionally be misdirected or misinformed, but in the long run he stands for what proves to be right.

These qualities are no happy accident. They have been fostered and strengthened by the objectives of our schools which, like home and church, are the repository of the ideals that make up the American dream of a better world. Truly, we have more often succeeded than failed as a people, and a substantial measure of credit for this success is due to the effectiveness of public education.

MODERN EDUCATION AND ITS CRITICS

Sidney Hook

Another type of criticism goes further than that so far considered. It underlines current strictures against modern education but is not content with a return merely to the conventional models. It substitutes a comprehensive conception of education —new in form but perennial in essence—to guide the remolding of our educational institutions. This conception, whose banner bearer is Mr. Hutchins, has been worked out in detail for liberal education of a specific kind—the only kind there is, we are assured—on the college level. The curriculum of the elementary and high schools is to be reorganized in such a way as to make this kind of liberal education possible for all students.

This view, whose most recent expression is found in *Conflicts in Education* (N.Y. 1953), is frankly and proudly nonempirical. It makes great play with deductions from axiomatic first principles and proposes to do what I have tried to show cannot be done, viz., validly to derive a desirable educational program from metaphysical premises.

Here I wish only to analyze some of the leading assumptions behind his position. The first assumption concerns the ends of education and how they are derived. The second concerns the curricular means by which these ends are to be achieved. The third, and most important, concerns the claim that to deny the adequacy of Mr. Hutchins' curricular means involves a denial of the democratic philosophy itself.

That the *central* aim of education should be the development of man's power of thought is, so far as I know, denied by nobody

---

SOURCE: "Modern Education and Its Critics," by Sidney Hook. Seventh Yearbook of the American Association of Colleges for Teacher Education, Oneonta, New York, 1954, pp. 141–143.

—provided we do not identify power of thought with a specific intellectual skill. But, whereas most educators justify the emphasis on thought because of its key role in the organization of impulse and feeling, the control of action, and the enrichment of the meanings of experience even when we cannot act, Mr. Hutchins derives it from a definition of man's fixed and essential nature.

Man is a rational animal. He is uniquely different from other animals by virtue of his power to think. Therefore, education must be directed exclusively to the cultivation of his intellect.

Now there are several things wrong with the deduction. First, even if we deny that other animals can think—and not all psychologists agree with this—the power to think is not the only differentiating feature of the human animal. There are other differentiating features. Man is the only animal who makes his tools. Man is the only animal with a sense of humor. If we were to derive our educational aims from these differentia, we should have to say that man's education must primarily be vocational or technological or that it must develop his power to crack jokes.

Second, the nature of a thing is not completely given by what differentiates it. It includes what it has in common with other species in its genus. Man is a creature of emotion, an organism which adapts to and modifies its environment. An education appropriate to the nature of man must be appropriate to the *whole* of man's nature. This would include some things which Mr. Hutchins excludes. The Greeks, whom Mr. Hutchins takes as his model, regarded the end of education, not exclusively intellectual development, but the harmonious development of all human faculties. For them a life of reason is no more identical with a reasoning life than a joy of life is identical with a life of joy.

Third, what do we mean by thought? Modern education, to the extent that it is inspired by Dewey, interprets it broadly as creative intelligence in the solution of problems which arise in *all* fields of human experience. But Mr. Hutchins seems to identify thought or reason with academic intellectuality, with verbal skills in the interpretation of texts.

This deductive approach from fallible first principles is carried over into discussion of the curriculum of education. Since by definition all men have a common nature, the education appropriate to that nature must be common, and the means of achieving it—the educational curriculum—must be common. Therefore education everywhere, at all times, and for all men (and women), must be the same. Contrast this with modern education which, not by deduction but by inquiry, discovers that men have a great many needs in common and yet vary greatly, that their differences in culture and time reflect themselves in the way their common needs are fulfilled, and that even in the same culture variations among them are appreciable. It therefore stresses the fact that their indisputable common need—the development of intelligence—may be achieved in different ways.

An analogy might make the point clearer. Everyone needs to be healthy. What it means to be healthy, i.e., the *definition* of health, is the same for all men. We might even concede that the *formal* requirements of a well-balanced diet necessary for health are the same for all men. But who will therefore deduce that all men must eat the same things at the same time, or exercise in the same way, in order to be healthy? If there are differences among men, if they live in different climates and must perform different tasks, to prescribe a *common* dietary regimen is to guarantee that not all of them will be healthy. Just as there are different dietary roads to health, so there are different curricular roads to educational maturity. Great segments of these roads, of course, will be common. . . .

Accused in the past of advocating an education irrelevant, if not hostile, to the needs of men in a democratic society, Mr. Hutchins is now contending that only those who agree with his conception of the best education can be considered consistent democrats. To have "strong faith in the political judgment of the masses with strong doubts of their intellectual capacities," i.e., of their intellectual capacities to acquire the best education, writes Mr. Hutchins, is a paradox. And in criticism of those who penned the report of the President's Commission on Education he says, "They most undemocratically assume that the mass of people are incapable of achieving such an education. . . ."

What Mr. Hutchins is really saying is this: either accept the rule of an élite or of intellectual experts and give up democracy or admit that the masses are all potential intellectual experts in a democracy and educate them to be experts. But it is not necessary to be an expert to judge the basic policies proposed by experts. One can choose his doctor wisely without a medical education. It is Mr. Hutchins who is inconsistent here. For, in addressing his appeal for the reform of education to the community, he himself admits that wise educational decisions may be made by those who are not educational experts or who have not been nurtured on the great books. If there are any experts in the wisdom of life, they cannot be mass produced by the same education. It is one thing to say that a healthy democracy rests upon some kind of common education. It is quite another to say that *all* education in a democracy must be common. And it is still something else again to assert that the content of a common education must be unchanging and identical in every respect. . . .

One final word. Modern education will always be on the defensive if it waits for criticisms from those who are hostile to its philosophy before facing its problems and correcting its defects. It is the modern educators themselves who should be the foremost critics of modern education.

Historical Foundations of Secondary Education

~~~~~~

"The understanding of the past," wrote John Dewey, "is the key to the understanding of the present."

The confusion and conflict which was discussed in the previous chapter is related to the fact that the concept of universal secondary education, as it is presently understood, was in an embryonic state prior to the twentieth century.

The first institution in American educational history deserving of the title "secondary school" was the Latin Grammar School, which enrolled students from ages seven through fourteen. Transplanted from England to the New England colonies in 1635, with its roots in Western European culture, this institution was essentially a college preparatory school, training selected boys for college, where they would become ministers and leaders in the early colonial theocracy. The curriculum of the Latin Grammar School emphasized the mastery of the classical languages. Because instruction was concentrated on the form rather than the substance of humanistic studies, the Latin Grammar School did not continue as the accepted pattern of secondary education beyond the colonial period. However, it was a part of England's

51

educational legacy to her errant colonies that education beyond the rudiments of Bible reading (as established by the early laws of Massachusetts) was essential for the development of the leadership necessary for colonial government.

The equalitarian and utilitarian spirit of eighteenth century America demanded that a new type of school be founded. In 1751 Benjamin Franklin proposed the establishment of the Academy, which broke from the traditions of the Latin Grammar School but continued to provide a Latin or classical curriculum as well as an expanded course of studies that included the teaching of English. Colonists insisted that the curriculum also include functional subjects (agriculture, navigation, and mechanics), which would enable them to cope more readily with the problems of a budding mercantile nation. They were also beginning to demand that these schools serve the middle class, that there be similar education for girls, and that these institutions be supported from public contributions. Finally they looked upon the Academy as the second phase of educational training based upon prior elementary school experience.

The Academies flourished; by 1859 they numbered more than 6,085. The contributions they made to the advancement of secondary education were many. Through them the concept of liberal education was introduced. Many of the teachers who taught in the elementary schools were trained there. However, the Academy did not fulfill its initial promise and began to decline after the Civil War. Even though functional subjects were listed in the curriculum, moral and intellectual instruction took precedence over them. In addition, the teachers in the Academies were unable to interpret effectively the multiple aims of the curriculum in the classroom. Finally the forces for social and political change in the nineteenth century contended that the control of secondary education should rest in the hands of local public officials rather than private or semiprivate administrators.

The factors which led to the American common or elementary school also affected the secondary school. The Academy because of its tendency toward exclusiveness and appeal to the middle class was subjected to attack by the advocates of a more democratic institution that would offer education to those children of the mercantile and mechanic class. Some of this opposition was expressed in the Massachusetts Law of 1827, which became the model for other similar state laws. As a result of this public opposition the Boston English Classical School was established in 1821 and three years later was renamed the English High School. At first this institution was thought of as a publicly supported Academy, an extension of the elementary school, and not as a competitor to the private Latin Grammar School.

The growth of the public high school was slow; in 1851 only a total of three hundred such institutions were functioning in some eighty cities. Before the high school was to become a permanent part of the American educational dream, it had to emerge victorious from its battle with the semiprivate Academy. There were those who opposed public support on financial grounds and others who could not yet envision the high school as an extension of the elementary school system. Supported by the Kalamazoo Decision, the concept of a universal public secondary school system did develop, in direct contrast to the selected secondary system practiced in Europe. By 1890 there were 2,526 public high schools in operation compared to 1,632 private high schools. The structural organization which has evolved permitted and demanded that every American boy or girl attend public school from the elementary through the secondary grades.

In the early part of the twentieth century, industrial, agricultural, and other vocational groups began to look to the public schools for assistance in training students for employment in an expanding industrial America. Further, schools were expected to assume responsibility for citizenship training and those functions usually associated with home and family. The major educational document that most clearly represents the tendency of Americans to react to the demands of a dynamic society was the Seven Cardinal Principles. In a larger sense the Progressive Education movement which followed was an effort to reconcile education with the problems or impact of the new urban industrialization of America.

What has been learned from this perusal of the history of secondary education? Subsequent chapters will reexamine the nature of the secondary curriculum and its ability to reflect effectively the societal demands put upon it. Acceptance of each major development in secondary education was neither wholehearted nor immediate. Even though certain educational milestones have been stressed in this historical review, it must not be assumed that all the issues have been settled. Should all secondary youth be educated? Should the high school respond to the pressures of the times? Should there be compulsory secondary education? Should all citizens be taxed for the support of the public secondary school? Should the parents of parochial youth be reimbursed or exempted from such taxation? Should the schools assume responsibility for the total education of high school students?

THE LATIN GRAMMAR SCHOOL

Elwood P. Cubberley

This ancient and venerable institution, so intimately connected with the early history of Boston, and of its learned men in generations that are past, seems to demand a moment's pause: *Res ipsa hortari videtur, quoniam de moribus civitatis tempus admonuit, supra repetere, ac, paucis, instituta majorum disserere.* It is grateful to look back on the picture of primitive, but enlightened simplicity exhibited in the early history of New England, and to arrest, as far as possible, the progress of decay by which its already indistinct lines are rapidly fading from our view.

*   *   *

The whole school house in School Street is now appropriated

SOURCE: Elwood P. Cubberley, *Readings in the History of Education* (Boston: Houghton Mifflin Company, 1920). Reprinted by permission.

to this school. The last catalogue contains *two hundred and twenty-five* scholars. These are distributed into six separate apartments, under the care of the same number of instructors; viz. a Principal, or head master, a sub-master, and four assistants. For admission, boys must be at least nine years old, able to read correctly and with fluency, and to write running hand; they must know all the stops, marks, and abbreviations, and have sufficient knowledge of English Grammar to parse common sentences in prose. The time of admission is the Friday and Saturday next preceding the Commencement at Cambridge, which two days are devoted to the examination of candidates. The regular course of instruction lasts five years; and the school is divided into five classes, according to the time of entrance.

When a class has entered, the boys commence the Latin Grammar all together, under the eye of the principal, where they continue until he has become in some degree acquainted with their individual characters and capacities. As they change their places at each recitation, those boys will naturally rise to the upper part of the class who are most industrious or who learn with the greatest facility. After a time a division of from twelve to fifteen boys is taken off from the upper end of the class; after a few days more, another division is in like manner taken off; and so on, till the whole class is separated into divisions of equal number; it having been found that from twelve to fifteen is the most convenient number *to drill* together.

In this way boys of like capacities are put together, and the evil of having some unable to learn the lesson which others get in half the time allowed is in some measure obviated. The class, thus arranged for the year, is distributed among the assistant teachers, a division to each . . . as writing is not taught in the school, the younger classes for the first two or three years are dismissed at eleven o'clock, an hour before school is done, that they may attend a writing school. . . .

* * *

Thus we have endeavored to give a view of the means, provided at the public expense, for the gratuitous instruction of the children of all classes of the citizens of Boston. They are offered equally to all. The poorest inhabitant may have his children instructed from the age of four to seventeen, at schools, some of which are already equal, if not *superior* to any private schools in our country; and *all* of them may be made so.

Indeed if a child be kept at a Primary School from four to seven, and then at one of the Grammar Schools until nine, and from that time till seventeen at the Latin, and the English Classical School, there is no question but he will go through a more *thorough* and *complete* course of instruction, and in *reality* enjoy greater advantages than are provided at many of the respectable colleges in the Union.

PROPOSALS RELATING TO THE EDUCATION OF YOUTH IN PENNSYLVANIA—PHILADELPHIA: PRINTED IN THE YEAR MDCCXLIX

Benjamin Franklin

ADVERTISEMENT TO THE READER

It has long been regretted as a misfortune to the youth of this province that we have no ACADEMY in which they might receive the accomplishments of a regular education. The following paper

SOURCE: Benjamin Franklin, "Proposals Relating to the Education of Youth in Pennsylvania, 1749. Reprinted by permission of the publishers from Robert Ulich, editor, *Three Thousand Years of Educational Wisdom: Selections from Great Documents,* Cambridge, Mass.: Harvard University Press, Copyright 1947, 1954, by the President and Fellows of Harvard College.

of hints toward forming a plan for that purpose is so far approved by some public-spirited gentlemen, to whom it has been privately communicated, that they have directed a number of copies to be made by the press and properly distributed in order to obtain the sentiments and advice of men of learning, understanding, and experience in these matters, and have determined to use their interest and best endeavors to have the scheme, when completed, carried gradually into execution, in which they have reason to believe they shall have the hearty concurrence and assistance of many who are wellwishers to their country. Those who incline to favor the design with their advice, either as to the parts of learning to be taught, the order of study, the method of teaching, the economy of the school, or any other matter of importance to the success of the undertaking, are desired to communicate their sentiments as soon as may be, by letter directed to B. Franklin, Printer, in Philadelphia.

PROPOSALS

The good education of youth has been esteemed by wise men in all ages as the surest foundation of the happiness both of private families and of commonwealths. Almost all governments have therefore made it a principal object of their attention to establish and endow with proper revenues such seminaries of learning as might supply the succeeding age with men qualified to serve the public with honor to themselves and to their country.

Many of the first settlers of these provinces were men who had received a good education in Europe, and to their wisdom and good management we owe much of our present prosperity. But their hands were full, and they could not do all things. The present race are not thought to be generally of equal ability; for though the American youth are allowed not to want capacity, yet the best capacities require cultivation, it being truly with them, as with the best ground, which unless well tilled and sowed with profitable seed, produces only ranker weeds.

That we may obtain the Advantages arising from an increase of knowledge, and prevent as much as may be the mischievous consequences that would attend a general ignorance among us, the following hints are offered toward forming a plan for the education of the youth of *Pennsylvania.*

It is proposed:

That some persons of leisure and public spirit apply for a charter by which they may be incorporated, with power to erect an academy for the education of youth, to govern the same, provide masters, make rules, receive donations, purchase lands, etc., and to add to their number, from time to time such other persons as they shall judge suitable.

That the members of the corporation make it their pleasure, and in some degree their business, to visit the academy often, encourage and countenance the youth, countenance and assist the masters, and by all means in their power advance the usefulness and reputation of the design; that they look on the students as in some sort their children, treat them with familiarity and affection, and, when they have behaved well, and gone through their studies, and are to enter the world, zealously unite and make all the interest that can be made to establish them, whether in business, offices, marriages, or any other thing for their advantage, preferably to all other persons whatsoever even of equal merit.

And if men may, and frequently do, catch such a taste for cultivating flowers, for planting, grafting, inoculating, and the like, as to despise all other amusements for their sake, why may not we expect they should acquire a relish for that *more useful* culture of young minds. Thompson says:

> 'Tis Joy to see the human Blossoms blow,
> When infant Reason grows apace, and calls
> For the kind Hand of an assiduous Care.
> Delightful Task! to rear the tender Thought,
> To teach the young Idea how to shoot;
> To pour the fresh Instruction o'er the Mind,
> To breathe th' enliv'ning Spirit, and to fix
> The generous Purpose in the glowing Breast.

That a house be provided for the academy, if not in the town, not many miles from it, the situation high and dry, and if it may be, not far from a river, having a garden, orchard, meadow, and a field or two.

That the house be furnished with a library (if in the country; if in the town, the town libraries may serve) with maps of all countries, globes, some mathematical instruments, an apparatus for experiments in natural philosophy, and for mechanics; prints of all kinds, prospects, buildings, machines, etc.

That the rector be a man of good understanding, good morals, diligent and patient, learned in the languages and sciences, and a correct pure speaker and writer of the English tongue, and to have such tutors under him as shall be necessary.

That the boarding scholars diet together, plainly, temperately, and frugally.

That, to keep them in health, and to strengthen and render active their bodies, they be frequently exercised in running, leaping, wrestling, and swimming, etc.

That they have peculiar habits to distinguish them from other youth, if the academy be in or near the town; for this, among other reasons, that their behavior may be the better observed.

PHILLIPS ANDOVER ACADEMY IS CHARTERED, 1780

Acts and Laws of Massachusetts

Whereas, the education of youth has ever been considered by the wise and good as an object of the highest consequence to the safety and happiness of a people; as at that period the mind easily receives and retains impressions, is formed with peculiar advantage to piety and virtue, and directed to the pursuit of the most useful knowledge; and, whereas the Honorable Samuel

SOURCE: *Acts and Laws of Massachusetts*, 1780.

Phillips of Andover, in the County of Essex, Esq., and the Honorable John Phillips of Exeter, in the County of Rockingham, and State of New Hampshire, Esq., on the first day of April, in the year of our Lord one thousand seven hundred and seventy-eight, by a legal instrument of that date, gave, granted, and assigned to the Honorable William Phillips, Esq., and others, therein named, and to their heirs, divers lots and parcels of land, in said Instrument described, as well as certain other estate, to the use and upon the trust following, namely, that the rents, profits, and interest thereof, be forever laid out and expended by the Trustees in the said Instrument named, for the support of a Public Free School or Academy, in the town of Andover: and, whereas the execution of the generous and important design of the grantors aforesaid will be attended with very great embarrassments, unless, by an act of incorporation, the Trustees, mentioned in the said Instrument, and their successors, shall be authorized to commence and prosecute actions at law, and transact such other matters in their corporate capacity, as the interest of the said Academy shall require.

ACADEMY ESTABLISHED

Be it therefore enacted by the Council and the House of Representatives in General Court assembled, and by the authorship of the same, that there be and hereby is established in the Town of Andover, and County of Essex, an Academy, by the name of *Phillips Academy*, for the purpose of promoting piety and virtue, and for the education of youth, in the English, Latin, and Greek languages, together with Writing, Arithmetic, Music, and the Art of Speaking; also practical Geometry, Logic and Geography, and such other of the liberal Arts and Sciences, or Languages, as opportunity may hereafter permit, and as the Trustees, hereinafter provided, shall direct.

❅   ❅   ❅

THE ESTABLISHMENT OF THE FIRST AMERICAN HIGH SCHOOL

Report of the School Committee to the Town Meeting of Boston

~~~~~~

Though the present system of public education, and the munificence with which it is supported, are highly beneficial and honorable to the town; yet, in the opinion of the Committee, it is susceptible of a greater degree of perfection and usefulness, without materially augmenting the weight of the public burdens. Till recently, our system occupied a middle station: it neither commenced with the rudiments of Education nor extended to the higher branches of knowledge. This system was supported by the Town at a very great expense, and to be admitted to its advantages, certain preliminary qualifications were required at individual cost, which have the effect of excluding many children of the poor and unfortunate classes of the community from the benefits of a public education. The Town saw and felt this inconsistency in the plan, and have removed the defect by providing Schools (Primary) in which the children of the poor can be fitted for admission into the public seminaries.

The present system, in the opinion of the Committee, requires still further amendment. The studies that are pursued at the English grammar schools are merely elementary, and more time than is necessary is devoted to their acquisition. A scholar is admitted at seven, and is dismissed at fourteen years of age; thus, seven years are expended in the acquisition of a degree of knowledge, which with ordinary diligence and a common capacity, may be easily and perfectly acquired in five. If then, a boy remain the

---

SOURCE: Report of the School Committee to the Town Meeting of Boston, "The Establishment of the First American High School," January, 1821.

usual term, a large portion of the time will have been idly or uselessly expended, as he may have learned all that he may have been taught long before its expiration. This loss of time occurs at that interesting and critical period of life, when the habits and inclinations are forming by which the future character will be fixed and determined. This evil, therefore, should be removed, by enlarging the present system, not merely that the time now lost may be saved, but that those early habits of industry and application may be acquired, which are so essential in leading to a future life of virtue and usefulness.

Nor are these the only existing evils. The mode of education now adopted, and the branches of knowledge that are taught at our English grammar schools, are not sufficiently extensive nor otherwise calculated to bring the powers of the mind into operation nor to qualify a youth to fill usefully and respectably many of those stations, both public and private, in which he may be placed. A parent who wishes to give a child an education that shall fit him for active life, and shall serve as a foundation for eminence in his profession, whether Mercantile or Mechanical, is under the necessity of giving him a different education from any which our public schools can now furnish. Hence, many children are separated from their parents and sent to private academies in this vicinity, to acquire that instruction which cannot be obtained at the public seminaries. Thus, many parents, who contribute largely to the support of these institutions, are subjected to heavy expense for the same object, in other towns.

The Committee, for these and many other weighty considerations that might be offered, and in order to render the present system of public education more nearly perfect, are of the opinion that an additional School is required. They therefore recommend the founding of a seminary which shall be called the English Classical School, and submit the following as a general outline of a plan for its organization and of the course of studies to be pursued.

1st. That the term of time for pursuing the course of studies proposed be three years.

2ndly. That the School be divided into three classes, and one year be assigned to the studies of each class.

3rdly. That the age of admission be not less than twelve years.

4thly. That the School be for Boys exclusively.

5thly. That candidates for admission be proposed on a given day annually; but scholars with suitable qualifications may be admitted at any intermediate time to an advanced standing.

6thly. That candidates for admission shall be subject to a strict examination, in such manner as the School Committee may direct, to ascertain their qualifications according to these rules.

7thly. That it be required of every candidate, to qualify him for admission, that he be well acquainted with reading, writing English grammar in all its branches, and arithmetic as far as simple proportion.

8thly. That it be required of the Masters and Ushers, as a necessary qualification, that they shall have been regularly educated at some University.

First Class: Composition; reading from the most approved authors; exercises in criticism, comprising critical analyses of the language, grammar, and style of the best English authors, their errors and beauties; Declamation; Geography; Arithmetic continued.

Second Class: Composition, Reading, Exercises in Criticism, Declamation; Algebra; Ancient and Modern History and Chronology; Logic; Geometry; Plane Trigonometry, and its application to mensuration of heights and distances; Navigation; Surveying; Mensuration of Surfaces and Solids; Forensic Discussions.

Third Class: Composition; Exercises in Criticism; Declamation; Mathematics; Logic; History, particularly that of the United States; Natural Philosophy, including Astronomy; Moral and Political Philosophy.

THE ENGLISH CLASSICAL SCHOOL (IN 1824 RENAMED AS THE ENGLISH HIGH SCHOOL)

The System of Education Pursued at the Free Schools in Boston

Public opinion and the wants of a large class of citizens of this town have long been calling for a school in which those, who have either not the desire or the means of obtaining a classical education, might receive instruction in many branches of great practical importance which have usually been taught only at the Colleges. This led to the establishment of the English Classical School.

This school was established by a vote of the town in 1820, expressly for the purpose of affording to lads, intending to become merchants or mechanics, better means of instruction than were provided at any of the public schools. A large building was erected, in a central part of the town, and an appropriation made of $2500, to furnish a philosophical apparatus. It was provided that there should be four instructors, viz. one Principal, one Sub-master, and two Ushers. A plan was reported for the studies of the course, including three years. This, however, was only an outline, and intended for the general guidance, rather than the particular direction of the instructors, as to the order in which the studies should be introduced, and the time which should be devoted to each. The instructors, accordingly, while they have adhered to the general intention, have, with the concurrence of the school committee, deviated from the plan in the disposition of the studies, and have introduced some studies not originally included.

The school went into operation in May, 1821; since which

source: The System of Education Pursued at the Free Schools in Boston, "The English Classical School," Boston, 1823.

time, one hundred and seventy-six boys have been admitted, of which number nearly one hundred are now in the school. The annual examination for admission is in August.

For admission, boys are examined in those branches which are taught at the Grammar schools, viz. Reading, Writing, English Grammar, and Arithmetic; and, as they are allowed to remain in the Grammar schools until fourteen, none are admitted to this school under twelve. Fourteen was fixed as the other limit, but it was found that this would operate unjustly on those boys who were just fourteen, and this had consequently not been strictly insisted on.

As there are many lads who cannot continue at school during a complete course, nor even remain long after they have become able to do something for their own support, it is desirable to arrange the studies in such a manner that those branches should fall in the first year, which are of the most essential importance. The course for the first year includes Intellectual and Written Arithmetic, Geography and the use of the Globes, exercises in Grammar, General History, and History of the United States, Book-keeping by single entry, Elements of some Arts and Sciences, Composition and Declamation. That for the second and third year embraces Geometry, Algebra, Trigonometry and its applications, Book-keeping by double entry, various branches of Natural Philosophy, Natural History, Chemistry, Moral Philosophy and Natural Theology, Rhetoric, Evidences of Christianity, Intellectual Philosophy, Political Economy, and Logic.

* * *

The establishment of this school forms an era in the history of Free Education in Boston. Its present high reputation and growing importance, while they render it an object of increasing interest, promise extensive and lasting utility; and furnish a gratifying proof of the wisdom of that policy which brings forward to places of high responsibility *young men of* talents and learning, who have a reputation and fortune to gain.

THE FIRST PUBLIC HIGH SCHOOL LAW IN THE UNITED STATES, 1827

Laws of Massachusetts

~~~~~~

Be it enacted, That each town or district within this Common-
wealth, containing fifty families, or householders, shall be provided with a teacher or teachers, of good morals, to instruct
children in orthography, reading, writing, English grammar,
geography, arithmetic, and good behavior, for such term of time
as shall be equivalent to six months for one school in each year;
and every town or district containing one hundred families or
householders, shall be provided with such teacher or teachers,
for such term of time as shall be equivalent to eighteen months,
for one school in each year. In every city, town, or district, containing five hundred families, or householders shall be provided
with such teacher or teachers for such term of time as shall be
equivalent to twenty-four months, shall also be provided with a
master of good morals, competent to instruct, in addition to the
branches of learning aforesaid, in the history of the United States,
bookkeeping by single entry, geometry, surveying, algebra; and
shall employ such master to instruct a school in such city, town,
or district, for the benefit of all the inhabitants thereof, at least
ten months in each year, exclusive of vacations, in such convenient places, or alternately at such places in such city, town,
or district, as said inhabitants, at their meeting in March, or
April, annually, shall determine; and in every city, or town, and

SOURCE: *Laws of Massachusetts,* January Session, 1827, Chapter XCLIII,
The First Public High School Law in the United States, 1827. In spite
of its mandatory provisions, this legislation was not well enforced until
the time of Horace Mann, who became Secretary of the State Board of
Education in 1837. See B. A. Hinsdale, *Horace Mann and the Common
School Revival in the United States;* also G. H. Martin, *The Evolution
of the Massachusetts Public School System.*

district, containing four thousand inhabitants, such master shall be competent in addition to all the foregoing branches, to instruct the Latin and Greek languages, history, rhetoric, and logic.

THIS WRETCHED MOCKERY OF EDUCATION IN MASSACHUSETTS, 1824

James G. Carter

~~~~~~

The pilgrims of Plymouth set the first example not only to our own country, but to the civilized world, of a system of free schools, at which were educated together, not by compulsion, but from mutual choice, all classes of the community—the high, the low, the rich, and the poor—a system, by which the state so far assumed the education of the youth, as to make all property responsible for the support of common schools for the instruction of all children. This institution was indeed the foster child, and has justly been the pride, of Massachusetts and of New England. Its influences were strong, and they still are strong, upon the moral and political character of the people. . . .

If the policy of the legislature in regard to free schools for the last twenty years be not changed, the institution which has been the glory of New England will, in twenty years more, be extinct. If the State continue to relieve itself of the trouble of providing for the instruction of the whole people, and to shift the responsibility upon the towns, and the towns upon the districts, and the districts upon individuals, each will take care of himself and

SOURCE: James G. Carter, "Essays on Popular Education." Given in *Old South Leaflets,* VI, No. 135, pp. 201, 220.

his own family as he is able, and as he appreciates the blessing of a good education. The rich will, as a class, have much better instruction than they now have, while the poor will have much worse or none at all. The academies and private schools will be carried to much greater perfection than they have been, while the public free schools will become stationary or retrograde, till at length they will be thrown for support upon the gratuitous and of course capricious and uncertain efforts of individuals; and then, like the lower schools of the crowded cities of Europe, they will soon degenerate into mere mechanical establishments, such as the famous *seminaries* of London, Birmingham, and Manchester, of which we hear so much lately, not for rational, moral, and intellectual instruction of human beings, but for training young animals to march, sing, and draw figures in sand—establishments in which the power of one man is so prodigiously multiplied that he can overlook, direct, and control the intellectual exercises of a thousand! And this wretched mockery of education they must be right glad to accept as a charity instead of inheriting as their birthright as good instruction as the country affords.

THE FIRST COMPULSORY SCHOOL LAW IN THE

UNITED STATES, 1852

Acts and Resolves Passed by the General Court of Massachusetts in the Year 1852

~~~~~~

AN ACT CONCERNING THE ATTENDANCE OF CHILDREN AT SCHOOL

Be it enacted by the Senate and House of Representatives in General Court assembled, and by the authority of the same, as follows:

Sect. 1. Every person who shall have any child under his control, between the ages of eight and fourteen years, shall send such child to some public school within the town or city in which he resides, during at least twelve weeks, if the public schools within such town or city shall be so long kept, in each and every year during which such child shall be under his control, six weeks of which shall be consecutive.

Sect. 2. Every person who shall violate the provisions of the first section of this act shall forfeit, to the use of such town or city, a sum not exceeding twenty dollars, to be recovered by complaint or indictment.

Sect. 3. It shall be the duty of the school committee in the several towns or cities to inquire into all cases of violation of the

---

SOURCE: *Acts and Resolves Passed by the General Court of Massachusetts in the Year 1852,* "The First Compulsory School Law in the United States, 1852," pp. 170–171. By an act of 1850 the General Court had given authority to cities and towns of Massachusetts "to make any needful provisions and arrangements concerning habitual truants and children not attending school, without any regular and lawful occupation, growing up in ignorance, between the ages of six and sixteen. . . ." *Acts and Resolves Passed by the General Court of Massachusetts in the Year 1850,* pp. 468–469.

first section of this act, and to ascertain of the persons violating the same, the reasons, if any, for such violation, and they shall report such cases, together with such reasons, if any, to the town or city in their annual report; but they shall not report any cases such as are provided for by the fourth section of this act.

Sect. 4. If, upon inquiry by the school committee, it shall appear, or if upon the trial of any complaint or indictment under this act it shall appear, that such child has attended some school, not in the town or city in which he resides, for the time required by this act, or has been otherwise furnished with the means of education for a like period of time, or has already acquired those branches of learning which are taught in common schools, or if it shall appear that his bodily or mental condition has been such as to prevent his attendance at school, or his acquisition of learning for such a period of time, or that the person having the control of such child, is not able, by reason of poverty, to send such child to school, or to furnish him with the means of education, then such person shall be held not to have violated the provisions of this act.

AN ARGUMENT AGAINST STATE SUPPORT OF EDUCATION, 1830

Philadelphia National Gazette

It is an old and sound remark that government cannot provide for the necessities of the People; that it is they who maintain the government, and not the latter the People. Education may

SOURCE: "An Argument Against State Support of Education, 1830," *Philadelphia National Gazette,* July 12, 1830.

be among their necessities; but it is one of that description which the state or national councils cannot supply, except partially and in a limited degree. They may endow public schools for the indigent, and colleges for the most comprehensive and costly scheme of instruction. To create or sustain seminaries for the tuition of all classes—to digest and regulate systems, to adjust and manage details, to render a multitude of schools effective —is beyond their province and power. Education in general must be the work of the intelligence, need, and enterprise of individuals and associations. At present, in nearly all the most populous parts of the United States, it is attainable for nearly all the inhabitants; it is comparatively cheap, and if not the best possible, it is susceptible of improvement and likely to be advanced. Its progress and wider diffusion will depend, not upon government, but upon the public spirit, information, liberality, and training of the citizens themselves, who may appreciate duly the value of the object as a national good, and as a personal benefit for their children. Some of our writers about universal public instruction and discipline seem to forget the constitution of modern society, and declaim as if our communities could receive institutions or habits like those of Sparta.

A SKETCH OF WOODWARD HIGH SCHOOL
IN CINCINNATI, 1856

American Journal of Education

〰〰〰〰〰〰〰〰〰〰〰〰〰〰〰〰〰〰〰〰〰〰〰

The System of Common Schools in Cincinnati was established in 1828–29 under a special act of the Legislature, by which a tax of $7000 was annually imposed for the building of school-houses, and a like amount, in addition to the state appropriation, for the support of schools. Under this act schoolhouses were erected, in point of location, size, and internal convenience, greatly in advance of the then generally received notions as to school architecture.

In 1834 the system was greatly extended, and in 1845 the trustees were authorized to establish schools of different grades, and in 1850 to appoint a superintendent.

In 1847 a central high school was organized, and in 1852 the Woodward Fund and the Hughes Fund, amounting to $300,000, and yielding over $5000 (the Woodward estate, in 1856, yielded $4510), were united for the purpose of sustaining two schools of this grade.

In 1853 a building was erected for the accommodation of the Hughes High School, at an expense, including lot, of about $40,-000, and in 1856, in an opposite section of the city, another building, at a cost of $50,000, for the Woodward High School. The latter, built in the Tudor style of architecture, was of brick and three stories high, with a high basement. The basement contained two Philosophical Rooms, 27¾ x 42¾ feet in size; and four furnaces. The first and second floors were alike and contained four classrooms each, while the third floor was given over to a Lecture Hall, 68¾ x 83¾ feet in size, a large platform, and two small ante-

SOURCE: "A Sketch of Woodward High School in Cincinnati, 1856," *American Journal of Education*, IV (1858), pp. 520–525.

rooms. The building was warmed by four hot-air furnaces, and lighted by gas.

AN EXAMPLE OF THE OPPOSITION TO HIGH SCHOOLS

John P. Gulliver

~~~~~~

. . . The lower schools up to the grade of the grammar school were well sustained. Men were to be found in all our communities who had been themselves educated up to that point, and understood, practically, the importance of such schools, in sufficient numbers to control popular sentiment, and secure for them ample appropriations and steady support. But the studies of the high school, Algebra, Geometry, Chemistry, Natural Philosophy, Ancient History, Latin, Greek, French and German, were a perfect "terra incognita" to the great mass of the people. While the High School was a new thing and while a few enlightened citizens had the control of it, in numerous instances it was carried to a high state of perfection. But after a time the burden of taxation would begin to be felt. Men would discuss the high salaries paid to the accomplished teachers which such schools demand, and would ask, "To what purpose is this waste?" Demagogues, keen-scented as wolves, would snuff the prey. "What do we want of a High School to teach rich men's children?" they would shout.

SOURCE: "An Example of the Opposition to High Schools," John P. Gulliver, *Norwich* (Connecticut) *Weekly Courier*, November 25, 1856.

THE KALAMAZOO DECISION

Stuart v. *School District No. 1 of Kalamazoo*

〰〰〰〰〰〰〰〰〰〰〰〰〰〰〰〰〰〰〰〰〰〰〰〰〰〰〰〰〰

(Mr. Justice Cooley delivered the opinion of the Court.)

The bill in this case is filed to restrain the collection of such portion of the school taxes assessed against complainants for the year 1872 as have been voted for the support of the high school in that village, and for the payment of the salary of the superintendent. While, nominally, this is the end sought to be attained by the bill, the real purpose of the suit is wider and vastly more comprehensive than this brief statement would indicate inasmuch as it seeks a judicial determination of the right of school authorities, in what are called union school districts of the state, to levy taxes upon the general public for the support of what in this state are known as high schools, and to make free by such taxation the instruction of children in other languages than the English. . . . It is, as we understand it, that there is no authority in this state to make the high schools free by taxation levied on the people at large. The argument is that while there may be no constitutional provision expressly prohibiting such taxation, the general course of legislation in the state and the general understanding of the people have been such as to require us to regard the instruction in the classics and in living modern languages in these schools as in the nature not of practical and therefore necessary instruction for the benefit of the people at large, but rather as accomplishments for the few to be sought after in the main by those best able to pay for them, and to be paid for by those who seek them, and not by general tax. And not only has this been the general state policy, but this higher learning of itself, when supplied by the state, is so far a matter

source: The Kalamazoo Decision, *Stuart* v. *School District No. 1 of Kalamazoo,* 30 Mich. 69 (1874).

of private concern to those who receive it that the courts ought to declare it incompetent to supply it wholly at the public expense. This is in substance, as we understand it, the position of the complainants in this suit. . . . We supposed it had always been understood in this state that education, not merely in the rudiments, but in an enlarged sense, was regarded as an important practical advantage to be supplied at their option to rich and poor alike, and not as something pertaining merely to culture and accomplishment to be brought as such within the reach of those whose accumulated wealth enabled them to pay for it.

Thus stood the law when the constitution of 1835 was adopted. The article on education in that instrument contained the following provisions:

"2. The legislature shall encourage by all suitable means the promotion of intellectual, scientifical and agricultural improvement. The proceeds of all lands that have been, or hereafter may be, granted by the United States to this state for the support of schools, which shall hereafter be sold or disposed of, shall be and remain a perpetual fund, the interest of which, together with the rents of all such unsold lands, shall be inviolably appropriated to the support of schools throughout the state.

"3. The legislature shall provide for a system of common schools, by which a school shall be kept up and supported in each school district at least three months in every year; and any school district neglecting to keep up and support such a school may be deprived of its equal proportion of the interest of the public fund."

The fifth section provided for the support of the university, "with such branches as the public convenience may hereafter demand for the promotion of literature, the arts and sciences," etc. Two things are specially noticeable in these provisions: *first*, that they contemplated provision by the state for a complete system of instruction, beginning with that of the primary school and ending with that of the university; *second*, that while the legislature was required to make provision for district schools for at least three months in each year, no restriction was imposed upon its power to establish schools intermediate the common district school and the university, and we find nothing to indicate an intent to limit their discretion as to the class or grade of schools to which the proceeds of school lands might be devoted, or as to the range of studies or grade of instruction which might be provided for in the district schools. It must suffice to say that the law of 1827, which provided for grammar schools as a grade of common schools, was adopted from laws which from a very early period had been in existence in Massachusetts, and which in like manner, under heavy penalties, compelled the support of these grammar schools in every considerable town.—See *Mass. Laws, 1789, p. 39;* compare *General Stat., 1860, p. 215, § 2.*

It now becomes important to see whether the constitutional convention and the people, in 1850, did anything to undo what previously had been accomplished towards furnishing high schools as a part of the primary school system. The convention certainly did nothing to that end. On the contrary, they demonstrated in the most unmistakable manner that they cherished no such desire or purpose. The article on education as originally reported, while providing for free schools to be kept in each district at least three months in every year, added that "the English language and no other shall be taught in such schools." Attention was called to this provision, and it was amended so as to read that instruction should be "conducted in the English language." The reason for the change was fully given, that as it was reported it might be understood to prohibit the teaching of other languages than the English in the primary schools; a result that was not desired. Judge Whipple stated in the convention that, in the section from which he came, French and German were taught, and "it is a most valuable improvement of the common school system." The late superintendent Pierce said that in some schools Latin was taught, and that he himself had taught Latin in a common school. He would not adopt any provision by which any knowledge would be excluded. "All that we ought to do is this: we should say the legislature shall establish primary schools." This, in his opinion, would give full power, and the details could be left to legislation.—See *Debates of the Convention, 269, 549.*

The instrument submitted by the convention to the people and adopted by them provided for the establishment of free schools in every school district for at least three months in each year, and for the university. By the aid of these we have every reason to believe the people expected a complete collegiate education might be obtained. The branches of the university had ceased to exist; the university had no preparatory department, and it must either have been understood that young men were to be prepared for the university in the common schools, or else that they should go abroad for the purpose, or be prepared in private schools. Private schools adapted to the purpose were almost unknown in the state, and comparatively a very few persons were at that time of sufficient pecuniary ability to educate their children abroad. The inference seems irresistible that the people expected the tendency towards the establishment of high schools in the primary school districts would continue until every locality capable of supporting one was supplied. And this inference is strengthened by the fact that a considerable number of our union schools date their establishment from the year 1850 and the two or three years following.

If these facts do not demonstrate clearly and conclusively a general state policy, beginning in 1817 and continuing until after the adoption of the present constitution, in the direction of free schools in which education, and at their option the elements of classical education, might be brought within the reach of all the children of the state, then, as it seems to us, nothing can demonstrate it.

We might follow the subject further, and show that the subsequent legislation has all concurred with this policy, but it would be a waste of time and labor. We content ourselves with the statement that neither in our state policy, in our constitution, or in our laws, do we find the primary school districts restricted in the branches of knowledge which their officers may cause to be taught, or the grade of instruction that may be given, if their voters consent in regular form to bear the expense and raise the taxes for the purpose.

It follows that the decree dismissing the bill was right, and should be affirmed.

The other Justices concurred.

EXTENT AND CAUSES OF PUPILS DROPPING OUT OF HIGH SCHOOL

A. C. Barker

~~~~~~

At the request of the executive committee of this Association, I undertook last spring to gather statistics to show the extent and causes of pupils dropping out of the high school. Inquiries were sent to all the public high schools in the state (California) asking how many of the pupils enrolled in the entering class of 1898–1899 have since left school, when, and for what reasons. The replies received from twenty-five principals indicate that approximately 30 percent have since then reached the senior year. For the rural schools the percentage is higher and for the city schools considerably lower, reaching in several cases a total of 20 percent. About 40 percent of these pupils left during the first year, 30 percent the second, and 10 percent the third. In regard to the time and reasons for leaving, the replies were in many cases, owing to the lack of systematic records, unsatisfactory. In some instances all records had disappeared with the change of principal. The Association, by adopting and recommending a record card for uniform use, would render a substantial service to the high schools of the State.

These replies show that 10 percent left on account of ill health. Nearly all of the cases reported were girls. In one high school 20 percent dropped out because of illness. The percentage of illness is certainly large enough to raise the question "Are not the requirements for graduation too high?" One school reports seventeen recitations per week as a regular requirement; seventeen require twenty; two, twenty-one; and two, twenty-five. These

SOURCE: A. C. Barker, "Extent and Causes of Pupils Dropping Out of the High School," *High School Association*, December 13, 1903, pp. 17–21.

requirements are in excess of those of Phillips Exeter and Andover, which rank among the best preparatory schools for boys in
this country. The public high school of today, however, is not
a boys' school; for it contains a much larger percentage of girls
than boys. The fact that girls cannot carry as many hours as boys
without undue danger to their health is too well established to
need discussion. The girls, to be sure, will do the required work,
yet many will break down under the strain. I have personally
known of several exceptionally bright girls who entered the high
school in robust health and left little better than physical wrecks.
Twenty hours (which seems to be the average requirement)
would not be excessive if a larger proportion of the time were
given to teaching or to actual instruction in the classroom rather
than to the hearing of recitations. In my opinion the high school
should not require more than fifteen prepared recitations per
week.

The reports again indicate that 29 percent left school on account of failure in studies. In two schools which had an enrollment of over two hundred, the failures exceed one half the whole
number of pupils. Fifty-two percent of these occurred in the first
year. Undoubtedly many failures were due to want of ability;
for the incompetent and unfortunate will always be with us.
But the fact that such a very large number occur during the first
year can be explained only by the lack of articulation between
elementary and high schools.

This gap between the lower grades and the high school seems
every year to be widening, owing to the fact that the former
have not kept pace in improvement with the latter. The work
of the last two years of the elementary school has too frequently
been a dead mechanical routine, possessing little interest and
requiring little or no mental effort except the exercise of the
memory. Professor Lyons declared that "the total permanent
result of the first eight years of the pupils' school life is the ability
to read but not the reading habit; the ability to spell and write
words, but no power of expression with the pen; a varying ability
to add, subtract, multiply and divide simple numbers, integral
and fractional, but much uncertainty in other operations; some
fragmentary book knowledge of names and places, and some
scrappy information relating to the history of the United States,

most of which information is found to be useless and is soon forgotten. The seventh and eighth years' curriculum is mainly a review of the sixth year, and it does not require serious application. During these years pupils are likely to acquire indolent habits which in the first year of the high school render failure almost certain. The introduction in the ninth year to four new and formal subjects will severely tax even the most diligent and ambitious student. When he passes from the elementary to the high school he finds an even greater change in teaching methods than in subject matter. For example, the instruction in English has so changed that it is to all purposes a new subject. Formal and mechanical reading has given way to a study of literature, and the pupil in consequence for the first few months flounders wretchedly. Of course it sometimes happens that high school teachers expect too much of beginners and many consequently fail or become discouraged and leave school. This is partly due to the fact that the teachers are frequently not conversant with the work of the grades and do not realize the difficulties with which beginners in the high school have to contend, partly to the change from the one teacher to the departmental system. There is undoubtedly too much explanation in the lower grades, the work is made too easy, and the habit of dependence is formed. Inexperienced high school teachers frequently assume that the pupils have acquired independent habits of study, and therefore often adopt methods better fitted for seniors than beginners. Each teacher is a specialist, a fact which naturally begets the idea that his subject is all important. Too often he does not know what is required of his pupils in other subjects. His own work must be done, or the pupil is mercilessly dropped. It is the old story of each one for himself and the devil take the last one.

~~~~~~

TEXT OF THE VOCATIONAL EDUCATION ACT
(Public, No. 347, Sixty-fourth Congress)
S. 703

An ACT to provide for the promotion of vocational education; to provide for cooperation with the States in the promotion of such education in curriculum and the trades and industries; to provide for cooperation with the States in the preparation of teachers of vocational subjects, and to appropriate money and regulate its expenditure. BE IT PROVIDED BY THE SENATE AND HOUSE OF REPRESENTATIVES OF THE UNITED STATES OF AMERICA IN CONGRESS ASSEMBLED, That there is hereby annually appropriated, sums of any money in the Treasury not otherwise appropriated, the sums provided in section two, three, and four of this Act to be paid to the respective States for the purpose of cooperating with the States in paying the salaries of teachers, supervisors, and directors of agricultural subjects, and teachers of trade, home economics and industrial subjects; and the sum provided for in section seven for the use of the Federal Board for Vocational Education for the administration of this Act and for the purpose of making studies, investigations, and reports to aid in the organization and conduct of vocational education, which sums shall be expended as hereinafter provided.

Sect. 12. That in order for any State to receive the benefits of the appropriation in this Act for the training of teachers, supervisors or directors of agricultural subjects, or of teachers of trade, industrial or home economics subjects, the State board of each State shall provide in its plan for such training that the same shall be given in schools or classes under public supervision or control; that such training shall be carried out under the supervision of the State board; that such training shall be given in schools or classes under public supervision or control; that such training shall be given only to persons who have had adequate vocational experience or contact in the line of work for which they are preparing themselves as teachers, supervisors or directors, or who are acquiring such experience or contact as a part of their training; and that the State board, with the approval of the Federal Board, shall establish minimum requirements for such experience or contact for teachers, supervisors, or directors of agricultural subjects and for teachers of trade, industrial, and home economics subjects that not more than sixty per centum nor less than twenty per centum of the money appropriated under the Act for the training of teachers of vocational subjects to any State for any year shall be expended for any one of the following purposes: For the preparation of teachers, supervisors, or directors of agricultural subjects, or the preparation of teachers of trade and industrial subjects, or the preparation of teachers of home economics subjects.

ENROLLMENT IN GRADES 9–12 IN PUBLIC AND NONPUBLIC SCHOOLS, COMPARED WITH POPULATION 14–17 YEARS OF AGE: CONTINENTAL UNITED STATES, 1889–90 TO 1957–58.

| School year | Enrollment, grades 9–12 and postgraduate | | Population, 14–17 years of age * | | Number enrolled per 100 persons 14–17 years of age |
	Number †	Percent increase over 1889–90	Number	Percent increase over 1889–90	
1889–90	359,949		5,354,653		6.7
1899–1900	699,403	94.3	6,152,231	14.9	11.4
1909–10	1,115,398	209.9	7,220,298	34.8	15.4
1919–20	2,500,176	594.6	7,735,841	44.5	32.3
1929–30	4,804,255	1,234.7	9,341,221	74.5	51.4
1939–40	7,123,009	1,878.9	'9,720,419	81.5	73.3
1949–50	6,453,009	1,692.8	8,404,768	57.0	76.8
1951–52	6,596,351	1,732.6	8,525,000 ‡	59.2	77.4
1953–54	7,108,973	1,875.0	8,878,000 ‡	65.8	80.1
1955–56	7,774,951	2,060.0	9,229,000 ‡	72.4	84.2
1957–58**	8,930,000		10,164,000 ‡		87.9

* Includes all persons residing in continental United States, but excludes Armed Forces overseas. Data shown are actual figures from the decennial censuses of population unless otherwise indicated.

† Includes pupils in schools operated by teacher-training institutions of higher education, in subcollegiate departments of institutions of higher education, and in residential schools for exceptional children. Beginning in 1949–50, also includes Federal schools.

‡ Estimated by the Bureau of the Census as of July 1 preceding the opening of the school year.

** Preliminary data.

Table compares enrollment in grades 9–12 with the population 14–17 years of age. The number enrolled per 100 persons 14–17 years of age has increased from 6.7 in 1889–90 to 87.9 in 1957–58.

SOURCE: U.S. Department of Health, Education, and Welfare, Office of Education, *Biennial Survey of Education in the United States.*

NUMBER OF HIGH SCHOOL GRADUATES * COMPARED WITH POPULATION 17 YEARS OF AGE: CONTINENTAL UNITED STATES, 1869–70 TO 1957–58.

Year	Population 17 years old †	High school graduates			Number graduated per 100 persons 17 years of age
		Total	Boys	Girls	
1869–70	815,000	16,000	7,064	8,936	2.0
1879–80	946,026	23,634	10,605	13,029	2.5
1889–90	1,259,177	43,731	18,549	25,182	3.5
1899–1900	1,489,146	94,883	38,075	56,808	6.4
1909–10	1,786,240	156,429	63,676	92,753	8.8
1919–20	1,855,173	311,266	123,684	187,582	16.8
1929–30	2,295,822	666,904	300,376	366,528	29.0
1939–40	2,403,074	1,221,475	578,718	642,757	50.8
1949–50	2,034,450	1,199,700	570,700	629,000	59.0
1951–52	2,040,800	1,196,500	569,200	627,300	58.6
1953–54	2,128,600	1,276,100	612,500	663,600	60.0
1955–56	2,270,000	1,414,800	679,500	735,300	62.3
1957–58 †	2,324,000	1,507,600	729,200	778,400	64.9

* Includes graduates from public and nonpublic schools.
† U.S. Bureau of the Census.
‡ Preliminary data.
This table compares high school graduates with population 17 years of age. The number graduating per 100 persons 17 years of age has increased from 2 in 1870 to approximately 65 in 1958.

SOURCE: U.S. Department of Health, Education, and Welfare, Office of Education, *Biennial Survey of Education in the United States.*

SCHOOL DISTRICTS AND EXPENDITURES

FOR EDUCATION

~~~~~~

INDEPENDENT * SCHOOL DISTRICTS: CONTINENTAL UNITED STATES,
1951–52 AND 1956–57.

Enrollment size	School districts					
	1951–52		1956–57		Changes in—	
	Number	Percent	Number	Percent	Number	Percent
United States total	67,346	100.0 †	50,440	100.0 †	−16,906	−25.1
Fewer than 50	44,393	65.9	30,312	60.0	−14,081	−31.7
50–150	7,902	11.7	5,903	11.7	−1,999	−25.3
150–300	5,047	7.5	3,883	7.7	−1,164	−23.1
300–600 †	5,379	8.0	3,745	7.4	−1,634	−30.4
600–1,200 ‡	2,294	3.4	2,861	5.7	567	24.7
1,200–3,000 ‡	1,300	1.9	2,305	4.6	1,005	77.3
3,000–6,000	611	.9	858	1.7	247	40.4
6,000–12,000	265	.4	383	.8	118	44.5
12,000–25,000	97	.1	112	.2	15	15.5
25,000 or more	58	.1	78	.2	20	34.5
Less than 600	62,721	93.1	43,843	86.9	−18,878	−30.1
More than 600	4,625	6.9	6,597	13.1	1,972	42.6

* Local districts are those classified by the Bureau of the Census as "independent."
Data omit "dependent" school districts or systems (2,409 in 1952 and 2,467 in 1957)
operated as part of State, county, municipal, town, and university governments rather
than by local school board.

† Because of rounding, percentages may not add to totals.

There was a decrease of almost 17,000 in the number of independent school districts
between 1952 and 1957. Most of the decrease may be attributed to the reorganization
and consolidation of districts with an enrollment of fewer than 50 pupils.

SOURCE: Bureau of the Census, *Governments in the United States in 1952—State
and Local Government,* Special Studies: No. 31, 1953, and *Governments in the
United States,* Vol. I, No. 1, 1957.

NATIONAL INCOME RELATED TO TOTAL EXPENDITURES * FOR EDUCATION:
CONTINENTAL UNITED STATES, 1929–30 TO 1957–58.

Calendar year	National income (in millions)	School year	Expenditures for education	
			Total (in thousands)	As a percent of national income
1929	$37,814	1929–30	$3,233,601	3.68
1931	59,708	1931–32	2,966,464	4.97
1933	40,159	1933–34	2,294,896	5.71
1935	57,057	1935–36	2,649,914	4.64
1937	73,618	1937–38	3,014,074	4.09
1939	72,753	1939–40	3,199,593	4.40
1941	104,710	1941–42	3,203,548	3.06
1943	170,310	1943–44	3,522,007	2.07
1945	181,248	1945–46	4,167,597	2.30
1947	198,177	1947–48	6,574,379	3.32
1949	217,690	1949–50	8,795,635	4.04
1951	279,313	1951–52	11,312,446	4.05
1953	305,573	1953–54	13,949,876	4.57
1955	330,206	1955–56	16,811,651	5.09
1957	366,503	1957–58	19,763,000 †	5.39

* Includes expenditures of public and nonpublic schools at all levels of education (elementary, secondary, and higher education).

† Estimated.

In 1957–58 the total national expenditure for education was three times the amount expended in 1947–48, whereas the national income had increased only 85 percent in the 10-year period. This is reflected in the greater percentage of national income spent for education in 1957–58 (5.39 percent) than was spent in 1947–48 (3.32 percent). The increase, in terms of a per capita expenditure based on the entire population of continental United States, was from $46 in 1947–48 to $116 in 1957–58, an increase of 153 percent.

SOURCE: U.S. Department of Health, Education, and Welfare, Office of Education, *Biennial Survey of Education in the United States;* U.S. Department of Commerce, Office of Business Economics, *Survey of Current Business,* July, 1958.

Philosophy of Secondary Education

~~~~~~

Historically, as noted in the preceding section, America's preoccupation with secondary education was with the establishment of a public high school which would best serve the democratic ideal. Legislative acts and institutions extended educational opportunities to most of the youth of the nation. Political philosophers such as Franklin and Jefferson maintained that an educated electorate was essential to the continuance of a democratic society.

A careful examination of the lives of the major educational figures of the eighteenth and nineteenth centuries would reveal that they were men of action rather than of ideas. Two of the most outstanding educators of the nineteenth century, Horace Mann and Henry Barnard, abandoned their law careers to become educational administrators because of their deep concerns about the inadequacies of the schools of the day.

This is not to say that American educators of this century have not been profoundly influenced by educational theorists, particularly those of Europe. Jean Jacques Rousseau's dramatic proposition that education was the chief instrument

89

whereby the child was emancipated, enunciated in *Emile*, was to have a far-reaching effect on educational theory, both in Europe and in the United States. John Amos Comenius, a Moravian bishop, impressed American educators by advocating that universal education was a human right and proposed a completely graded system based upon the natural psychological development of the pupil. His reputation was so prominent that Harvard College was reputed to have invited him to become president of that institution in 1745. John Locke, more widely known for his political treatises, was recognized by Franklin as an eminent educator and was quoted by him frequently. Johann Heinrich Pestalozzi's educational theories were internationally acclaimed, and his schools in Switzerland were meccas for American educators in the late nineteenth century.

Among the most widely read and discussed European philosophers was Frederick Herbart, who protested the mental discipline educational concept which was the predominant educational psychological theory of the nineteenth century. Herbart's ideas were accepted intellectually and put into practice by many teachers in this country.

The time preceding World War I was ideal for the emergence of an American educational philosophy. Pedagogy as a subject made its way into the university, combined, in some instances, with either philosophy or psychology. However, it must not be inferred that the academicians welcomed educationists into their ranks. The major spokesman of American educators, who synthesized some of the European theories with his own genius, was John Dewey, later to win international acclaim as an educator, philosopher, and psychologist.

Dewey was able to assess the tremendous changes in American life that had created problems of a social, economic, and political nature and prescribe an educational philosophy which, as he saw it, would weld together the diverse elements of a growing United States population. The Dewey position, which was the essence of the Progressive Movement, had obvious and immediate appeal to an educationally hungry America. Dewey and his followers, William Heard Kilpatrick, John L. Childs, Boyd H. Bode, George Counts, and Carleton Washburne, in spite of their differences, had one belief in common; intellectual and individual freedom should be combined with the social needs of society.

The tide of Progressivism was opposed as early as the first decade of the century by a group of philosophers who held the idealist and realist positions, who became known as Essentialists. Unfortunately an oversimplification of the controversy between the Essentialists and the Progressives centered around systematic training in the traditional subjects as opposed to activity methods. The more sophisticated students of educational philosophy recognize that the conflict is much more complex and reflects serious differences in attitude toward the problems of American society. The differences that exist among the adherents of the Progressive position exist as well among the Essentialists. The student of education would do well to examine carefully these differences as revealed by the readings in this section.

The word *education* does not appear in the Constitution of the United States; administration of the schools remains essentially a state prerogative guaranteed by the Tenth Amendment. The evolution of the schools in America has been such that the local districts have remained virtually autonomous, determining their own philosophic bases for operation. This independence has been in direct contrast with the centralized European system, which provides no means for local districts to exert their philosophical positions. In the United States there may be as many different educational, philosophical positions as there are local school districts. Whether such a condition is advantageous or not is speculative. For example, it encourages the critics of education to attack the public school on many fronts because of the multiplicity of educational philosophies.

American secondary education, then, has no single universally accepted philosophy. Changes that have occurred in the curricular patterns have more likely been the result of social, economic, and political pressures rather than from the implementation of philosophic contemplation. Various commissions and conferences have promulgated formulations of objectives and aims of education, but it is questionable whether these formulations have been predicated on any common philosophic basis.

More and more frequently American educators have been asking the question, What are the aims and purposes, the ends and means, of education? Recently there has been a greater focus on this problem because of the attacks on education by lay critics. Accrediting teams visiting high schools have requested that faculties seriously discuss the philosophy of their particular institutions.

The purpose of this section is to present to the reader a series of philosophical positions. There is strenuous debate about each of the points of view presented and their efficacy for American secondary education. Each of the writers included implies that his philosophy is the most desirable. The reader must constantly keep in mind these questions: For what purpose are the youth of the high schools in America being educated? Which of the philosophies presented is closest to the truth? Is the truly American philosophy of education still to be developed? What part will the student of education play in its formulation?

THE GREAT DIDACTIC

John Amos Comenius

~~~~~~

CHRISTIAN STATE. In these schools all youth of both sexes, without exception, can be instructed in the sciences, improved in their morals, filled with piety, and, in suchwise, be equipped in early years for all that belongs to the life here and beyond. This will be done by a concise, agreeable, and thorough form of instruction which:

derives its reasons from the genuine nature of things,
proves its truth by dint of adequate examples taken from the
    mechanical arts,

SOURCE: John Amos Comenius, "The Great Didactic." Reprinted by permission of the publishers from Robert Ulich, editor, *Three Thousand Years of Educational Wisdom: Selections from Great Documents,* Cambridge, Mass.: Harvard University Press, Copyright 1947, 1954, by the President and Fellows of Harvard College.

Title-Page of Comenius's *Great Didactic*

(First English edition, from the original Latin edition. Edited by M. W. Keatinge London, 1896)

The following title-page indicates well the nature of the treatise

The Great Didactic *

Setting forth

The whole Art of Teaching all Things to all Men

or

A certain Inducement to found such Schools in all
the Parishes, Towns, and Villages of every
Christian Kingdom, that the entire
Youth of both Sexes, none
being excepted, shall

Quickly, Pleasantly, & Thoroughly

Become learned in the Sciences, pure in Morals,
trained to Piety, and in this manner
instructed in all things necessary
for the present and for
the future life,

in which, with respect to everything that is suggested,

ITS FUNDAMENTAL PRINCIPLES are set forth from the essential
nature of the matter,
ITS TRUTH is proved by examples from the several
mechanical arts,
ITS ORDER is clearly set forth in years, months, days, and
hours, and, finally,
AN EASY AND SURE METHOD is shown, by which it can
be pleasantly brought into existence.

arranges the sequence of instruction by years, months, days, and
   hours, and finally,

shows an easy and safe way for the happy pursuit of all these
   suggestions.

The Beginning and End of our Didactic will be:

To seek and find a method by which the teachers teach less
and the learners learn more, by which the schools have less noise,
obstinacy, and frustrated endeavor, but more leisure, pleasant-
ness, and definite progress, and by which the Christian State will
suffer less under obscurity, confusion, and conflict, and will enjoy
a greater amount of light, order, peace, and quiet.

* * *

CHAPTER 2. MAN'S ULTIMATE GOAL LIES OUT-
SIDE THIS LIFE. . . . All our doing and suffering tells us
that we do not achieve our ultimate goal here on earth, but that
all that is in us and we ourselves aim farther. For what we are,
do, think, talk, contemplate, acquire, and possess is only a kind
of ladder, on which we always climb toward a higher rung, but
never reach the top. After man has begun his life in the form of
an amorphous mass he gradually takes on the contours of a body
and later on begins to move. After birth the senses awake, then
knowledge arises as a consequence of observation, and finally,
will assumes the office of the pilot by addressing itself to certain
things and going away from other things.

Also within the single levels of development we discover a
definite improvement. Just as the rays of the rising sun emerge
out of darkness so knowledge of things gradually increases, and
as long as life lasts more and more light is added. Also our actions
are insignificant, feeble, and awkward at the beginning; but
gradually the faculties of the soul unfold together with the faculties of the body, and in a noble mind all this aspires higher and
higher without limits; for in this life there is no fulfillment for
our wishes and desires. . . .

2. There should be taught all that can make men wise, honest,
and pious.

3. Education, which is preparation for life, should be finished
before adulthood.

4. Education should be carried out not with beating, severity

and any kind of coercion, but easily, pleasantly, and, so to speak, by its own momentum.

5. Not a semblance of education ought to be provided, but genuine education, not a superficial but thorough education; that means the rational animal man should be led by his own rather than a foreign reason. He should get accustomed to penetrating to the real roots of things and to take into himself their true meaning and usage, rather than read, perceive, memorize, and relate other people's opinions. The same ought to be the case with respect to morality and piety.

6. Education ought not to be painful but as easy as possible, everyday only four hours ought to be spent for public instruction, and this in such a way that one teacher should suffice for the simultaneous instruction of a hundred pupils. And he should do that ten times more easily than is now done with one pupil. . . .

SOME THOUGHTS ON EDUCATION

John Locke

~~~~~~

DEDICATION TO EDWARD CLARKE, OF CHIPLEY, ESQU.

. . . I myself have been consulted of late by so many who profess themselves at a loss how to breed their children, and the early corruption of youth is now become so a complaint, that he

SOURCE: John Locke, "Some Thoughts on Education." Reprinted by permission of the publishers from Robert Ulich, *Three Thousand Years of Educational Wisdom: Selections from Great Documents,* Cambridge, Mass.: Harvard University Press, Copyright 1947, 1954, by the President and Fellows of Harvard College.

cannot be thought wholly impertinent who brings the consideration of this matter on the stage, and offers something, if it be
but to excite others, or afford matter of correction. For errors in
education should be less indulged than any: these, like faults in
the first concoction, that are never mended in the second or third,
carry their afterwards-incorrigible taint with them through all
the parts and stations of life. . . .

But my business is not to recommend this treatise to you, whose
opinion of it I know already; nor it to the world, either by your
opinion or patronage. The well educating of their children is so
much the duty and concern of parents, and the welfare and prosperity of the nation so much depends on it, that I would have
every one lay it seriously to heart; and after having well examined and distinguished what fancy, custom, or reason advises in
the case, set his helping hand to promote everywhere that way
of training up youth, with regard to their several conditions,
which is the easiest, shortest, and likeliest to produce virtuous,
useful, and able men in their distinct callings; though that most
to be taken care of is the gentleman's calling. For if those of that
rank are by their education once set right, they will quickly bring
all the rest into order. . . .

1. A sound mind in a sound body is a short but full description
of a happy state in this world: he that has these two has little
more to wish for; and he that wants either of them will be but
little the better for anything else. Men's happiness or misery is
most part of their own making. He whose mind directs not wisely
will never take the right way; and he whose body is crazy and
feeble will never be able to advance in it. . . .

2. I imagine the minds of children as easily turned this or that
way as water itself; and though this be the principal part, and our
main care should be about the inside, yet the clay cottage is not
to be neglected. I shall therefore begin with the case and consider first the health of the body as that which perhaps you may
be rather expect from that study I have been thought more
peculiarly to have applied myself to; and that also which will be
soonest despatched, as lying, if I guess not amiss, in a very little
compass. . . .

* * *

27. As the strength of the body lies chiefly in being able to endure hardship, so also does that of the mind. And the great principle and foundation of all virtue and worth is placed in this, that a man is able to deny himself his own desires, cross his own inclinations, and purely follow what reason directs as best, though the appetite lean the other way. . . .

28. The great mistake I have observed in people's breeding their children has been that this has not been taken care enough of in its due season; that the mind has not been made obedient to discipline, and pliant to reason, when at first it was most tender, most easy to be bowed. Parents being wisely ordained by nature to love their children are very apt, if reason watch not that natural affection very warily, are apt, I say, to let it run into fondness. They love their little ones, and it is their duty: but they often with them cherish their faults too. They must not be crossed, forsooth; they must be permitted to have their wills in all things; and they being in their infancies not capable of great vices, their parents think they may safely enough indulge their little irregularities, and make themselves sport with that pretty perverseness, which they think well enough becomes that innocent age. But to a fond parent, that would not have his child corrected for a perverse trick, but excused it, saying it was a small matter, Solon very well replied, "Ay, but custom is a great one." . . .

✿   ✿   ✿

40. On the other side, if the mind be curbed, and humbled too much in children; if their spirit be abased and broken much, by too strict an hand over them; they lose all their vigor and industry and are in a worse state than the former. For extravagant young fellows that have liveliness and spirit come sometimes to be set right, and so make able and great men; but dejected minds, timorous and tame, and low spirits, are hardly ever to be raised, and very seldom attain to any thing. To avoid the danger that is on either hand is the great art; and he that has found a way how to keep up a child's spirit, easy, active, and free, and yet, at the same time, to restrain him from many things that are uneasy to him; he, I say, that knows how to reconcile these seeming contradictions, has, in my opinion, got the true secret of education. . . .

57. But if a right course be taken with children, there will not be so much need of the application of the common rewards and punishments, as we imagined, and as the general practice has established. For all their innocent folly, playing, and childish actions are to be left perfectly free and unrestrained, as far as they can consist with the respect due to those that are present, and that with the greatest allowance. If these faults of their age, rather than of the children themselves were, as they should be, left only to time and imitation and riper years to cure, children would escape a great deal of misapplied and useless corrections; which either fails to overpower the natural disposition of their childhood, and so, by an ineffectual familiarity, makes correction in other necessary cases of less use; or else if it be of force to restrain the natural gaiety of that age, it serves only to spoil the temper both of body and mind. If the noise and bustle of their play prove at any time inconvenience, or unsuitable to the place or company they are in (which can only be where their parents are) a look or a word from the father or mother, if they have established the authority they should, will be enough either to remove or quiet them for that time. But this gamesome humor, which is wisely adapted by nature to their age and temper, should rather be encouraged, to keep up their spirits and improve their strength and health, than curbed or restrained; and the chief art is to make all that they have to do sport and play too. . . .

*   *   *

60. But pray remember, children are not to be taught by rules, which will be always slipping out of their memories. What you think necessary for them to do, settle in them by an indispensable practice, as often as the occasion returns; and, if it be possible, make occasions. This will beget habits in them, which, being once established, operate of themselves easily and naturally, without the assistance of the *memory!* . . .

EMILE; OR A TREATISE OF EDUCATION

Jean Jacques Rousseau

BOOK I

All things are good as they come out of the hands of their Creator, but every thing degenerates in the hands of man. He compels one soil to nourish the productions of another, and one tree to bear the fruits of another. He blends and confounds elements, climates, and seasons: he mutilates his dogs, his horses, and his slaves: he defaces, he confounds every thing: he delights in deformity and monsters. He is not content with any thing in its natural state, not even with his own species. His very offspring must be trained up for him, like a horse in the menage, and be taught to grow after his own fancy, like a tree in his garden.

Without this, matters would be still worse than they are, and our species would not be civilized but by halves. Should a man, in a state of society, be given up, from the cradle, to his own notions and conduct, he would certainly turn out the most preposterous of human beings. The influence of prejudice, authority, necessity, example, and all those social institutions in which we are immerged, would stifle in him the emotions of nature, and substitute nothing in their place. His humanity would resemble a shrub, growing by accident in the high way, which would soon be destroyed by the casual injuries it must receive from the frequent passenger.

At twelve or thirteen years of age, the faculties of a child display themselves more rapidly than his wants. The most impetuous, the most coercive of all physical necessities he hath not yet

SOURCE: From the book *Emile* by Jean Jacques Rousseau. Translated by Barbara Foxley. Everyman's Library Edition. Reprinted by permission of E. P. Dutton & Co., Inc., New York, and J. M. Dent & Sons, Ltd., London.

experienced. The very organs that provide for its gratification are as yet imperfect, and seem to wait the exertion of the will to capacitate them for action. Unaffected by the inclemency of the weather, or the change of seasons, his natural heat supplies the artificial warmth of apparel, and his keenness of appetite the provocatives of fauces. At his age, whatever is but nourishing is good; if he be drowsy, he stretches himself on the ground, and falls asleep. Whatever he hath occasion for is within his reach; he craves not after imaginary dainties; he feels no disgust from prepossession. His desires confined within the sphere of his abilities, he is not only capable of providing for himself, but possess superfluous faculties for which he has no use. This, however, is the only time, during life, in which he will be in such a situation.

Let us convert our sensations into ideas; but let us not fly at once from sensible to intellectual objects. It is by a due and rational attention to the former we can only attain the latter. In the first operations of the understanding, let our senses then always be our guide, the world our only book, and facts our sole preceptors. Children, when taught to read, learn that only; they never think; they gain no information; all their learning consists in words.

Direct the attention of your pupil to the phaenomena of nature, and you will soon awaken his curiosity; but to keep that curiosity alive, you must be in no haste to satisfy it. Put questions to him adapted to his capacity, and leave him to resolve them. Let him take nothing on trust from his preceptor, but on his own comprehension and conviction: he should not learn, but invent the sciences. If ever you substitute authority in the place of argument, he will reason no longer; he will be ever afterwards bandied like a shuttlecock between the opinions of others. . . .

Talk not to children in a language they do not comprehend; make use of no pompous descriptions, no flowers of speech, no tropes and figures, no poetry; taste and sentiment are at present quite out of the question: simplicity, gravity, and precision are all that are yet required; the time will come but too soon when we must assume a different style.

A pupil educated agreeable to these maxims, and accustomed to receive no assistance till he has discovered his own inabilities, will examine every new object with a long and silent attention.

He will be thoughtful without asking questions. Content yourself, therefore, with presenting proper objects opportunely to his notice, and when you see they have sufficiently excited his curiosity, drop from leading laconic questions, which may put him in the way of discovering the truth.

*   *   *

The child who is taught, as the most important lesson, to know nothing but what is useful to him, will interrogate with the views of a Socrates: he will not put a question without having an answer ready to that which he knows will be put to him before his own is resolved.

*   *   *

Never point out anything to a child which is beyond his views. While he is a stranger to the relations and duties of humanity, as you cannot raise his comprehension to the state of manhood, you should bring down the state of manhood to a level with his capacity. In projecting what may be useful to him hereafter, speak to him directly only of what is apparently useful to him at present. . . .

Since we must have books, there is one already, which, in my opinion, affords a complete treatise on natural education. This book shall be the first Émile shall read. In this, indeed, will, for a long time, consist his whole library, and it will always hold a distinguished place among others. It will afford us the text, to which all our conversations on the objects of natural science will serve only as a comment. It will serve as our guide during our progress to a state of reason; and will even afterwards give us constant pleasure, unless our taste be totally vitiated. You ask impatiently, what is the title of this wonderful book? Is it Aristotle, Pliny, or Buffon? No. It is Robinson Crusoe.

Johann Heinrich Pestalozzi

The higher purpose of education is to prepare the individual to make free and self-reliant use of all the faculties with which the Creator has endowed him, and so to direct these faculties that they may perfect all human life; each individual, in his proper place, should be able to act as the instrument of the omnipotent, all-knowing Power that has called him into being.

The essence of training man's nature is to educate mankind to understanding love.

What else is education but the reverent joining of the past to the gloom of the future by making wise use of the present?

Education is an unbroken chain of measures that all spring from the same principle, namely, an understanding of the immutable laws that govern our nature. These measures are undertaken in a uniform spirit of good will and firmness, and they all lead to the same end, which is to exalt mankind to a dignity in keeping with his nature.

The material with which the educator works, which he must be able to mold in true creative fashion, is man himself, the masterpiece of Creation. It is man whom the educator must understand—man in his full scope and power—as a gardener wisely tends the rarest plants, from their first sprouting to the maturing of their fruit. The teacher must be capable of watching man's development, whatever direction it may take, whatever the circumstances. No profession on earth calls for a deeper under-

SOURCE: Johann Heinrich Pestalozzi, "The Education of Man: Aphorism" (New York: Philosophical Library, 1951). Reprinted by permission.

standing of human nature, nor for greater skill in guiding it
properly.

Teaching, by itself and in itself, does not make for love, any
more than it makes for hatred. That is why teaching is by no
means the essence of education. It is love that is its essence.
Love alone is the eternal effluvium of the divinity that is en-
throned within us. It is the central point from which the essentials of education flow.

Without love, neither the physical nor the intellectual powers
of the child will develop naturally. That is only human.

Nature has enclosed man's higher aptitudes as in a shell; if
you break the shell before it opens on its own, you will find only
a budding pearl. You will have destroyed the treasure you should
have preserved for your child.

You must bend your children in the direction they must go
almost before they know the difference between right and left.
They will thank you to the end of their days that they have
been trained for good ends and fitted to the yoke of our wretched
life, before they knew why it was being done.

In the world as it is, a man will learn only through necessity
or through conviction.

A man will never properly learn his trade in jest and fun.

The foundation for a good school is like that for any kind of
happiness; it is nothing else but true wisdom in living.

If a child is to learn more than his father can teach him, his
teacher must fit his supplementary instruction into what the
father does at home, much as a weaver works an ornamental
flower into the pattern of his cloth.

In my opinion, school instruction that fails to include the full
spirit education demands, and that ignores the circumstances in
the home in their entirety, is little more than a method for
shriveling up our generation.

The instruction of the young must in every aspect be directed
more toward developing their abilities than toward the enrichment of their knowledge.

Ignorance is better than knowledge that is but prejudice, a
glass through which to view the world. To arrive at knowledge
slowly, by one's own experience, is better than to learn by rote,
in a hurry, facts that other people know, and then, glutted with

words, to lose one's own free, observant and inquisitive ability to study.

The man who has much knowledge must be guided more intently and artfully than his less learned fellow toward understanding himself, toward harmonizing his knowledge with his circumstances, and toward developing all his intellectual powers uniformly. If this is not done, his knowledge will be but a will-o'-the-wisp that will disrupt his inner life and deprive him of the essential satisfactions which a simple, straightforward purpose in harmony with itself vouchsafes the most common man.

Not art, not books, but life itself is the true basis of teaching and education.

Knowing and doing condition each other like a river and a spring. Without knowledge there can be no action. But as the hidden spring comes to light in the river, diffusing its blessings wherever its waters flow, so must a man's knowledge come to the surface in his actions, spreading its beneficence wherever it takes effect.

A man learns by action and is cheered by action—have done with words!

O holy action, mother of deeds! It is inaction that begets misdeeds.

All that a man does bears fruit; inaction alone is barren. This is the motto of noble minds and nowhere does it apply so strikingly as in the case of children.

Our powers of understanding are best developed in business affairs, where every blunder and every omission shows up on the spot, for which men should thank God. In matters of opinion and literature, on the other hand, we can go on for all eternity, twisting and turning the words in our mouths.

Real truth, and genuine cheerfulness, are made up of perfection—perfection means completion. Whoever carries anything, let it be ever so little, to perfection, is secure for life.

Frederick Herbart

~~~~~~

CHAPTER XII—ON EDUCATION. 103 . . . Even for an adult it is not always easy to acquire and maintain a desirable attitude toward the problems of life. All the more one has to refrain from demanding indiscriminatingly that the teacher impart to his pupil the right attitude for the rest of his life. . . .

The simple duty of the teacher at any moment of his work is to preserve his pupil's natural vigor. To create or transform the personality is beyond the teacher's power; but what he can do and what we may demand from him is to ward off dangers from his pupil and to abstain from ill-handling him.

104. To this vigor belongs particularly the natural cheerfulness of youth; but man from his youth onward must voluntarily accept restrictions, particularly as he has to live a communal life. Hence, first: Children must learn to obey. Their natural exuberance must meet enough resistance to avert offense.

Immediately we meet a new difficulty. The easy means for a child not to offend his parents or teachers is concealment and lying!

To cut the knot some teachers assume at once that children always lie if they can. Hence they have to be so closely supervised and watched, and kept so busy from morning to evening that they have no time for trickery. There is some truth in this, but if it is carried out with too much harshness and exactness one may fail in the first fundamental postulate we have set up, that children's vigor must be preserved! For this they need free-

SOURCE: Frederick Herbart, *Brief Encyclopaedia of Practical Philosophy.* Reprinted by permission of the publishers from Robert Ulich, editor, *Three Thousand Years of Educational Wisdom: Selections from Great Documents,* Cambridge, Mass.: Harvard University Press, Copyright 1947, 1954, by the President and Fellows of Harvard College.

dom! Those teachers who restrict freedom to such a degree that all the children's actions are calculated to please the observer educate babies. Such creatures will have to learn how to use their powers when they are grown up—and in spite of all their endeavors they will remain timid, helpless, and inferior to free personalities, until eventually they will try to compensate in whatever way they can.

Consequently, as such a restricting form of education is dangerous something better must be combined with supervision and occupation.

One says rightly that well-bred children have not the heart to deceive their father and mother. Why not? They are used to rely on truth and confidence. This, then, becomes the keynote of their lives. Thus we have the third pedagogical postulate. Children must be accustomed to satisfy the need for confidential communication not only among themselves but also in relation to their teacher. Otherwise they will never learn to detest lying. If this attitude is deeply rooted, then they will betray occasional lies immediately by showing shame. Only if such conditions prevail the teacher may demand complete sincerity; otherwise this demand only enhances the child's disposition to lie.

WHAT KNOWLEDGE IS OF MOST WORTH?

Herbert Spencer

~~~~~~

. . . How to live?—that is the essential question for us. Not how to live in the mere material sense only, but in the widest sense. The general problem which comprehends every special problem is—the right ruling of conduct in all directions under all circumstances. In what way to treat the body; in what way to treat the mind; in what way to manage our affairs; in what way to bring up a family; in what way to behave as a citizen; in what way to utilize all those resources of happiness which nature supplies how to use all our faculties to the greatest advantage of ourselves and others—how to live completely. And this being the great thing needful for us to learn, is, by consequence, the great thing which education has to teach. To prepare us for complete living is the function which education has to discharge; and the only rational mode of judging of any educational course is to judge in what degree it discharges such function. . . .

Our first step must obviously be to classify, in the order of their importance, the leading kinds of activity which constitute human life. They may be naturally arranged into: (1) Those activities which directly minister to self-preservation; (2) those activities which, by securing the necessaries of life, indirectly minister to self-preservation; (3) those activities which have for their end the rearing and discipline of offspring; (4) those activities which are involved in the maintenance of proper social and political relations; (5) those miscellaneous activities which

SOURCE: Herbert Spencer, *Education: Intellectual, Moral and Physical* (New York: Appleton-Century-Crofts, Inc., 1897), pp. 30–32, 37–49, 51, 52, 54–60, 62, 64, 65, 67–75. First published in 1861. Reprinted by permission.

make up the leisure part of life, devoted to the gratification of the tastes and feelings.

If any one doubts the importance of an acquaintance with the fundamental principles of physiology as a means to complete living, let him look around and see how many men and women he can find in middle or later life who are thoroughly well. Occasionally only do we meet with an example of vigorous health continued to old age; hourly do we meet with examples of acute disorder, chronic ailment, general debility, premature decrepitude. Scarcely is there one to whom you put the question who has not, in the course of his life, brought upon himself illnesses which a little knowledge would have saved him from. Here is a case of heart disease consequent on a rheumatic fever that followed reckless exposure. There is a case of eyes spoiled for life by overstudy. . . . Now we hear of an irremediable injury that followed some silly feat of strength; and, again, of a constitution that has never recovered from the effects of excessive work needlessly undertaken. While on all sides we see the perpetual minor ailments which accompany feebleness. Not to dwell on the natural pain, the weariness, the gloom, the waste of time and money thus entailed, only consider how greatly ill-health hinders the discharge of all duties—makes business often impossible, and always more difficult; produces an irritability fatal to the right management of children; puts the functions of citizenship out of the question; and makes amusement a bore. Is it not clear that the physical sins—partly our forefathers' and partly our own —which produce this ill-health, deduct more from complete living than anything else? and to a great extent make life a failure and a burden instead of a benefaction and a pleasure?

To all which add the fact, that life, besides being thus immensely deteriorated, is also cut short. It is not true, as we commonly suppose, that a disorder or disease from which we have recovered leaves us as before. . . . Through the accumulation of small injuries it is that constitutions are commonly undermined, and break down, long before their time. And if we call to mind how far the average duration of life falls below the possible duration, we see how immense is the loss. . . .

Hence, knowledge which subserves direct self-preservation by preventing this loss of health, is of primary importance. . . . We infer that as vigorous health and its accompanying high spirits are larger elements of happiness than any other things whatever, the teaching how to maintain them is a teaching that yields in moment to no other whatever. And therefore we assert that such a course of physiology as is needful for the comprehension of its general truths, and their bearings on daily conduct, is an all-essential part of a rational education.

We need not insist on the value of that knowledge which aids indirect self-preservation by facilitating the gaining of a livelihood. This is admitted by all; and, indeed, by the mass is perhaps too exclusively regarded as the end of education. But while every one is ready to endorse the abstract proposition that instruction fitting youths for the business of life is of high importance, or even to consider it of supreme importance; yet scarcely any inquire what instruction will so fit them. It is true that reading, writing, and arithmetic are taught with an intelligent appreciation of their uses; but when we have said this we have said nearly all. While the great bulk of what else is acquired has no bearing on the industrial activities, an immensity of information that has a direct bearing on the industrial activities is entirely passed over.

For, leaving out only some very small classes, what are all men employed in? They are employed in the production, preparation, and distribution of commodities. And on what does efficiency in the production, preparation, and distribution of commodities depend? It depends on the use of methods fitted to the respective natures of these commodities; it depends on an adequate knowledge of their physical, chemical, or vital properties, as the case may be; that is, it depends on Science. . . .

For all the higher arts of construction, some acquaintance with Mathematics is indispensable. The village carpenter, who, lacking rational instruction, lays out his work by empirical rules learnt in his apprenticeship, equally with the builder of a Britannia Bridge, makes hourly reference to the laws of quantitative relations. . . .

And similarly with the harbours, docks, piers, and various engineering and architectural works that fringe the coasts and overspread the face of the country; as well as the mines that run underneath it. Out of geometry, too, as applied to astronomy, the art of navigation has grown; and so, by this science, has been made possible that enormous foreign commerce which supports a large part of our population, and supplies us with many necessaries and most of our luxuries. . . . And then let it be remembered that according as the principles of mechanics are well or ill used to these ends comes success or failure—individual and national.

Pass next to Physics. Joined with mathematics, it has given us the steam-engine, which does the work of millions of labourers. That section of physics which deals with the laws of heat has taught us how to economize fuel in our various industries; how to increase the produce of our smelting furnaces by substituting the hot for the cold blast; how to ventilate our mines; how to prevent explosions by using the safety-lamp, and, through the thermometer, how to regulate innumerable processes.

While in the details of indoor life, from the improved kitchen-range up to the stereoscope on the drawing-room table, the applications of advanced physics underlie our comforts and gratifications.

Still more numerous are the bearings of Chemistry on those activities by which men obtain the means of living. The bleacher, the dyer, the calico-printer, are severally occupied in processes that are well or ill done according as they do or do not conform to chemical laws.

And then the science of life—Biology: does not this, too, bear fundamentally upon these processes of indirect self-preservation? With what we ordinarily call manufactures, it has, indeed, little connection; but with the all-essential manufacture—that of food —it is inseparably connected. As agriculture must conform its methods to the phenomena of vegetable and animal life, it follows necessarily that the science of these phenomena is the rational basis of agriculture. . . .

Yet one more science have we to note as bearing directly on industrial success—the Science of Society. Without knowing it, men who daily look at the state of the money market, glance over prices current, discuss the probable crops of corn, cotton, sugar, wool, silk, weigh the chances of war, and from all those data decide on their mercantile operations, are students of social science. . . .

Not only the manufacturer and the merchant must guide their transactions by calculations of supply and demand, based on numerous facts; but even the retailer must do the like, his prosperity very greatly depending upon the correctness of his judgments respecting the future wholesale prices and the future rates of consumption. Manifestly, all who take part in the entangled commercial activities of a community are vitally interested in understanding the laws according to which those activities vary.

Thus, to all such as are occupied in the production, exchange, or distribution of commodities, acquaintance with science in some of its departments is of fundamental importance. Whoever is immediately or remotely implicated in any form of industry (and few are not) has a direct interest in understanding something of the mathematical, physical, and chemical properties of things; perhaps, also, has a direct interest in biology; and certainly has in sociology. Whether he does or does not succeed well in that indirect self-preservation which we call getting a good livelihood depends in a great degree on his knowledge of one or more of these sciences: not, it may be, a rational knowledge; but still a knowledge, though empirical. For what we call learning a business really implies learning the science involved in it, though not perhaps under the name of science. And hence a grounding in science is of great importance, both because it prepares for all this and because rational knowledge has an immense superiority over empirical knowledge. . . .

That which our school courses leave almost entirely out we thus find to be that which most nearly concerns the business of life. All our industries would cease were it not for that information which men begin to acquire as they best may after their education is said to be finished. And were it not for this information that has been from age to age accumulated and spread by unofficial means, these industries would never have existed. . . .

The vital knowledge—that by which we have grown as a nation to what we are, and which now underlies our whole existence, is a knowledge that has got itself taught in nooks and corners, while the ordained agencies for teaching have been mumbling little else but dead formulas.

We come now to the third great division of human activities—a division for which no preparation whatever is made. If by some strange chance not a vestige of us descended to the remote future save a pile of our school books or some college examination papers, we may imagine how puzzled an antiquary of the period would be on finding in them no indication that the learners were ever likely to be parents. "This must have been the *curriculum* for their celibates," we may fancy him concluding. "I perceive here an elaborate preparation for many things: especially for reading the books of extinct nations and of co-existing nations (from which indeed it seems clear that these people had very little worth reading in their own tongue); but I find no reference whatever to the bringing up of children. . . .

Seriously, is it not an astonishing fact that though on the treatment of offspring depend their lives or deaths, and their moral welfare or ruin, yet not one word of instruction on the treatment of offspring is ever given to those who will hereafter be parents? Is it not monstrous that the fate of a new generation should be left to the chances of unreasoning custom, impulse, fancy—joined with the suggestions of ignorant nurses and the prejudiced counsel of grandmothers.

. . . that parents should begin the difficult task of rearing children without ever having given a thought to the principles—physical, moral, or intellectual—which ought to guide them excites neither surprise at the actors nor pity for their victims.

And then the culture of the intellect—is not this, too, mismanaged in a similar manner? Grant that the phenomena of intelligence conform to laws; grant that the evolution of intelligence in a child also conforms to laws; and it follows inevitably that education can be rightly guided only by a knowledge of these laws. To suppose that you can properly regulate this process of forming and accumulating ideas, without understanding the nature of the process, is absurd. How widely, then, must teaching as it is differ from teaching as it should be; when hardly any parents, and but few teachers, know anything about psychology. . . . See the results. What with perceptions unnaturally dulled by early thwarting, and a coerced attention to books—what with the mental confusion produced by teaching subjects before they can be understood, and in each of them giving generalizations

before the facts of which these are the generalizations—what
with making the pupil a mere passive recipient of others' ideas,
and not in the least leading him to be an active inquirer or self-
instructor—and what with taxing the faculties to excess; there
are very few minds that become as efficient as they might be.
Examinations being once passed, books are laid aside; the greater
part of what has been acquired, being unorganized, soon drops
out of recollection; what remains is mostly inert—the art of applying knowledge not having been cultivated; and there is but
little power either of accurate observation or independent thinking. To all which add that while much of the information gained
is of relatively small value, an immense mass of information of
transcendent value is entirely passed over.

Thus we find the facts to be such as might have been inferred
a priori. The training of children—physical, moral, and intellectual
—is dreadfully defective. And in great measure it is so because
parents are devoid of that knowledge by which this training can
alone be rightly guided. . . .

From the parental functions let us pass now to the functions
of the citizen. We have here to inquire what knowledge best fits
a man for the discharge of these functions. It cannot be alleged,
as in the last case, that the need for knowledge fitting him for
these functions is wholly overlooked; for our school courses contain certain studies which, nominally at least, bear upon political
and social duties. Of these the only one that occupies a prominent
place is history.

But, as already more than once hinted, the historic information
commonly given is almost valueless for purposes of guidance.
Scarcely any of the facts set down in our school histories, and
very few even of those contained in the more elaborate works
written for adults, give any clue to the right principles of political
action. The biographies of monarchs (and our children commonly
learn little else) throw scarcely any light upon the science of
society. . . .

That which it really concerns us to know, is the natural history
of society. We want all facts which help us to understand how
a nation has grown and organized itself. Among these, let us of
course have an account of its government; with as little as may
be of gossip about the men who officered it, and as much as pos-

sible about the structure, principles, methods, prejudices, corruptions, etc., which it exhibited, and let this account not only include the nature and actions of the central government but also those of local governments, down to their minutest ramification.

Let us at the same time be informed of the control exercised by class over class, as displayed in all social observances—in titles, salutations, and forms of address. Let us know, too, what were all the other customs which regulated the popular life out of doors and indoors: including those which concern the relations of the sexes, and the relations of parents to children. The superstitions, also, from the more important myths down to the charms in common use, should be indicated. Next should come a delineation of the industrial system: showing to what extent the division of labour was carried; how trades were regulated, whether by caste, guilds, or otherwise; what was the connection between employers and employed; what were the agencies for distributing commodities; what were the means of communication; what was the circulating medium. Accompanying all which should be given an account of the industrial arts technically considered, stating the processes in use, the quality of the products. Further, the intellectual condition of the nation in its various grades should be depicted, not only with respect to the kind and amount of education, but with respect to the progress made in science, and the prevailing manner of thinking. The degree of aesthetic culture, as displayed in architecture, sculpture, painting, dress, music, poetry, and fiction, should be described. Nor should there be omitted a sketch of the daily lives of the people —their food, their homes, and their amusements. And lastly, to connect the whole, should be exhibited the morals, theoretical and practical, of all classes: as indicated in their laws, habits, proverbs, deeds. . . . Such alone is the kind of information respecting past times, which can be of service to the citizen for the regulation of his conduct. The only history that is of practical value is what may be called descriptive sociology. And the highest office which the historian can discharge is that of so narrating the lives of nations as to furnish materials for a comparative sociology; and for the subsequent determination of the ultimate laws to which social phenomena conform. . . .

And now we come to that remaining division of human life

which includes the relaxations, pleasures, and amusements filling leisure hours. After considering what training best fits for self-preservation, for the obtainment of sustenance, for the discharge of parental duties, and for the regulation of social and political conduct; we have now to consider what training best fits for the miscellaneous ends not included in these—for the enjoyments of nature, of literature, and of the fine arts, in all their forms. Postponing them as we do to things that bear more vitally upon human welfare, and bringing everything, as we have, to the test of actual value, it will perhaps be inferred that we are inclined to slight these less essential things. No greater mistake could be made, however. We yield to none in the value we attach to aesthetic culture and its pleasures. Without painting, sculpture, music, poetry, and the emotions produced by natural beauty of every kind, life would lose half its charm. So far from thinking that the training and gratification of the tastes are unimportant, we believe the time will come when they will occupy a much larger share of human life than now. When the forces of Nature have been fully conquered to man's use—when the means of production have been brought to perfection—when labour has been economized to the highest degree—when education has been so systematized that a preparation for the more essential activities may be made with comparative rapidity—and when, consequently, there is a great increase of spare time; then will the poetry, both of art and nature, rightly fill a large space in the minds of all.

But it is one thing to admit that aesthetic culture is in a high degree conducive to human happiness; and another thing to admit that it is a fundamental requisite to human happiness. However important it may be, it must yield precedence to those kinds of culture which bear more directly upon the duties of life. . . .

And here we see most distinctly the vice of our educational system. It neglects the plant for the sake of the flower. In anxiety for elegance, it forgets substance. While it gives no knowledge conducive to self-preservation—while of knowledge that facilitates gaining a livelihood it gives but the rudiments, and leaves the greater part to be picked up anyhow in after life—while for the discharge of parental functions it makes not the slightest provision—and while for the duties of citizenship it prepares by imparting a mass of facts, most of which are irrelevant, and the rest without key; it is diligent in teaching everything that adds to refinement, polish, éclat. However fully we may admit that extensive acquaintance with modern languages is a valuable accomplishment, which, through reading, conversation, and travel, aids in giving a certain finish; it by no means follows that this result is rightly purchased at the cost of that vitally important knowledge sacrificed to it. Supposing it true that classical education conduces to elegance and correctness of style; it cannot be said that elegance and correctness of style are comparable in importance to a familiarity with the principles that should guide the rearing of children. Grant that the taste may be greatly improved by reading all the poetry written in extinct languages; yet it is not to be inferred that such improvement of taste is equivalent in value to an acquaintance with the laws of health. Accomplishments, the fine arts, *belles-lettres,* and all those things which, as we say, constitute the efflorescence of civilization should be wholly subordinate to that knowledge and discipline in which civilization rests. *As they occupy the leisure part of life, so should they occupy the leisure part of education.* . . .

APPLICATIONS IN EDUCATION

John Dewey

. . . There is nothing peculiar about educational aims. They are just like aims in any directed occupation. The educator, like the farmer, has certain things to do, certain resources with which

SOURCE: Reprinted with permission of the publisher from *Democracy and Education* by John Dewey. Copyright 1916 by The Macmillan Company. Renewed 1944 by John Dewey.

to do, and certain obstacles with which to contend. The conditions with which the farmer deals, whether as obstacles or resources, have their own structure and operation independently of any purpose of his. Seeds sprout, rain falls, the sun shines, insects devour, blight comes, the seasons change. His aim is simply to utilize these various conditions; to make his activities and their energies work together, instead of against one another. It would be absurd if the farmer set up a purpose of farming, without any reference to these conditions of soil, climate, characteristic of plant growth, etc. His purpose is simply a foresight of the consequences of his energies connected with those of the things about him, a foresight used to direct his movements from day to day. Foresight of possible consequences leads to more careful and extensive observation of the nature and performances of the things he had to do with, and to laying out a plan—that is, of a certain order in the acts to be performed.

It is the same with the educator, whether parent or teacher. It is as absurd for the latter to set up their "own" aims as the proper objects of the growth of the children as it would be for the farmer to set up an ideal of farming irrespective of conditions. Aims mean acceptance of responsibility for the observations, anticipations, and arrangements required in carrying on a function—whether farming or educating. Any aim is of value so far as it assists observation, choice, and planning in carrying on activity from moment to moment and hour to hour; if it gets in the way of the individual's own common sense (as it will surely do if imposed from without or accepted on authority) it does harm.

And it is well to remind ourselves that education as such has no aims. Only persons, parents, and teachers, etc., have aims, not an abstract idea like education. And consequently their purposes are indefinitely varied, differing with different children, changing as children grow and with the growth of experience on the part of the one who teaches. Even the most valid aims which can be put in words will, as words, do more harm than good unless one recognizes that they are not aims, but rather suggestions to educators as to how to observe, how to look ahead, and how to choose in liberating and directing the energies of the concrete situations in which they find themselves. As a recent writer has said: "To lead this boy to read Scott's novels instead of old Sleuth's stories; to teach this girl to sew; to root out the habit of bullying from John's make up; to prepare this class to study medicine—these are samples of the millions of aims we have actually before us in the concrete work of education."

Bearing these qualifications in mind, we shall proceed to state some of the characteristics found in all good educational aims. (1) An educational aim must be founded upon the intrinsic activities and needs (including original instincts and acquired habits) of the given individual to be educated. The tendency of such an aim as preparation is, as we have seen, to omit existing powers, and find the aim in some remote accomplishment or responsibility. In general, there is a disposition to take considerations which are dear to the hearts of adults and set them up as ends irrespective of the capacities of those educated. There is also an inclination to propound aims which are so uniform as to neglect the specific powers and requirements of an individual, forgetting that all learning is something which happens to an individual at a given time and place. The larger range of perception of the adult is of great value in observing the abilities and weaknesses of the young, in deciding what they may amount to. Thus the artistic capacities of the adult exhibit what certain tendencies of the child are capable of; if we did not have the adult achievements we should be without assurance as to the significance of the drawing, reproducing, modeling, coloring activities of childhood. So if it were not for adult language, we should not be able to see the import of the babbling impulses of infancy. But it is one thing to use adult accomplishments as a context in which to place and survey the doings of childhood and youth; it is quite another to set them up as a fixed aim without regard to the concrete activities of those educated.

(2) An aim must be capable of translation into a method of cooperating with the activities of those undergoing instruction. It must suggest the kind of environment needed to liberate and to organize *their* capacities. Unless it lends itself to the construction of specific procedures, and unless these procedures test, correct, and amplify the aims, the latter is worthless. Instead of helping the specific task of teaching, it prevents the use of ordinary judgment in observing and sizing up the situation. It op-

erates to exclude recognition of everything except what squares up with the fixed end in view. Every rigid aim just because it is rigidly given seems to render it unnecessary to give careful attention to concrete conditions. Since it *must* apply anyhow, what is the use of noting details which do not count?

The vice of externally imposed ends has deep roots. Teachers receive them from superior authorities; these authorities accept them from what is current in the community. The teachers impose them upon children. As a first consequence, the intelligence of the teacher is not free; it is confined to receiving the aims laid down from above. Too rarely is the individual teacher so free from the dictation of authoritative supervisor, textbook on methods, prescribed course of study, etc., that he can let his mind come to close quarters with the pupil's mind and the subject matter. This distrust of the teacher's experience is then reflected in lack of confidence in the responses of pupils. The latter receive their aims through a double or treble external imposition, and are constantly confused by the conflict between the aims which are natural to their own experience at the time and those in which they are taught to acquiesce. Until the democratic criterion of the intrinsic significance of every growing experience is recognized, we shall be intellectually confused by the demand for adaptation to external aims.

(3) Educators have to be on their guard against ends that are alleged to be general and ultimate. Every activity, however specific, is, of course, general in its ramified connections, for it leads out indefinitely into other things. So far as a general idea makes us more alive to these connections, it cannot be too general. But "general" also means "abstract," or detached from all specific context. And such abstractness means remoteness, and throws us back, once more, upon teaching and learning as mere means of getting ready for an end disconnected from the means. That education is literally and all the time its own reward means that no alleged study or discipline is educative unless it is worth while in its own immediate having. A truly general aim broadens the outlook; it stimulates one to take more consequences (connections) into account. This means a wider and more flexible observation of means. The more interacting forces, for example, the farmer takes into account, the more varied will be his im-

mediate resources. He will see a greater number of possible starting places, and a greater number of ways of getting at what he wants to do. The fuller one's conception of possible future achievements, the less his present activity is tied down to a small number of alternatives. If one knew enough, one could start almost anywhere and sustain his activities continuously and fruitfully.

Understanding then the term *general or comprehensive aim* simply in the sense of a broad survey of the field of present activities, we shall take up some of the larger ends which have currency in the educational theories of the day, and consider what light they throw upon the immedate concrete and diversified aims which are always the educator's real concern. We premise (as indeed immediately follows from what has been said) that there is no need of making a choice among them or regarding them as competitors. When we come to act in a tangible way we have to select or choose a particular act at a particular time, but any number of comprehensive ends may exist without competition, since they mean simply different ways of looking at the same scene. One cannot climb a number of different mountains simultaneously, but the views had when different mountains are ascended supplement one another: they do not set up incompatible, competing worlds. Or, putting the matter in a slightly different way, one statement of an end may suggest certain questions and observations, and another statement another set of questions, calling for other observations. Then the more general ends we have, the better. One statement will emphasize what another slurs over. What a plurality of hypotheses does for the scientific investigator, a plurality of stated aims may do for the instructor.

DARE THE SCHOOL BUILD A NEW SOCIAL ORDER?

George S. Counts

~~~~~~

That the existing school is leading the way to a better social order is a thesis which few informed persons would care to defend. Except as it is forced to fight for its own life during times of depression, its course is too serene and untroubled. Only in the rarest of instances does it wage war on behalf of principle or ideal. Almost everywhere it is in the grip of conservative forces and is serving the cause of perpetuating ideas and institutions suited to an age that is gone. But there is one movement above the educational horizon which would seem to show promise of genuine and creative leadership. I refer to the Progressive Education movement. Surely in this union of two of the great faiths of the American people, the faith in progress and the faith in education, we have reason to hope for light and guidance. Here is a movement which would seem to be completely devoted to the promotion of social welfare through education.

Even a casual examination of the program and philosophy of the Progressive schools, however, raises many doubts in the mind. To be sure, these schools have a number of large achievements to their credit. They have focused attention squarely upon the child; they have recognized the fundamental importance of the interest of the learner; they have defended the thesis that activity lies at the root of all true education; they have conceived learning in terms of life situations and growth of character; they have championed the rights of the child as a free personality. Most of this is excellent, but in my judgment it is not enough. It constitutes too narrow a conception of the mean-

SOURCE: Copyright 1932 by George S. Counts. Reprinted from *Dare the School Build a New Social Order?* by George S. Counts by permission of The John Day Company, Inc., publisher.

ing of education; it brings into the picture but one half of the landscape.

If an educational movement, or any other movement, calls itself progressive, it must have orientation; it must possess direction. The word itself implies moving forward, and moving forward can have little meaning in the absence of clearly defined purposes. We cannot, like Stephen Leacock's horseman, dash off in all directions at once. Nor should we, like our presidential candidates, evade every disturbing issue and be all things to all men. Also we must beware lest we become so devoted to motion that we neglect the question of direction and be entirely satisfied with movement in circles. Here, I think, we find the fundamental weakness, not only of Progressive Education, but also of American education generally. Like a baby shaking a rattle, we seem to be utterly content with action, provided it is sufficiently vigorous and noisy. In the last analysis a very large part of American educational thought, inquiry, and experimentation is much ado about nothing. And, if we are permitted to push the analogy of the rattle a bit further, our consecration to motion *is* encouraged and supported in order to keep us out of mischief. At least we know that so long as we thus busy ourselves we shall not incur the serious displeasure of our social elders.

THE CONCEPT OF NEEDS IN EDUCATION

Boyd H. Bode

~~~~~~

All this is but a roundabout way of saying that needs refer to ends or aims. In specific situations where the end in view may be taken for granted, it is entirely appropriate to speak of needs, since the end or purpose furnishes a point of reference for judging the needs. But to undertake to build an educational program by starting with needs is quite another matter. Unless we assume that there is a predestined end for human living and that we are in on the know as to what this end is, there is no justification whatsoever for talking so blithely about needs. An authoritarian scheme of education could make excellent use of a doctrine of needs, for it would be in a position to know at every point what it was talking about. In a democratic system of education the center of the plot must always be the continuous rebuilding of the scheme of values, the underlying philosophy or social outlook, by the pupil, as a basis for determining his needs. At first the social and material environment can only furnish an opportunity to choose between alternative conceptions of needs—and even this opportunity is largely dependent on cooperation by the school in supplying the conditions for making an intelligent choice.

The point at issue is far more than the verbal question of how the "need" is to be employed. It concerns the question of what education should be primarily concerned to achieve. The failure to emancipate ourselves completely from Rousseauism and the instinct psychology is responsible for most, if not all, the weaknesses of the progressive movement in education. The attitude of superstitious reverence for childhood is still with us.

SOURCE: Boyd H. Bode, "The Concept of Needs in Education," *Progressive Education*, Vol. 15, January, 1938, pp. 7–9. Reprinted by permission.

The insistence that we must stick like a leech at all times to the "needs" of childhood has bred a spirit of anti-intellectualism, which is recognized in the reliance on improvizing instead of long-range organization, in the overemphasis of the here and now, in the indiscriminate tirades against "subjects," in the absurdities of pupil planning, and in the lack of continuity in the educational program. It has frequently resulted in an unhealthy attitude towards children, an attitude which suggests that there is no such thing as a normal child, and that we must be everlastingly exploring his insides, like a Calvinist taking himself apart day after day to discover evidences of sin.

It is a commonplace that the infant's only chance to grow into a human being is through social relationships. This is only another way of saying that growth is not directed from within but by the "patterns" embodied in the social order. If we believe in progress, in a democratic sense, we must believe that these patterns require continuous revision. As they actually exist in our complex modern world, they not only present conflicting types, but the basic patterns are severally incoherent and internally contradictory. In business, for example, we accept both the profit motive and the ideal of social service; in government we hold to both rugged individualism and the ideal of social security; in the field of esthetics we find that standards are both absolute and relative. Yet these are the patterns which must serve as instrumentalities for "growth." In a properly organized educational system this confusion in our cultural heritage will be the constant point of reference, instead of being merely appended, like the tail to the kite, as an additional item after we have set up the program in terms of "needs," the concept of needs thus making a red herring drawn across the trail. What we need is a moratorium on needs, so that we can get down to serious business and bring to fruition the splendid promise that is contained in the philosophy of progressive education.

PHILOSOPHY OF EDUCATION AS
PHILOSOPHY OF POLITICS

Theodore Brameld

~~~~~~

. . . In short, education in its comprehensive sense should become the copartner of politics—the politics of comprehending and implementing popular government on a world-wide scale. The philosophy of education thereby becomes primarily concerned with the foundations upon which this copartnership functions.

If, however, we are to dedicate ourselves to this objective, our initial duty is to assess realistically and to devise strategies for overcoming the obstacles in our way. Three such obstacles may be chosen for brief analysis.

The first is the inference . . . that, because mass understanding always lags behind social accomplishment, therefore workable self-government in the foreseeable future is impossible, on the one hand, and a professedly benevolent dictatorship of indefinite duration is inevitable, on the other hand. This point of view, as we know, exerts vast influence upon our generation; indeed, it has slowly become the single most compelling adversary of the democratic conviction that the average person even now can learn how and for what purposes to engage in popular rule. . . .

A second resistance in the path of government by and for an educated people is the hard realization that understanding of social processes and structures is by no means assuredly increasing at a rate commensurate with popular requirements—that, rather, it may be in many cases actually decreasing. Moreover,

SOURCE: From *Education for an Emerging Age* by Theodore Brameld. Copyright 1950 by Harper & Brothers; copyright © 1961 by Theodore Brameld. Reprinted with the permission of Harper & Row, Publishers, Incorporated.

to a great extent technology is again ironically responsible: we are thinking here, of course, of our powerful engines of public opinion. Nor can we dispute the fact that the newspaper, magazine, photograph, motion picture, radio, and television are in largest part rigidly controlled by forces benefiting by as wide a disparity as possible between mass comprehension and social import. So dextrously indeed do they now manipulate the average mind that one may even inquire whether they are not, in actuality, perhaps more determinative of popular attitudes and habits than is the whole of organized formal education.

That public opinion sometimes serves to awaken people to their own larger interests should also, of course, be recognized. Partly because of it, though more largely for such other reasons as the rapid growth of self-enlightening mass movements, the oppressed millions in countries like India and Africa are gradually becoming more articulate, more restless, more indignant than ever before in recorded history. Yet, at the same time, this phenomenon of mass awareness nervously incites those so largely in control of public opinion to develop all the more ingenious techniques for keeping the chasm wide.

The last obstacle chosen to illustrate the scope of our key problem is the present status of education itself. Despite the commendable pronouncements of American school leaders, an astounding array of evidence can be mustered to show how often democratic ideals become hypocritical shibboleths concealing autocratic types of practice. Observe, too, the alacrity with which the ordinary school helps to oil and fuel the very engines of public opinion to which we have referred.

Nor are the obstacles induced by the status of current education confined to such misguided practices. Educational theory, also, frequently renders conscious or unconscious support to misunderstanding rather than understanding, to social acquiescence rather than activity. Here again we are limited to merely one or two examples. One is the sort of philosophy, whatever its name, that helps at least indirectly to undermine full confidence in self-government by assuming that men are not, after all, sufficient judges of what is good for them—that accordingly some transcendental fountainhead of goodness is required upon which men may draw when desperate or doubtful of their own sovereign capacity. A second, quite different from the first, is the sort of philosophy which limits itself chiefly to methodological considerations; and which, therefore, despite its more consistent respect for man's right to serve as his own exclusive governor, discourages the full exercise of that right by shunning commitment to those concrete cultural designs that are both compulsions and symbols of political maturity. . . .

We in educational philosophy, no less than those in psychology or other foundational studies, need now to establish much more active association, not only with experts in curriculum, in method, in adult education, but also with experts in other fields like politics itself.

Such association should include more thorough experimentation with semantics, propaganda analysis, and other techniques leading in turn both to ruthless exposure and to democratic direction of the devices now threatening to destroy the brain cells of popular mentality. It should provide literally thousands of opportunities for the practice of learning through and toward the achievement of wide consensuses, themselves the symbol of public rule of the deeper organic significance I have been trying to imply. It should encourage communication with the educational philosophers of countries beyond America, looking toward influencing such potentially important agencies of international understanding as UNESCO. It should lead to action on all community levels in order to strengthen our grasp of conflicting social forces, of the meaning of the state, of the structures and processes of government. It should stimulate cultural designing as an indispensable way of building inductive commitment to the axiological and institutional patterns demanded by the new world that is being born.

Finally, such association should include relentless examination of the chief alternatives. One is offered . . . because mass understanding remains below that of objective conditions, therefore rule by the few—albeit an ostensibly well-intentioned few—becomes inescapable, at least until some nebulous if not receding future. The second great alternative is, of course, the tyranny of minorities concerned only with manipulating people to maintain their own entrenched power, their private gains, even if the cost is world-wide bloodshed or starvation.

The third solution is that for which I plead. That difficulties in its way are staggering is indisputable. Yet education, hand in hand with politics, can and should become the one remaining power greater than the power of the atom. To bridge the chasm, to bring public understanding to its rightful heritage of full public control, this is the primary task of reconstructed theory expressed in militant democratic practice.

THE ESSENTIALIST PHILOSOPHY OF EDUCATION

William C. Bagley

∼∼∼∼∼∼∼∼∼∼∼∼∼∼∼∼∼∼∼∼∼∼∼∼∼∼∼∼∼∼∼∼∼∼∼∼∼

. . . Hence a primary function of American education will be to safeguard and strengthen these ideals of American democracy with especial emphasis upon freedom of speech, freedom of the press, freedom of assembly, and freedom of religion. It is clear enough now that whenever any one of these is permitted to collapse, the whole democratic structure will topple like a house of cards. These, then, are among the first essentials in the platform of the Essentialist.

11. This problem is far more than merely personal or individual in its reference. A democratic society has a vital, collective stake in the informed intelligence of every individual citizen. That a literate electorate is absolutely indispensable not only to its welfare but to its very survival is clearly demonstrated by the sorry fate that so speedily overtook every unschooled and il-

SOURCE: William C. Bagley, "An Essentialist's Platform for the Advancement of American Education," *Educational Administration and Supervision,* Vol. 24, April, 1938, pp. 241–256. Reprinted by permission.

130 PHILOSOPHY OF SECONDARY EDUCATION

literate democracy founded as a result of the War that was to "Make the world safe for democracy."

And literacy in this sense means, of course, far more than the mere ability to translate printed letters into spoken words; it means the development and expansion of ideas; it means the basis for intelligent understanding and for the collective thought and judgment which are the essence of democratic institutions. These needs are so fundamental to an effective democracy that it would be folly to leave them to the whim or caprice of either learner or teacher.

Among the essentials of the Essentialist, then, is a recognition of the right of the immature learner to guidance and direction when these are needed either for his individual welfare or for the welfare and progress of the democratic group. The responsibility of the mature for the instruction and control of the immature is the biological meaning of the extended period of human immaturity and necessary dependence. It took the human race untold ages to recognize this responsibility. It is literally true that until this recognition dawned man remained a savage. Primitive societies, as numerous students have observed (and their testimony seems to be unanimous), pamper and indulge their young. Freedom of children from control, guidance, and discipline is with them a rule so nearly universal that its only brief but significant exception during the nearly universal savage ceremonies marking the adolescent onset of maturity is regarded as the first faint beginning of consciously directed human education.

It would be futile to deny that control and discipline may be stupid and brutal and used for unworthy ends. It would be futile to deny the need for the development of self-discipline and for the relaxation of external discipline with the growth of volitional maturity. But all this does not alter the fundamental truth that freedom must go hand in hand with responsibility, and that responsible freedom is always a conquest, never a gift.

12. An effective democracy demands a community of culture. Educationally this means that each generation be placed in possession of a common core of ideas, meanings, understandings, and ideals representing the most precious elements of the human heritage.

There can be little question as to the essentials. It is by no means a mere accident that the arts of recording, computing, and measuring have been among the first concerns of organized education. They are basic social arts. Every civilized society has been founded upon these arts, and when these arts have been lost, civilization has invariably and inevitably collapsed. Egypt, Asia Minor, and Mesopotamia are strewn with the ruins of civilizations that forgot how to read and write. Contemporary civilization, for the first time in history has attempted to insure its continuance by making these arts in so far as possible the prerogative of all.

Nor is it at all accidental that a knowledge of the world that lies beyond one's immediate experience has been among the recognized essentials of universal education, and that at least a speaking acquaintance with man's past and especially with the story of one's own country was early provided for in the program of the universal school. Widening the space horizon and extending the time perspective are essential if the citizen is to be protected from the fallacies of the local and the immediate.

Investigation, invention, and creative art have added to the heritage and the list of recognized essentials has been extended and will be further extended. Health instruction and the inculcation of health practices are now basic phases of the work of the lower schools. The elements of natural science have their place. Neither the fine arts nor the industrial arts are neglected.

13. A specific program of studies including these essentials should be the heart of a democratic system of education. In a country like ours with its highly mobile population there should be an agreement as to the order and grade-placement of subjects and especially of crucial topics. There is no valid reason for the extreme localism that has come to characterize American education. There is no valid reason for the failure of the American elementary school to lay as firm a foundation in the fundmentals of education as do the elementary schools of other democracies. It is especially regrettable that contemporary educational theory should in effect condone and rationalize scamped work by ridiculing such traits as thoroughness, accuracy, persistence, and the ideal of good workmanship for its own sake. One may be very sure that democracy schooled to the easy way will have short

shrift in competition or conflict with any social order dominated by objectives which, however reprehensible, are clear-cut and appealing, and are consequently embraced even by disenfranchised masses.

THE INTELLECTUAL VIRTUES

Robert M. Hutchins

In this chapter I should like to talk about content, not about method. I concede the great difficulty of communicating the kind of education I favor to those who are unable or unwilling to get their education from books. I insist, however, that the education I shall outline is the kind that everybody should have, that the answer to it is not that some people should not have it, but that we should find out how to give it to those whom we do not know how to teach at present. You cannot say my content is wrong because you do not know the method of transmitting it. Let us agree upon content if we can have faith that the technological genius of America will solve the problem of communication.

Economic conditions require us to provide some kind of education for the young, and for all the young, up to about their twentieth year. Probably one third of them cannot learn from books. This is no reason why we should not try to work out a better course of study for the other two thirds. At the same time we should continue our efforts and experiments to find

SOURCE: Robert M. Hutchins, "The Intellectual Virtues," *The Higher Learning in America* (New Haven, Conn.: Yale University Press, 1936). Reprinted by permission.

out how to give a general education to the hand-minded and the functionally illiterate. Even these attempts may be somewhat simplified if we know what a general education is.

Please do not tell me that the general education I propose should not be adopted because the great majority of those who pass through it will not go on to the university. The scheme that I advance is based on the notion that general education is education for everybody, whether he goes on to the university or not. It will be useful to him in the university; it will be equally useful if he never goes there. I will admit that it will not be useful to him outside the university in the popular sense of utility. It may not assist him to make money or to get ahead. It may not in any obvious fashion adjust him to his environment or fit him for the contemporary scene. It will, however, have a deeper, wider utility: it will cultivate the intellectual virtues.

The trouble with the popular notion of utility is that it confuses immediate and final ends. Material prosperity and adjustment to the environment are good more or less, but they are not good in themselves and there are other goods beyond them. The intellectual virtues, however, are good in themselves and good as means to happiness. By the intellectual virtues I mean good intellectual habits. The ancients distinguish five intellectual virtues: the three speculative virtues of intuitive knowledge, which is the habit of induction; of scientific knowledge, which is the habit of demonstration; and of philosophical wisdom, which is scientific knowledge, combined with intuitive reason, of things highest by nature, first principles and first causes. To these they add the two virtues of the practical intellect: art, the capacity to make according to a true course of reasoning, and prudence, which is right reason with respect to action.

In short, the intellectual virtues are habits resulting from the training of the intellectual powers. An intellect properly disciplined, an intellect properly habituated, is an intellect able to operate well in all fields. An education that consists of the cultivation of the intellectual virtues, therefore, is the most useful education, whether the student is destined for a life of contemplation or a life of action.

I shall not be attentive when you tell me that the plan of

general education I am about to present is remote from real life, that real life is in constant flux and change, and that education must be in constant flux and change as well. I do not deny that all things are in change. They have a beginning, and a middle, and an end. Nor will I deny that the history of the race reveals tremendous technological advances and great increases in our scientific knowledge. But we are so impressed with scientific and technological progress that we assume similar progress in every field. We renounce our intellectual heritage, read only the most recent books, discuss only current events, try to keep the schools abreast or even ahead of the times, and write elaborate addresses on Education and Social Change. Our erroneous notion of progress has thrown the classics and the liberal arts out of the curriculum, overemphasized the empirical sciences, and made education the servant of any contemporary movements in society, no matter how superficial. In recent years this attitude has been accentuated by the world-wide depression and the highly advertised political, social, and economic changes resulting from it. We have been very much upset by all these things. We have felt that it was our duty to educate the young so that they would be prepared for further political, social, and economic changes. Some of us have thought we should try to figure out what the impending changes would be and frame a curriculum that embodied them. Others have even thought that we should decide what changes are desirable and then educate our students not merely to anticipate them, but also to take part in bringing them about. One purpose of education is to draw out the elements of our common human nature. These elements are the same in any time or place. The notion of educating a man to live in any particular time or place, to adjust him to any particular environment, is therefore foreign to a true conception of education.

Education implies teaching. Teaching implies knowledge. Knowledge is truth. The truth is everywhere the same. Hence education should be everywhere the same. I do not overlook the possibilities of differences in organization, in administration, in local habits and customs. These are details. I suggest that the heart of any course of study designed for the whole people will be, if education is rightly understood, the same at any time, in any place, under any political, social, or economic conditions.

Even the administrative details are likely to be similar because all societies have generic similarity.

If education is rightly understood, it will be understood as the cultivation of the intellect. The cultivation of the intellect is the same good for all men in all societies. It is, moreover, the good for which all other goods are only means. Material prosperity, peace and civil order, justice and the moral virtues are means to the cultivation of the intellect. So Aristotle says in the *Politics:* "Now, in men reason and mind are the end toward which nature strives, so that the generation and moral discipline of the citizens ought to be ordered with a view to them." An education which served the means rather than their end would be misguided.

I agree, of course, that any plan of general education must be such as to educate the student for intelligent action. It must, therefore, start him on the road toward practical wisdom. But the question is what is the best way for education to start him and how far can it carry him. Prudence or practical wisdom selects the means toward the ends that we desire. It is acquired partly from intellectual operations and partly from experience. But the chief requirement for it is correctness in thinking. Since education cannot duplicate the experiences which the student will have when he graduates, it should devote itself to the developing correctness in thinking as a means to practical wisdom, that is, to intelligent action. A modern heresy is that all education is formal education and that formal education must assume the total responsibility for the full development of the individual. The Greek notion that the city educates the man has been forgotten. Everything that educated the man in the city has to be imported into our schools, colleges, and universities. We are beginning to behave as though the home, the church, the state, the newspapers, the radio, the movies, the neighborhood club, and the boy next door did not exist. All the experience that is daily and hourly acquired from these sources is overlooked, and we set out to supply imitations of it in educational institutions. The experience once provided by some of these agencies may be attenuated now; but it would be a bold man who would assert that the young person today lived a life less full of experience than the youth of yesterday. Today as yesterday we may leave experience to other institutions and influences and emphasize in education the contribution that it is supremely fitted to make, the intellectual training of the young. The life they lead when they are out of our hands will give them experience enough. We cannot try to give it to them and at the same time perform the task that is ours and ours alone.

Young people do not spend all their time in school. Their elders commonly spend none of it there. Yet their elders are, we hope, constantly growing in practical wisdom. They are, at least, having experience. If we can teach them while they are being educated how to reason, they may be able to comprehend and assimilate their experience. It is a good principle of educational administration that a college or university should do nothing that another agency can do as well. This is a good principle because a college or university has a vast and complicated job if it does what only it can do. In general education, therefore, we may wisely leave experience to life and set about our job of intellectual training.

If there are permanent studies which every person who wishes to call himself educated should master, if those studies constitute our intellectual inheritance, then those studies should be the center of a general education. They cannot be ignored because they are difficult, or unpleasant, or because they are almost totally missing from our curriculum today. The child-centered school may be attractive to the child, and no doubt is useful as a place in which the little ones may release their inhibitions and hence behave better at home. But educators cannot permit the students to dictate the course of study unless they are prepared to confess that they are nothing but chaperons, supervising an aimless, trial-and-error process which is chiefly valuable because it keeps young people from doing something worse. The free elective system as Mr. Eliot introduced it at Harvard and as Progressive Education adapted it to lower age levels amounted to a denial that there was content to education. Since there was no content to education, we might as well let students follow their own bent. They would at least be interested and pleased and would be as well educated as if they had pursued a prescribed course of study. This overlooks the fact that the aim of education is to connect man with man, to connect the present with the past, and to advance the thinking of the race. If this is the aim of education, it cannot be left to the sporadic, spontaneous interests of children or even of undergraduates.

It cannot be assumed that students at any age will always select the subjects that constitute education. If we permit them to avoid them, we cannot confer upon them insignia which certify to the public that they are in our opinion educated. In any field the permanent studies on which the whole development of the subject rests must be mastered if the student is to be educated.

The variations that should be encouraged fall not in the realm of content but in that of method. Allowances for individual differences should be provided for by abolishing all requirements except the examinations and permitting the student to take them whenever in his opinion he is ready to do so. The cultivation of independent thought and study, now almost wholly missing from our program, may thus be somewhat advanced. And this may be done without sacrificing the content of education to the obsessions of the hour or the caprices of the young.

If we are educators we must have a subject matter, and a rational, defensible one. If that subject matter is education, we cannot alter it to suit the whims of parents, students, or the public. . . .

In general education we are interested in drawing out the elements of our common human nature; we are interested in the attributes of the race, not the accidents of individuals.

If our course of study reflects today an interest in the accidents of individuals; if the permanent studies are conspicuous by their absence from it, I can only say that these are the reasons why our course of study is bad. We know that our course of study leads to the most unfortunate results in the organization of education, in the qualities and activities of professors and students, and in the cultivation of our people. It is surely not a criticism of the permanent studies that they have had no share in producing these results.

By insisting on the permanent studies as the heart of a general education I do not mean to insist that they are the whole of it. We do not know enough to know whether certain technological work, for example, may not have certain subsidiary value in general education for some students. Nor do I overlook the fact that since by hypothesis general education may be terminal for most students, it must connect them with the present and future as well as with the past. It is as important for them to know that thinking is still going on as it is for them to know what has been thought before.

The question whether certain technical work shall be allowed to be a part of general education is rather a question of method than of content, a question how to teach rather than what. Technology as such has no place in general education. If it can be justified at all, it can only be because we discover that certain principles can best be communicated through technical work. The question of present thought is largely answered by saying that it is impossible to think of a teacher who contented himself with elucidating the thought of the past without intimating that these ideas have a history running to the present day. . . .

Let us avoid all questions of administration and method. Let us assume that we have an intelligible organization of education under which there is a four-year unit, beginning at about the beginning of the junior year in high school and ending at about the end of the sophomore year in college. Let us assume that we are going to try to teach in that unit everybody who can learn from books. Let us assume further that the conclusion of their work in this unit will mark the end of formal instruction for most students. They will not go on to the university. Nevertheless we must have a curriculum which will, in the main, do as well for those who are going on as those who are not. What shall this curriculum be?

We have excluded body building and character building. We have excluded the social graces and the tricks of trades. We have suggested that the curriculum should be composed principally of the permanent studies. We propose the permanent studies because these studies draw out the elements of our common human nature, because they connect man with man, because they connect us with the best that man has thought, because they are basic to any further study and to any understanding of the world. What are the permanent studies?

They are in the first place those books which have through the centuries attained to the dimensions of classics. Many such books,

I am afraid, are in the ancient and medieval period. But even these are contemporary. A classic is a book that is contemporary in every age. That is why it is a classic. The conversations of Socrates raise questions that are as urgent today as they were when Plato wrote. In fact they are more so, because the society in which Plato lived did not need to have them raised as much as we do. We have forgotten how important they are.

Such books are then a part, and a large part, of the permanent studies. They are so in the first place because they are the best books we know. How can we call a man educated who has never read any of the great books in the western world? Yet today it is entirely possible for a student to graduate from the finest American colleges without having read any of them, except possibly Shakespeare. Of course, the student may have heard of these books, or at least of their authors. But this knowledge is gained in general through textbooks, and textbooks have probably done as much to degrade the American intelligence as any single force. If the student should know about Cicero, Milton, Galileo, or Adam Smith, why should he not read what they wrote? Ordinarily what he knows about them he learns from texts which must be at best secondhand versions of their thought.

In the second place these books are an essential part of general education because it is impossible to understand any subject or to comprehend the contemporary world without them. If we read Newton's *Principia*, we see a great genius in action; we make the acquaintance of a work of unexampled simplicity and elegance. We understand, too, the basis of modern science. The false starts, the backing and filling, the wildness, the hysteria, the confusion of modern thought and the modern world result from the loss of what has been thought and done by earlier ages. The Industrial Revolution begins our study of history and the social sciences. Philosophy begins with Descartes and Locke and psychology with Wundt and William James. Natural science originates with the great experimenters of the nineteenth century. . . .

You will observe that the great books of the western world cover every department of knowledge. The *Republic* of Plato is basic to an understanding of the law; it is equally important as education for what is known as citizenship. The *Physics* of Aristotle, which deals with change and motion in nature, is fundamental to the natural sciences and medicine, and is equally important to all those who confront change and motion in nature, that is, to everybody. Four years spent partly in reading, discussing and digesting books of such importance would, therefore, contribute equally to preparation for specialized study and to general education of a terminal variety. Certainly four years is none too long for this experience. It is an experience which will, as I have said, serve as preparation for advanced study and as general education designed to help the student understand the world. It will also develop habits of reading and standards of taste and criticism that will enable the adult, after his formal education is over, to think and act intelligently about the thought and movements of contemporary life. It will help him to share in the intellectual activity of his time.

In order to read books one must know how to do it. The degeneracy of instruction in English grammar should not blind us to the fact that only through grammatical study can written works be understood. Grammar is the scientific analysis of language through which we understand the meaning and force of what is written. Grammar disciplines the mind and develops the logical faculty. It is good in itself and as an aid to reading the classics. It has a place in general education in connection with the classics and independently of them. For those who are going to learn from books learning the art of reading would seem to be indispensable.

I do not suggest that learning the languages or the grammar in which the ancient classics were written is necessary to general education. Excellent translations of almost all of them now exist. Unless it can be shown that the study of Greek and Latin grammar is essential to the study of English grammar or that the mastery of the Greek and Latin languages is essential to mastery of our own, I see no reason for insisting on these languages as part of general education. The modern languages, of course, are no necessary part of it. Time should be allowed for students to acquire them, but the examinations reflecting general education should not contain them. They are an extracurriculum accomplishment or a tool for advanced work rather than a fundamental portion of general education.

I add to grammar, or the rules of reading, rhetoric, and logic, or the rules of writing, speaking, and reasoning. The classics provide models of excellence; grammar, rhetoric, and logic are means of determining how excellence is achieved. We have forgotten that there are rules for speaking. And English composition, as it is commonly taught, is a feeble and debased imitation of the classical rules of writing, placing emphasis either on the most trivial details or on what is called self-expression. Self-expression as here understood is, of course, the exact reverse of the discipline which rhetoric in all ages up to the present was used to give. Logic is a statement in technical form of the conditions under which reasoning is rigorously demonstrative. If the object of general education is to train the mind for intelligent action, logic cannot be missing from it.

Logic is a critical branch of the study of reasoning. It remains only to add a study which exemplifies reasoning in its clearest and most precise form. That study is, of course, mathematics, and of the mathematical studies chiefly those that use the type of exposition that Euclid employed. In such studies the pure operation of reason is made manifest. The subject matter depends on the universal and necessary processes of human thought. It is not affected by differences in taste, disposition, or prejudice. It refutes the common answer of students who, conformable to the temper of the time, wish to accept the principles and deny the conclusions. Correctness in thinking may be more directly and impressively taught through mathematics than in any other way.[1] It is depressing that in high schools and junior colleges mathematics is not often taught in such a way as to achieve these ends. Arithmetic and geometry are there usually presented to the student as having great practical value, as of course they have.[2] But I have had students in the freshman year in college who had never heard that they had any other value, and who were quite unwilling to consider mathematical questions until their practical

---

[1] " 'You see, then, my friend,' said I, 'that this branch of study really seems to be indispensable for us since it plainly compels the souls to employ pure thought with a view to truth itself.' " Plato, *Republic*, Book VII.

[2] Plato on geometers: "Their language is most ludicrous, though they cannot help it, for they speak as if they were doing something and as if all their words were directed toward action. For all their talk is of squaring and applying and adding and the like, whereas the real object of the entire study is pure thought." *Ibid.* See also Aristotle, *Ethics*, 2098a.

possibilities had been explained. To this pass has our notion of utility brought us.

We have then for general education a course of study consisting of the greatest books of the western world and the arts of reading, writing, thinking, and speaking, together with mathematics, the best exemplar of the processes of human reason. If our hope has been to frame a curriculum which educes the elements of our common human nature, this program should realize our hope. If we wish to prepare the young for intelligent action, this course of study should assist us; for they will have learned what has been done in the past, and what the greatest men have thought. They will have learned how to think themselves. If we wish to lay a basis for advanced study, that basis is provided. If we wish to secure true universities, we may look forward to them, because students and professors may acquire through this course of study a common stock of ideas and common methods of dealing with them. All the needs of general education in America seem to be satisfied by this curriculum.

What, then, are the objections to it? They cannot be educational objections; for this course of study appears to accomplish the aims of general education. One objection may be that the students will not like it, which is, as we have seen, irrelevant. But even if it were relevant, it is not true. Since the proposed curriculum is coherent and comprehensible, and since it is free from the triviality that now afflicts our program, students will respond to it if the teachers will give them a chance to do it.

It may be said that the course of study is too difficult. It is not too difficult for students who can read or who can be taught to do so. For ease of reading, as well as other qualities, *The Federalist*, an American classic, is superior to some recent treatises on government and public administration; Herodotus is more sprightly than most modern historians of the ancient world; and Plato and Aristotle are as intelligible as contemporary philosophers.

No, the students can do the work if the faculties will let them. Will the faculties let them? I doubt it. The professors of today have been brought up differently. Not all of them have read all the books they would have to teach. Not all of them are ready to change the habits of their lives. Meanwhile they are bringing up their successors in the way they were brought up, so that the next crop will have the habits they have had themselves. And the love of money, a misconception of democracy, a false notion of progress, a distorted idea of utility, and the anti-intellectualism to which all these lead conspire to confirm their conviction that no disturbing change is needed. The times call for the establishment of a new college or for an evangelistic movement in some old ones which shall have for its object the conversion of individuals and finally of the teaching profession to a true conception of general education. Unless some such demonstration or some such evangelistic movement can take place, we shall remain in our confusion; we shall have neither general education nor universities; and we shall continue to disappoint the hopes of our people.

THE CHRISTIAN EDUCATION OF YOUTH

Pope Pius XI

~~~~~~

. . . Hence it is that in this proper object of her mission, that is, "in faith and morals, God Himself has made the Church sharer in the divine magisterium and, by a special privilege, granted her immunity from error; hence she is the mistress of men, supreme and absolutely sure, and she has inherent in herself an inviolable right to freedom in teaching." By necessary consequence the Church is independent of any sort of earthly power as well in the origin as in exercise of her mission as educator, not merely in regard to

SOURCE: Pope Pius XI, Five Great Encyclicals *The Christian Education of Youth* (New York: Paulist Press, 1929), pp. 39–45, 48, 50–51, 61–62, 65–68. Reprinted by permission.

her proper end and object, but also in regard to the means necessary and suitable to attain that end. Hence with regard to every other kind of human learning and instruction, which is the common patrimony of individuals and society, the Church has an independent right to make use of it, and above all to decide what may help or harm Christian education. And this must be so, because the Church as a perfect society has an independent right to the means conducive to its end, and because every form of instruction, no less than every human action, has a necessary connection with man's last end, and therefore cannot be withdrawn from the dictates of the divine law, of which the Church is guardian, interpreter and infallible mistress. . . .

The Rights of the Church. Therefore with full right the Church promotes letters, science, art, in so far as necessary or helpful to Christian education, in addition to her work for the salvation of souls; founding and maintaining schools and institutions adapted to every branch of learning and degree of culture. Nor may even physical culture, as it is called, be considered outside the range of her maternal supervision, for the reason that it also is a means which may help or harm Christian education.

And this work of the Church in every branch of culture is of immense benefit to families and nations which without Christ are lost, as St. Hilary points out correctly: "What can be more fraught with danger for the world than the rejection of Christ?" Nor does it interfere in the least with the regulations of the State, because the Church in her motherly prudence is not unwilling that her schools and institutions for the education of the laity be in keeping with the legitimate dispositions of civil authority; she is in every way ready to cooperate with this authority and to make provision for a mutual understanding, should difficulties arise.

Again it is the inalienable right as well as the indispensable duty of the Church, to watch over the entire education of her children, in all institutions, public or private, not merely in regard to the religious instruction there given, but in regard to every other branch of learning and every regulation in so far as religion and morality are concerned.

Nor should the exercise of this right be considered undue interference, but rather maternal care on the part of the Church in protecting her children from the grave danger of all kinds of doctrinal and moral evil. Moreover, this watchfulness of the Church not merely can create no real inconvenience, but must on the contrary confer valuable assistance in the right ordering and well-being of families and of civil society; for it keeps far away from youth the moral poison which at that inexperienced and changeable age more easily penetrates the mind and more rapidly spreads its baneful effects. For it is true, as Leo XIII has wisely pointed out, that without proper religious and moral instruction "every form of intellectual culture will be injurious; for young people not accustomed to respect God, will be unable to bear the restraint of a virtuous life, and never having learned to deny themselves anything, they will easily be incited to disturb the public order."

The Church's Mission. The extent of the Church's mission in the field of education is such as to embrace every nation, without exception, according to the command of Christ: "Teach ye all nations"; and there is no power on earth that may lawfully oppose her or stand in her way. In the first place, it extends over all the Faithful, of whom she has anxious care as a tender mother. For these she has throughout the centuries created and conducted an immense number of schools and institutions in every branch of learning. . . .

Curriculum Developments and Issues

Secondary education in the United States in the eighteenth and nineteenth centuries was the privilege of less than 10 percent of the eligible school population. The concept of educating all the youth of secondary-school age was developing slowly, and it would take three to four decades into the twentieth century before this idea became universally accepted. After 1890, when the youth of high school age began to stream into the schools—a sevenfold increase in twenty years—the problem as to what shall be taught in the secondary school became a major issue of discussion among concerned educators and the public at large.

Today there seems to be general consensus that the curriculum of the comprehensive high school recommended by James B. Conant should be the pattern of the high school of the future. In many communities the Conant Report has stimulated boards of education to reappraise their programs using Conant's recommendations as criteria. Such action, however, does not mean that the comprehensive high school, as he has endorsed it, has been accepted unanimously.

Uncertainty still exists as to the validity of the comprehensive high school. The historical conflicts between progressivism and traditionalism, vocationalism and general education, have not been adequately resolved. Would the comprehensive high school's curriculum be able successfully to meet the demands of our contemporary society? Prominent educational leaders have voiced objections to the comprehensive high school and have given their interpretations to the concept of the new American high school.

What should be taught in the high school is the complex and rhetorical question that must be raised continually. The purpose of this text is not to suggest a final answer, but to encourage the student of curriculum to evaluate those forces that have created our present high school course structure and to recognize those conditions that might lead to its revitalization.

The proposition that there be a standardized curriculum for all secondary-school students was one of the major issues prompting the formation of the historically significant Committee of Ten (1893). After noting the inconsistencies of course offerings throughout the country, this Committee sought to ameliorate the situation by suggesting a curriculum pattern that was to dominate the high school curriculum for the next fifty years.

As a corollary to the recommendations of the Committee of Ten, the Carnegie Foundation, by defining educational units, reinforced the effect of the Committee by allowing the colleges and universities to grant credit for those courses that they deemed acceptable for admission to their institutions.

Fifty-eight years after Herbert Spencer had published "What Knowledge Is of Most Worth?" the Commission on the Reorganization of Secondary Education, accepting Spencer's ideas, issued "Cardinal Principles of Secondary Education." Its pronouncements, which one writer characterized as the Declaration of Independence of secondary education, provided the frame of reference for many of the theories and practices in schools from 1918 to the present time. The

Cardinal Principles were formulated because the Commission recognized the fact that the secondary curriculum must meet the diversified needs of a heterogeneous school population, and therefore departed from the limited concept of the classical curriculum given strong support by the Committee of Ten.

The junior high school, America's unique contribution to education, a reflection of both standardization and differentiation, is generally conceded to be an outgrowth of the deliberations of the Committee of Ten and the Committee on College Entrance Requirements. Organized originally for the purpose of economy of time, that is, standardizing the high school curriculum as a six-year course of study, educators realized that if this institution was to flourish, it would have to broaden its objectives and functions, a development which has marked its progress. Whether the junior high school has fulfilled the expectations of its early advocates and present supporters is still a matter of conjecture.

Attempts to modify the classical curriculum were in evidence as part of the Progressive Education Movement. The most dramatic of these efforts began with the question "How can the high school improve its service to American youth?" Some thirty schools addressed themselves to this question, reported in *The Story of the Eight-Year Study*. The evidence indicated quite conclusively (despite some criticism of the design of the experiment) that the high school students who had been exposed to a variety of curricular offerings could succeed in college. The implications of the Eight-Year Study and concurrent and subsequent programs of what became known as core teaching heightened the battle between the advocates of this curricular approach and those who supported the more traditional curricular programs.

Other educational spokesmen issued formulations of objectives for the needs of the youth of modern America. Highly regarded were the "Ten Imperative Needs" written by the Educational Policies Commission of the National Education

Association in 1944 and revised in 1952 and 1961. These statements were an extension of the Seven Cardinal Principles.

Also commanding considerable attention concurrently with Progressive Education was the Life Adjustment movement. The success of Charles Prosser and his followers in promoting his historic resolution of 1945 gave rise to debate as to whether or not life adjustment education was the answer. The problem of the high school youth who is confronted with a classical, college preparatory curriculum remains as a continuing one in American education.

The various organizations, associations, and individuals grappling with the problem of what should be taught in the high school have stimulated considerable experimentation, implementation, and opinion. They have raised as well as answered many questions in the search for a reasonable solution. The final answer is still in the future.

BOSTON LATIN GRAMMAR SCHOOL (FOUNDED 1635)—

COURSE OF STUDY—1773

*Report of the Commissioner of Education
for the Year 1903*

~~~~~~

The United States
BUREAU OF EDUCATION
Created as a department March 2, 1867
Made an Office of the Interior Department July 1, 1869

COMMISSIONERS

Henry Barnard, LL.D.
March 14, 1867 to March 15, 1870

SOURCE: "Boston Latin Grammar School," Report of the Commissioner of Education for the Year 1903, Vol. 1 (Washington, D.C.: U.S. Bureau of Education, 1905).

John Eaton, Ph.D., LL.D.
   March 16, 1870 to August 5, 1886
Nathaniel H. R. Dawson, L.H.D.
   August 6, 1886, to September 3, 1903
Wm. T. Harris, Ph.D., LL.D.
   September 12, 1889 to date [1903]

COURSE OF STUDY OF THE BOSTON LATIN SCHOOL JUST BEFORE THE REVOLUTION

(No regular curriculum of the school has come down to us from the colonial period. What follows is arranged from the published reminiscences of old-time pupils, and chiefly from those of Harrison Gray Otis, who entered the school in 1773.)

The pupils entered at the age of 7, having already learned to read English.

FIRST YEAR: 7 years of age
   Cheever's *Accidence*
   "A small Nomenclature"
   Corderius's *Colloquies*

SECOND YEAR: 8 years of age
   Aesop's *Fables*   During these three years the
   Eutropius   pupils spent the hour from 11
   Ward's Lilly's grammar   to 12 each day in a writing
                             school, in which arithmetic was
                             studied as far as the "rule
                             three" (simple proportion).

THIRD YEAR: 9 years of age
   Eutropius and grammar
     continued
   Clarke's *Introduction to*
     Writing Latin

FOURTH YEAR: 10 years of age
   Subjects of the third year
     continued

FOURTH YEAR (*continued*):
Caesar's *Commentaries*
"Making Latin"

FIFTH YEAR: 11 years of age
Tully's *Orations*
"Making Latin"

SIXTH YEAR: 12 years of age
The first books of Vergil's
Æneid with Trappe's and
Dryden's translation
"Making Latin"
Ward's Greek grammar
Greek Testament with
Beza's Latin translation

SEVENTH YEAR: 13 years of age
Horace
Latin verse composition
with the Gradus ad
Parnassum
Five or six books of
Homer's *Iliad* with
Clarke's translation
(Ovid's *Metamorphoses*,
Vergil's *Georgics*, and
something of Xenophon
were read by some
classes)

PROPOSALS RELATING TO THE EDUCATION OF
YOUTH IN PENNSYLVANIA, 1749

Benjamin Franklin

~~~~~~

. . . As to their studies, it would be well if they could be taught everything that is useful and everything that is ornamental; but art is long, and their time is short. It is therefore proposed that they learn those things that are likely to be most useful and most ornamental, regard being had to the several professions for which they are intended.

All should be taught to write a fair hand, and swift, as that is useful to all. And with it may be learned something of drawing, by imitation of prints, and some of the first principles of perspective. Arithmetic, accounts, and some of the first principles of geometry and astronomy. The English language might be taught by grammar; in which some of our best writers, as Tillotson, Addison, Pope, Algernon Sidney, Cato's *Letters*, etc., should be classics, the styles principally to be cultivated, being the clear and the concise. Reading should also be taught, and pronouncing, properly, distinctly, emphatically, not with an even tone, which underdoes, nor a theatrical, which overdoes, nature.

To form their style they should be put to writing letters to each other, making abstracts of what they read or writing the same things in their own words; telling or writing stories lately read, in their own expressions. All to be revised and corrected by the tutor who should give his reasons, explain the force and import of words, etc.

To form their pronunciation, they may be put on making

SOURCE: From *Educational Views of Benjamin Franklin* by Thomas Woody, editor. Copyright 1931. McGraw-Hill Book Company. Used by permission.

NOTE: All footnotes in this selection have been omitted.

declamations, repeating speeches, delivering orations, etc., the tutor assisting at the rehearsals, teaching, advising, correcting their accent, etc.

But if history be made a constant part of their reading, such as the translations of the Greek and Roman historians and the modern histories of ancient Greece and Rome, etc., may not almost all kinds of useful knowledge be that way introduced to advantage, and with pleasure to the student? As:

Geography, by reading with maps and being required to point out the places where the greatest actions were done, to give their old and new names, with the bounds, situation, extent of the countries concerned, etc.

Chronology, by the help of Helvicus or some other writer of the kind who will enable them to tell when those events happened, what princes were contemporaries, what states or famous men flourished about that time, etc., the several principal epochs to be first well fixed in their memories.

Ancient customs, religious and civil, being frequently mentioned in history, will give occasion for explaining them, in which the prints of medals, bas-reliefs and ancient monuments will greatly assist.

Morality, by descanting and making continual observations on the causes of the rise or fall of any man's character, fortune, power, etc., mentioned in history; the advantages of temperance, order, frugality, industry, perseverance, etc. etc. Indeed the general natural tendency of reading good history must be to fix in the minds of youth deep impressions of the beauty and usefulness of virtue of all kinds, public spirit, fortitude, etc.

History will show the wonderful effects of oratory in governing, turning and leading great bodies of mankind, armies, cities, nations. When the minds of youth are struck with admiration at this, then is the time to give them the principles of that art, which they will study with taste and application. Then they may be made acquainted with the best models among the ancients, their beauties being particularly pointed out to them. Modern political oratory being chiefly performed by the pen and press, its advantages over the ancient in some respects are to be shown, as that its effects are more extensive, more lasting, etc.

History will also afford frequent opportunities of showing the necessity of a public religion, from its usefulness to the public; the advantage of a religious character among private persons; the mischiefs of superstition, etc., and the excellency of the Christian religion above all others ancient or modern.

History will also give occasion to expatiate on the advantage of civil orders and constitutions, how men and their properties are protected by joining in societies and establishing government, their industry encouraged and rewarded, arts invented, and life made more comfortable: the advantages of liberty, mischiefs of licentiousness, benefits arising from good laws and a due execution of justice, etc. Thus may the first principles of sound politics be fixed in the minds of youth. Natural history will also afford opportunities of introducing many observations relating to the preservation of health, which may be afterwards of great use. Arbuthnot on air and aliment, Sanctorius on perspiration, Lemery on foods and some others, may now be read, and a very little explanation will make them sufficiently intelligible to youth.

While they are reading natural history might not a little gardening, planting, grafting, inoculating, etc., be taught and practiced and now and then excursions made to the neighboring plantations of the best farmers, their methods observed and reasoned upon for the information of youth, the improvement of agriculture being useful to all, and skill in it no disparagement to any?

The history of commerce, of the invention of arts, rise of manufactures, progress of trade, change of its seats, with the reasons, causes, etc., may also be made entertaining to youth, and will be useful to all. And this, with the accounts in other history of the prodigious force and effect of engines and machines used in war, will naturally introduce a desire to be instructed in mechanics, and to be informed of the principles of that art by which weak men perform such wonders, labor is saved, manufactures expedited, etc. This will be the time to show them prints of ancient and modern machines, to explain them, to let them be copied, and to give lectures in mechanical philosophy.

With the whole should be constantly inculcated and cultivated that benignity of mind, which shows itself in searching for and seizing every opportunity to serve and to oblige, and is the foundation of what is called good breeding, highly useful to the possessor, and most agreeable to all.

The idea of what is true merit should also be often presented to youth, explained and impressed on their minds, as consisting in an inclination joined with an ability to serve mankind, one's country, friends and family; which ability is (with the blessing of God) to be acquired or greatly increased by true learning, and should indeed be the great aim and end of all learning.

COURSE OF STUDY—CHICAGO HIGH SCHOOL (CENTRAL)

John Addison Clement

~~~~~~

SYNOPSIS OF THE GENERAL COURSE (1861)

Years	First Term	Second Term	Third Term
I.	Algebra German or Latin Descriptive Geography	Algebra German or Latin English Grammar and Analysis	Arithmetic German or Latin Physical Geography
II.	Algebra German or Latin Universal History	Geometry German or Latin Universal History	Geometry German or Latin Universal History, Botany
III.	Geometry French, Latin or German, or Physiology Rhetoric	Trigonometry French, Latin or German Natural Philosophy English Literature	Mensuration, Navigation and Surveying German, Latin or French Natural Philosophy English Literature

SOURCE: John Addison Clement, *Principles and Practices of Secondary Education* (New York: Appleton-Century-Crofts, Inc., 1924), pp. 188–189. Reprinted by permission.

SYNOPSIS OF THE GENERAL COURSE (1861) (*Continued*)

Years	First Term	Second Term	Third Term
IV.	Astronomy German, Latin or French Intellectual Philosophy, Constitution, United States	Chemistry German, Latin or French, Logic Political Economy	Geology and Mineralogy German, Latin or French Moral Science Political Economy

Reading during the first and second years. Drawing during the second, third, and fourth years. Composition and Declamation during the entire course.

SYNOPSIS OF THE CLASSICAL COURSE (1861)

Years	First Term	Second Term	Third Term
I.	Algebra Harkness' 1st Latin Book Descriptive Geography	Algebra Harkness' 1st Latin Book English Grammar and Analysis	Arithmetic Latin Reader Physical Geography
II.	Algebra Latin Reader Universal History	Geometry Cæsar Universal History	Geometry Cæsar Universal History, Botany
III.	Greek Cæsar or Cicero Physiology	Greek Cicero Natural Philosophy	Greek, Anabasis Cicero, Natural Philosophy
IV.	Greek, Anabasis Virgil, Eclogues Cicero Latin Prose	Greek Virgil, Æneid and Georgics Latin Prose	Greek, Iliad Virgil, Æneid Review of Latin

Reading during the first and second years. Drawing during the second, third, and fourth years. Composition and Declamation during the entire course. Classical Antiquities, Military affairs, during the second year. Classical Antiquities, Civic Affairs, during the second year. Classical Antiquities, Mythology, during the fourth year.

Chicago High School Program of Studies After 1875. In 1884 in harmony with the reclassification of schools in 1880, a new course of study was adopted by the Board for the full course of four years. As can be observed by comparing the courses of study for 1861 and for 1884, there is some change in the general nature of subjects offered, in the sequence, length of the unit of some of the subjects, and in the total amount offered.

HIGH SCHOOL DEPARTMENT FULL COURSE
FOUR YEARS (Adopted in 1884)

	First Term	*Second Term*	*Third Term*
1st Year	Algebra Physiology Latin or German	Algebra Physical Geography Latin or German Physiology	Algebra Physical Geography Latin or German
2nd Year	Geometry History Latin or German Natural History	Geometry History Latin or German Natural History Botany	Geometry History Latin or German Botany

3rd Year	Natural Philosophy
	Rhetoric
	Latin, German, or
	   French
	Chemistry
		Natural Philosophy
		English Literature
		Latin, German, or
		   French
		Chemistry
			Natural Philosophy
			English Literature
			Latin, German, or
			   French

4th Year	Astronomy
	Civil Government
	Latin, German, or
	   French
	Study of Authors
		Astronomy
		Geology
		Mental Science
		Latin, German, or
		   French
		Reviews
			Geology
			Political Economy
			Latin, German, or
			   French
			Reviews

Composition, Declamation and Select Readings through the course. Drawing and Singing optional through the course. Greek elective after the first year. Bookkeeping optional during the last year.

CLASSICAL COURSE—THREE YEARS

	First Term	Second Term	Third Term
1st Year	Algebra Latin Reader Greek	Algebra Latin Reader Greek	Algebra Latin Reader Greek
2nd Year	Geometry Latin—Cæsar Latin—Cæsar or Greek—Anabasis	Geometry Latin—Cæsar or Cicero Greek—Anabasis	Trigonometry Latin—Cicero Greek—Anabasis
3rd Year	Latin—Virgil Latin Composition Greek—Iliad Greek Composition	Latin—Virgil Latin Composition Greek—Iliad Greek Composition Reviews	Latin—Virgil Latin Composition Greek Reviews

Composition, Declamation, and Select Readings through the course.
Drawing and Singing optional through the course.

THE COMMITTEE OF TEN PROPOSES A
PROGRAM FOR SECONDARY SCHOOLS

Report of the Committee of Ten on Secondary School Studies

~~~~~~

Year	Classical		Latin-Scientific	
	Three foreign languages (one modern)		Two foreign languages (one modern)	
	Latin	5p.	Latin	5p.
	English	4p.	English	4p.
I.	Algebra	4p.	Algebra	4p.
	History	4p.	History	4p.
	Physical Geography	3p.	Physical Geography	3p.
		20p.		20p.
	Latin	5p.	Latin	5p.
	English	2p.	English	2p.
	German [1] (or French) begun	4p.	German (or French begun)	4p.
II.	Geometry	3p.	Geometry	3p.
	Physics	3p	Physics	3p.
	History	3p.	Botany or Zoology	3p.
		20p.		20p.

[1] In any school in which Greek can be better taught than a modern language, or in which local public opinion or the history of the school makes it desirable to teach Greek in an ample way, Greek may be substituted for German or French in the second year of the Classical programme.

SOURCE: "The Committee of Ten—Proposals for a Program for Secondary Schools," *Report of the Committee of Ten on Secondary School Studies* (Washington, D.C.: United States Bureau of Education, 1893), pp. 46, 47.

	Latin	4p.	Latin	4p.
	Greek ¹	5p.	English	3p.
	English	3p.	German (*or* French)	4p
III.	German (*or* French)	4p.	Mathematics {Algebra 2 / Geometry 2}	4p.
	Mathe-matics {Algebra 2 / Geometry 2}	4p.	Astronomy ½ yr. & Meteorology ½ yr.	3p.
		—	History	2p.
		20p.		—
				20p.

	Latin	4p.	Latin	4p.
	Greek	5p.	English {as in Classical 2 / additional 2}	4p.
	English	2p.	German (*or* French)	3p.
	German (*or* French)	3p.	Chemistry	3p.
IV.	Chemistry	3p.	Trigonometry & Higher Algebra *or* History }	3p.
	Trigonometry & Higher Algebra *or* History }	3p.	Geology or Physiography ½ yr. and Anatomy, Physiology, & Hygiene ½ yr.	3p.
		—		—
		20p.		20p.

	Modern Languages Two foreign languages (both modern)		*English* One foreign language (ancient or modern)	
	French (*or* German) begun	5p.	Latin, or German, or French	5p.
	English	4p.	English	4p.
I.	Algebra	4p.	Algebra	4p.
	History	4p.	History	4p.
	Physical Geography	3p.	Physical Geography	3p.
		20p.		20p.
	French (*or* German)	4p.	Latin, or German, or French	5 or 4p.
	English	2p.	English	3 or 4p.
II.	German (*or* French) begun	5p.	Geometry	3p.
	Geometry	3p.	Physics	3p.
	Physics	3p.	History	3p.
	Botany or Zoology	3p.	Botany or Zoology	3p.
		20p.		20p.

III.

French (*or* German)	4p.	Latin, or German, or		
English	3p.	French		4p.
German (*or* French)	4p.	English { as in others 3 / additional 2 }		5p.
Mathe- { Algebra 2 / matics { Geometry 2 }	4p.	Mathematics { Algebra 2 / Geometry 2 }		4p.
Astronomy ½ yr. &		Astronomy ½ yr. &		
Meteorology ½ yr.	3p.	Meteorology ½ yr.		3p.
History	2p	History { as in the Latin- / Scientific 2 / additional 2 }		4p.
	20p.			20p.

IV.

French (*or* German)	3p.	Latin, or German, or	
English { as in Classi- / cal / additional 2 }	4p.	French	4p.
		English { as in Classical 2 / additional 2 }	4p.
German (*or* French)	4p.	Chemistry	3p.
Chemistry	3p.	Trigonometry & Higher	
Trigonometry & Higher / Algebra / *or* / History	3p.	Algebra	3p.
		History	3p.
		Geology or Physiography ½ yr. and	
Geology or Physiography ½ yr. and		Anatomy, Physiology, & Hygiene ½ yr.	3p.
Anatomy, Physiology, & Hygiene ½ yr.	3p.		20p.
	20p.		

THE COMMITTEE OF TEN ON REQUIREMENTS FOR ADMISSION TO COLLEGE

Report of the Committee of Ten on
Secondary School Studies

One of the subjects which the Committee of Ten were directed to consider was requirements for admission to college; and particularly they were expected to report on uniform requirements for admission to colleges, as well as on a uniform secondary school program. Almost all the Conferences have something to say about the best mode of testing the attainments of candidates at college admission examinations; and some of them, notably the Conferences on History and Geography, make very explicit declarations concerning the nature of college examinations. The improvements in the secondary schools, the various subjects which enter into the course will be found clearly described under each subject in the several Conference reports; but there is a general principle concerning the relation of the secondary schools to colleges which the Committee of Ten, inspired and guided by the Conferences, feel it their duty to set forth with all possible distinctness.

The secondary schools of the United States, taken as a whole, do not exist for the purpose of preparing boys and girls for colleges. Only an insignificant percentage of the graduates of these schools go to colleges or scientific schools. Their main function is to prepare for the duties of life that small proportion of all the children in the country—a proportion small in number, but very important to the welfare of the nation—who show themselves

SOURCE: Report of the Committee of Ten on Secondary School Studies "The Committee of Ten on Requirements for Admission to College, 1893" (Washington, D.C.: United States Office of Education, 1893), pp. 51–53.

able to profit by an education prolonged to the eighteenth year, and whose parents are able to support them while they remain so long at school. There are, to be sure, a few private or endowed secondary schools in the country, which make it their principal object to prepare students for the colleges and universities; but the number of these schools is relatively small. A secondary school program intended for national use must therefore be made for those children whose education is not to be pursued beyond the secondary school. The preparation of a few pupils for college or scientific school should in the ordinary secondary school be the incidental, and not the principal, object. At the same time, it is obviously desirable that the colleges and scientific schools should be accessible to all boys or girls who have completed creditably the secondary school course. Their parents often do not decide for them, four years before the college age, that they shall go to college, and they themselves may not, perhaps, feel the desire to continue their education until near the end of their school course. In order that any successful graduate of a good secondary school should be free to present himself at the gates of the college or scientific school of his choice, it is necessary that the colleges and scientific schools of the country should accept for admission to appropriate courses of their instruction the attainments of any youth who has passed creditably through a good secondary school course, no matter to what group of subjects he may have mainly devoted himself in the secondary school. As secondary school courses are now too often arranged, this is not a reasonable request to prefer to the colleges and scientific schools; because the pupil may now go through a secondary school course of a very feeble and scrappy nature—studying a little of many subjects and not much of any one, getting, perhaps, a little information in a variety of fields, but nothing which can be called a thorough training. Now the recommendations of the nine Conferences, if well carried out, might fairly be held to make all the main subjects taught in the secondary schools of equal rank for the purposes of admission to college or scientific school. They would all be taught consecutively and thoroughly, and would all be carried on in the same spirit; they would all be used for training the powers of observation, memory, expression, and reasoning; and they would all be good to that end, although differing among themselves in quality and substance. In preparing the programs, the Committee had in mind that the requirements for admission to colleges might, for schools which adopted a program derived from that table, be simplified to a considerable extent, though not reduced. A college might say, We will accept for admission any groups of studies taken from the secondary school program, provided that the sum of the studies in each of the four years amounts to sixteen, or eighteen, or twenty periods a week—as may be thought best—and provided, further, that in each year at least four of the subjects presented shall have been pursued at least three periods a week, and that at least three of the subjects shall have been pursued three years or more. For the purposes of this reckoning, natural history, geography, meteorology, and astronomy might be grouped together as one subject. Every youth who entered college would have spent four years in studying a few subjects thoroughly; and, on the theory that all the subjects are to be considered equivalent in educational rank for the purposes of admission to college, it would make no difference which subjects he had chosen from the program—he would have had four years of strong and effective mental training. The Conferences on Geography and Modern Languages make the most explicit statement to the effect that college requirements for admission should coincide with high school requirements for graduation. The Conference on English is of opinion "that no student should be admitted to college who shows in his English examination and his other examinations that he is very deficient in ability to write good English." This recommendation suggests that an ample English course in the secondary school should be required of all persons who intend to enter college. It would of course be possible for any college to require for admission any one subject, or any group of subjects, in the table, and the requirements of different colleges, while all kept within the table, might differ in many respects; but the Committee are of opinion that the satisfactory completion of any one of the four years' courses of study embodied in the foregoing programs should admit to corresponding courses in colleges and scientific schools. They believe that this close articulation between the secondary schools and the higher institutions would be advantageous alike for the schools, the colleges, and the country.

First Annual Report of the President and Treasurer

The terms *college* and *university* have, as yet, no fixed meaning on this continent. It is not uncommon to find flourishing high schools which bear one or the other of these titles. To recognize institutions of learning without some regard to this fact would be to throw away whatsoever opportunity the Foundation has for the exertion of educational influence.

The trustees have, therefore, adopted for the present an arbitrary definition of what constitutes a college, one framed very closely after that adopted in the revised ordinances of the State of New York. This definition is expressed in the rules of the Foundation as follows:

"An institution to be ranked as a college, must have at least six (6) professors giving their entire time to college and university work, a course of four full years in liberal arts and sciences, and should require for admission, not less than the usual four years of academic or high school preparation, or its equivalent, in addition to the preacademic or grammar school studies."

In order to judge what constitutes "four years of academic or high school preparation" the officers of the Foundation have made

---

SOURCE: "The Carnegie Foundation's Definition of Educational 'Units,' 1906," The Carnegie Foundation for the Advancement of Teaching, *First Annual Report of the President and Treasurer*, 1906, Pp. 38–39. "Thus the unit triumphed, both in the examining and in the certificating colleges. . . . It may not be entirely an accident that the automobile and the unit system were invented at about the same time and were perfected and popularized almost simultaneously." R. L. Duffus, *Democracy Enters College: A Study of the Rise and Decline of the Academic Lockstep* (New York, Charles Scribner's Sons, 1936), p. 51. Used by permission.

use of a plan commonly adopted by college entrance examination boards. By this plan college entrance requirements are designated in terms of units, a unit being a course of five periods weekly throughout an academic year of the preparatory school. For the purposes of the Foundation the units in each branch of academic study have also been quantitatively defined, the aim being to assign values to the subjects in accordance with the time usually required to prepare adequately upon them for college entrance. Thus, plane geometry, which is usually studied five periods weekly throughout an academic year of the preparatory school, is estimated as one unit. In other words, the value of the unit is based upon the actual amount of work required and not upon the time specified for the preparation of the work.

A difficulty, however, arises in estimating by this method the entrance requirements of the various colleges and universities. The large majority of institutions accept the certificates of "approved" preparatory schools and academies. In the courses of these "approved" schools it frequently happens that there is a marked discrepancy between the amount of work required and the time specified for the preparation of the work, when judged by the definitions of the units as adopted by the officers of the Foundation. For example, plane geometry may be accepted as an entrance requirement by an institution, although that subject has been studied in the preparatory school for only two periods weekly throughout an academic year. In such cases the officers of the Foundation will credit the institution with plane geometry solely upon the basis of the time given to the preparation of the subject. Thus, plane geometry, studied two periods weekly throughout an academic year, would be counted as two fifths of a unit and not as one unit. Or, if the time given to the preparation of the academic course is generally below the standard, the officers of the Foundation reserve the right to consider such work as altogether unsatisfactory unless adequate explanation is offered.

Fourteen units constitute the minimum amount of preparation which may be interpreted as "four years of academic or high school preparation." The definitions of the units, are in close accordance with the requirements of the College Entrance Examination Board.

CARDINAL PRINCIPLES OF SECONDARY EDUCATION

Commission on the Reorganization of Secondary Education

~~~~~~

THE NEED FOR REORGANIZATION

Secondary education should be determined by the needs of the society to be served, the character of the individuals to be educated, and the knowledge of educational theory and practice available. These factors are by no means static. Society is always in process of development; the character of the secondary-school population undergoes modifications; and the sciences on which educational theory and practice depend constantly furnish new information. Secondary education, however, like any other established agency of society, is conservative and tends to resist modification. Failure to make adjustments when the need arises leads to the necessity for extensive reorganization at irregular intervals. The evidence is strong that such a comprehensive reorganization of secondary education is imperative at the present time. . . .

THE GOAL OF EDUCATION IN A DEMOCRACY

Education in the United States should be guided by a clear conception of the meaning of democracy. It is the ideal of democracy that the individual and society may find fulfillment each in the other. Democracy sanctions neither the exploitation of the individual by society, nor the disregard of the interests of society by the individual. More explicitly—

SOURCE: Commission on the Reorganization of Secondary Education, National Education Association, *Cardinal Principles of Secondary Education,* (Washington, D.C., Government Printing Office Bulletin, No. 35, 1918), pp. 7–16.

The purpose of democracy is so to organize society that each member may develop his personality primarily through activities designed for the well-being of his fellow members and of society as a whole.

This ideal demands that human activities be placed upon a high level of efficiency; that to this efficiency be added an appreciation of the significance of these activities and loyalty to the best ideals involved; and that the individual choose that vocation and those forms of social service in which his personality may develop and become most effective. For the achievement of these ends democracy must place chief reliance upon education.

Consequently, education in a democracy, both within and without the school, should develop in each individual the knowledge, interests, ideals, habits, and powers whereby he will find his place and use that place to shape both himself and society toward ever nobler ends. . . .

THE ROLE OF SECONDARY EDUCATION IN ACHIEVING THESE OBJECTIVES

The objectives outlined above apply to education as a whole— elementary, secondary, and higher. It is the purpose of this section to consider specifically the role of secondary education in achieving each of these objectives.

For reasons stated in Section X, this commission favors such reorganization that secondary education may be defined as applying to all pupils of approximately 12 to 18 years of age.

1. *Health.* Health needs cannot be neglected during the period of secondary education without serious danger to the individual and the race. The secondary school should therefore provide health instruction, inculcate health habits, organize an effective program of physical activities, regard health needs in planning work and play, and cooperate with home and community in safeguarding and promoting health interests.

To carry out such a program it is necessary to arouse the public to recognize that the health needs of young people are of vital importance to society, to secure teachers competent to ascertain and meet the needs of individual pupils and able to inculcate in the entire student body a love for clean sport, to furnish adequate equipment for physical activities, and to make the school building, its rooms and surroundings, conform to the best standards of hygiene and sanitation.

2. *Command of Fundamental Processes.*   Much of the energy of the elementary school is properly devoted to teaching certain fundamental processes, such as reading, writing, arithmetical computations, and the elements of oral and written expression. The facility that a child of 12 or 14 may acquire in the use of these tools is not sufficient for the needs of modern life. This is particularly true of the mother tongue. Proficiency in many of these processes may be increased more effectively by their application to new material than by the formal reviews commonly employed in grades seven and eight. Throughout the secondary school, instruction and practice must go hand in hand, but as indicated in the report of the committee on English, only so much theory should be taught at any one time as will show results in practice.

3. *Worthy Home-membership.*   Worthy home-membership as an objective calls for the development of those qualities that make the individual a worthy member of a family, both contributing to and deriving benefit from that membership.

This objective applies to both boys and girls. The social studies should deal with the home as a fundamental social institution and clarify its relation to the wider interests outside. Literature should interpret and idealize the human elements that go to make the home. Music and art should result in more beautiful homes and in greater joy therein. The coeducational school with a faculty of men and women should, in its organization and its activities, exemplify wholesome relations between boys and girls and men and women.

Home membership as an objective should not be thought of solely with reference to future duties. These are the better guaranteed if the school helps the pupils to take the right attitude toward present home responsibilities and interprets to them the contribution of the home to their development.

In the education of every high school girl, the household arts should have a prominent place because of their importance to the girl herself and to others whose welfare will be directly in her keeping. The attention now devoted to this phase of education is inadequate, and especially so for girls preparing for occupations not related to the household arts and for girls planning for higher institutions. The majority of girls who enter wage-earning occupations directly from the high school remain in them for only a few years, after which home making becomes their lifelong occupation. For them the high school period offers the only assured opportunity to prepare for that lifelong occupation, and it is during this period that they are most likely to form their ideals of life's duties and responsibilities. For girls planning to enter higher institutions—

> our traditional ideals of preparation for higher institutions are particularly incongruous with the actual needs and future responsibilities of girls. It would seem that such high school work as is carefully designed to develop capacity for, and interest in, the proper management and conduct of a home should be regarded as of importance at least equal to that of any other work. We do not understand how society can properly continue to sanction for girls high school curriculums that disregard this fundamental need, even though such curriculums are planned in response to the demands made by some of the colleges for women.[1]

In the education of boys, some opportunity should be found to give them a basis for the intelligent appreciation of the value of the well-appointed home and of the labor and skill required to maintain such a home, to the end that they may cooperate more effectively. For instance, they should understand the essentials of food values, of sanitation, and of household budgets.

4. *Vocation.* Vocational education should equip the individual to secure a livelihood for himself and those dependent on him, to serve society well through his vocation, to maintain the right relationships toward his fellow workers and society, and, as far as possible, to find in that vocation his own best development.

This ideal demands that the pupil explore his own capacities and aptitudes, and make a survey of the world's work, to the end that he may select his vocation wisely. Hence, an effective program of vocational guidance in the secondary school is essential.

[1] Report of the Committee on the Articulation of High School and College, 1911.

Vocational education should aim to develop an appreciation of the significance of the vocation to the community, and a clear conception of right relations between the members of the chosen vocation, between different vocational groups, between employer and employee, and between producer and consumer. These aspects of vocational education, heretofore neglected, demand emphatic attention.

The extent to which the secondary school should offer training for a specific vocation depends upon the vocation, the facilities that the school can acquire, and the opportunity that the pupil may have to obtain such training later. To obtain satisfactory results those proficient in that vocation should be employed as instructors and the actual conditions of the vocation should be utilized either within the high school or in cooperation with the home, farm, shop, or office. Much of the pupil's time will be required to produce such efficiency.

5. *Civic Education.* Civic education should develop in the individual those qualities whereby he will act well his part as a member of neighborhood, town or city, State, and Nation, and give him a basis for understanding international problems.

For such citizenship the following are essential: A many-sided interest in the welfare of the communities to which one belongs; loyalty to ideals of civic righteousness, practical knowledge of social agencies and institutions; good judgment as to means and methods that will promote one social end without defeating others; and as putting all these into effect, habits of cordial cooperation in social undertakings.

The school should develop the concept that the civic duties of men and women, while in part identical, are also in part supplementary. Differentiation in civic activities is to be encouraged, but not to the extent of loss of interest in the common problems with which all should cope.

Among the means for developing attitudes and habits important in a democracy are the assignment of projects and problems to groups of pupils for cooperative solution and the socialized recitation whereby the class as a whole develops a sense of collective responsibility. Both of these devices give training in collective thinking. Moreover, the democratic organization and administration of the school itself, as well as the cooperative relations of pupils and teacher, pupil and pupil, and teacher and teacher, are indispensable.

While all subjects should contribute to good citizenship, the social studies—geography, history, civics, and economics—should have this as their dominant aim. Too frequently, however, does mere information, conventional in value and remote in its bearing, make up the content of the social studies. History should so treat the growth of institutions that their present value may be appreciated. Geography should show the interdependence of men while it shows their common dependence on nature. Civics should concern itself less with constitutional questions and remote governmental functions, and should direct attention to social agencies close at hand and to the informal activities of daily life that regard and seek the common good. Such agencies as child-welfare organizations and consumers' leagues afford specific opportunities for the expression of civic qualities by the older pupils.

The work in English should kindle social ideals and give insight into social conditions and into personal character as related to these conditions. Hence the emphasis by the committee on English on the importance of a knowledge of social activities, social movements, and social needs on the part of the teacher of English.

The comprehension of the ideals of American democracy and loyalty to them should be a prominent aim of civic education. The pupil should feel that he will be responsible, in cooperation with others, for keeping the Nation true to the best inherited conceptions of democracy, and he should also realize that democracy itself is an ideal to be wrought out by his own and succeeding generations.

Civic education should consider other nations also. As a people we should try to understand their aspirations and ideals that we may deal more sympathetically and intelligently with the immigrant coming to our shores, and have a basis for a wiser and more sympathetic approach to international problems. Our pupils should learn that each nation, at least potentially, has something of worth to contribute to civilization and that humanity would be incomplete without that contribution. This means a study of specific nations, their achievements and possibilities, not ignoring their limitations. Such a study of dissimilar contributions in the light of the ideal of human brotherhood should help to establish a genuine internationalism, free from sentimentality, founded on fact, and actually operative in the affairs of nations.

6. *Worthy Use of Leisure.* Education should equip the individual to secure from his leisure the re-creation of body, mind, and spirit, and the enrichment and enlargement of his personality.

This objective calls for the ability to utilize the common means of enjoyment, such as music, art, literature, drama, and social intercourse, together with the fostering in each individual of one or more special avocational interests.

Heretofore the high school has given little conscious attention to this objective. It has so exclusively sought intellectual discipline that it has seldom treated literature, art, and music so as to evoke right emotional response and produce positive enjoyment. Its presentation of science should aim, in part, to arouse a genuine appreciation of nature.

The school has failed also to organize and direct the social activities of young people as it should. One of the surest ways in which to prepare pupils worthily to utilize leisure in adult life is by guiding and directing their use of leisure in youth. The school should, therefore, see that adequate recreation is provided both within the school and by other proper agencies in the community. The school, however, has a unique opportunity in this field because it includes in its membership representatives from all classes of society and consequently is able through social relationships to establish bonds of friendship and common understanding that can not be furnished by other agencies. Moreover, the school can so organize recreational activities that they will contribute simultaneously to other ends of education, as in the case of the school pageant or festival.

7. *Ethical Character.* In a democratic society ethical character becomes paramount among the objectives of the secondary school. Among the means for developing ethical character may be mentioned the wise selection of content and methods of instruction in all subjects of study, the social contacts of pupils with one another and with their teachers, the opportunities afforded by the organization and administration of the school for the development on the part of pupils of the sense of personal responsibility

and initiative, and, above all, the spirit of service and the principles of true democracy which should permeate the entire school
—principal, teachers, and pupils.

Specific consideration is given to the moral values to be obtained from the organization of the school and the subjects of
study in the report of this commission entitled "Moral Values in
Secondary Education." That report considers also the conditions
under which it may be advisable to supplement the other activities of the school by offering a distinct course in moral instruction.

DEMOCRACY AND EDUCATION

John Dewey

~~~~~~

It is fatal for a democracy to permit the formation of fixed
classes. Differences of wealth, the existence of large masses of
unskilled laborers, contempt for work with the hands, inability
to secure the training which enables one to forge ahead in life,
all operate to produce classes, and to widen the gulf between
them. Statesmen and legislation can do something to combat
those evil forces. Wise philanthropy can do something. But the
only fundamental agency for good is the public school system.
Every American is proud of what has been accomplished in the
past in fostering among very diverse elements of population a
spirit of unity and of brotherhood so that the sense of common
interests and aims have prevailed over the strong forces working
to divide our people into classes. The increasing complexity of

SOURCE: Reprinted with permission of the publisher from *Democracy
and Education* by John Dewey. Copyright 1916 by The Macmillan
Company. Renewed 1944 by John Dewey.

our life, with the great accumulation of wealth at one social extreme and the conditions of almost dire necessity at the other makes the task of democracy constantly more difficult. The days are rapidly passing when the simple provision of a system in which all individuals mingle is enough to meet the need. The subject-matter and the methods of teaching must be positively and aggressively adapted to that end.

There must not be one system for the children of parents who have more leisure and another for the children of those who are wage-earners. The physical separation forced by such a scheme, while unfavorable to the development of a proper mutual sympathy, is the least of its evils. Worse is the fact that the over-bookish education for some and the over-"practical" education for others brings about a division of mental and moral habits, ideal and outlook.

The academic education turns out future citizens with no sympathy for work done with the hands, and with absolutely no training for understanding the most serious of present-day social and political difficulties. The trade training will turn future workers who may have greater immediate skill than they would have had without their training, but who have no enlargement of mind, no insight into the scientific and social significance of the work they do, no education which assists them in finding their way on or in making their own adjustments. A division of the public school system into one part which pursues traditional methods, with incidental improvements, and another which deals with those who are to go into manual labor means a plan of social predestination totally foreign to the spirit of a democracy.

The democracy which proclaims equality of opportunity as its ideal requires an education in which learning and social application, ideas and practice, work and recognition of the meaning of what is done are united from the beginning and for all. Schools such as we have discussed in this book—and they are rapidly coming into being in large numbers all over the country—are showing how the ideal of equal opportunity for all is to be transmuted into reality.

A STATEMENT OF THE PRINCIPLES

OF PROGRESSIVE EDUCATION

Progressive Education

~~~~~~

I. FREEDOM TO DEVELOP NATURALLY.

The conduct of the pupil should be governed by himself according to the social needs of his community, rather than by arbitrary laws. Full opportunity for initiative and self-expression should be provided, together with an environment rich in interesting material that is available for the free use of every pupil.

II. INTEREST, THE MOTIVE OF ALL WORK.

Interest should be satisfied and developed through: (1) Direct and indirect contact with the world and its activities, and the use of the experience thus gained. (2) Application of knowledge gained, and correlation between different subjects. (3) The consciousness of achievement.

III. THE TEACHER A GUIDE, NOT A TASK-MASTER.

It is essential that teachers should believe in the aims and general principles of Progressive Education and that they should have latitude for the development of initiative and originality.

Progressive teachers will encourage the use of all the senses, training the pupils in both observation and judgment; and instead of hearing recitations only, will spend most of the time teaching how to use various sources of information, including life activities

SOURCE: "A Statement of the Principles of Progressive Education, 1924," *Progressive Education: A Quarterly Review of the Newer Tendencies in Education*, Vol. 1, No. I April, 1924, p. 2. Reprinted by permission.

as well as books; how to reason about the information thus acquired; and how to express forcefully and logically the conclusions reached.

Ideal teaching conditions demand that classes be small, especially in the elementary school years.

IV. SCIENTIFIC STUDY OF PUPIL DEVELOPMENT.

School records should not be confined to the marks given by the teachers to show the advancement of the pupils in their study of subjects, but should also include both objective and subjective reports on those physical, mental, moral and social characteristics which affect both school and adult life, and which can be influenced by the school and the home. Such records should be used as a guide for the treatment of each pupil, and should also serve to focus the attention of the teacher on the all-important work of development rather than on simply teaching subject matter.

V. GREATER ATTENTION TO ALL THAT AFFECTS THE CHILD'S PHYSICAL DEVELOPMENT.

One of the first considerations of Progressive Education is the health of the pupils. Much more room in which to move about, better light and air, clean and well-ventilated buildings, easier access to the out-of-doors and greater use of it, are all necessary. There should be frequent use of adequate playgrounds. The teachers should observe closely the physical condition of each pupil and, in cooperation with the home, make abounding health the first objective of childhood.

VI. COOPERATION BETWEEN SCHOOL AND HOME TO MEET THE NEEDS OF CHILDLIFE.

The school should provide, with the home, as much as is possible of all that the natural interests and activities of the child demand, especially during the elementary school years. These conditions can come about only through intelligent cooperation between parents and teachers.

*VII. THE PROGRESSIVE SCHOOL A LEADER IN
EDUCATIONAL MOVEMENTS.*

The Progressive School should be a leader in educational movements. It should be a laboratory where new ideas, if worthy,
meet encouragement; where tradition alone does not rule, but
the best of the past is leavened with the discoveries of today,
and the result is freely added to the sum of educational knowledge.

A SUGGESTED NEW SECONDARY CURRICULUM

William Heard Kilpatrick

The proposals for remaking the curriculum discussed in the
preceding chapters have found readier acceptance in the elementary school than in the secondary. Probably it is the existence
of departmentalized teaching that has opposed the spread of the
"activity" movement to the high school. Many secondary-school
people admit readily enough a strong argument in favor of basing
education on the life process as hereinbefore discussed, but they
do not see how they can give up the concentration and specialization that departmentalization of teaching allows. So far these
have accordingly been unwilling to follow a procedure that
ignores subject-matter lines.

Without discussing here how much of this devotion to teaching
by distinct subjects is the inertia of tradition and how much of

SOURCE: William Heard Kilpatrick, *Remaking the Curriculum* (New
York: Newson and Co., 1936). Reprinted by permission.

it is justified on sounder grounds, let us admit outright that some pupils can and will profit by at least some of the concentration and specialization which is permitted by existing high school departmentalization. But it does not follow that all pupils profit equally by such a regime nor that any pupils of secondary age need to have their whole school time so split into separate subjects. For one thing, there are strong reasons why some one teacher should have such continual and extended acquaintance with each distinct pupil as to permit a degree of personal counseling and guidance denied under a complete regime of departmentalization. It appears exceedingly doubtful that demands either of mental hygiene or of proper educational guidance can be adequately safeguarded on the usual basis of departmental teaching.

Furthermore there are many high school pupils for whom the need for extended specialization is far from clear. Especially is this true where anything like all pupils of high school age continue in school. If the considerations advanced in the preceding chapters for remaking the curriculum are granted to hold for the elementary school, as they increasingly are so granted, there appears no obvious reason why the argument should suddenly fail of cogency as children get to be around twelve or fourteen years of age. In fact if the arguments hold for the elementary school, the burden of proof would seem to lie with those who claim a difference for the secondary school.

It is from these considerations that the proposals are herein made for a new type of secondary school. The aim is to contrive a school program that will keep education for all the pupils on a basis of living for most of each day at the beginning of the high school period and grant the privilege of specialization only as an affirmative case is made out for each individual concerned.

To fix ideas, suppose the 6–3–3 plan is in operation with the elementary school run on the basis advocated in the preceding chapters. In the sixth grade the teacher has had charge of all the pupils certainly most of the day, and this teacher has tried to manage the education of her pupils on a thoroughgoing living process as has been discussed. This means that the various sides and aspects of life suitable for rounding out life for pupils of this age have been cared for by the ongoing curriculum. And the teacher has sought to have the pupils grow each in ever more adequate self-direction as they have faced the successive situation experiences that had constituted the activity curriculum. Each pupil has meanwhile been to the teacher a distinct personality, studied and guided as such, so that always the "whole child" might grow best into ever fuller and more adequate participation in the surrounding cultural life. As the children have thus been studied, the teacher has learned that they had different abilities and widely varying tastes and interests. Within certain social-moral limitations, it has been a definite aim of the teacher to cultivate each such individuality for all it was worth. James has been encouraged to study electricity, and Henry butterflies, while Mary has been encouraged to follow her special interest in music and Susie her interest in drawing and Lizzie her wish to write poetry. All such special interests have been cherished and cultivated as choice instances of budding individual life.

Now according to the plan herein proposed the seventh grade would be run in much the same way as was the sixth. One teacher will be in principal charge of all children. The main part of the class, perhaps three fourths of it, will be common to all the pupils and this will be guided, as was done the year before, so as to care for all the sides and aspects of the well-ordered life. There are two differences between the seventh grade this year and the sixth grade last year: one, the pupils are a year older and have got farther along in knowing and managing life; the other, some of the pupils are ready by special taste and aptitude to take up seriously one or more lines of specialization. James wishes to carry his electricity further in the direction of a more general science and John wishes to join him. Henry's butterflies now call for a wider study of biology. Mary's music is ready for further and more consistent study, as is Susie's art work. Lizzie's poetry now reaches out into a closer study of literature as well as more adequate writing. Other pupils wish to begin algebra, and some others typewriting.

Those pupils who have as yet found no special task or interest will continue to work together during the specializing period at any matter that seems best to teacher and pupils, possibly in one large group, possibly in smaller groups, possibly at individual projects. It is the business of the seventh-grade teacher to help the pupils here as elsewhere and always to use their time to best advantage.

When the same pupils reach the eighth grade, they will find the same general state of affairs. They are now a year older and still farther along in insight into and control over life. More will have developed individual tastes and interests worthy of specialized pursuit, and some will need more extended periods of study. Possibly one third of the day may now be devoted to these approved specialized interests. And similarly for each succeeding year to the last, always for a large part of the day all the pupils are together under one home-room teacher, while an increasing proportion of the time will be available for approved specialization. What proportion of the work of grade twelve will be common may well be debated. My own opinion is that from one third to one fourth may well be so spent. For pupils going on to colleges which are still so backward as to specify precisely their entrance requirements, possibly a large part of the day given to departmentalized work may be needed. But this now seems, to me at any rate, not the best use of their time.

Such an arrangement as that here sketched contemplates that practically all pupils of secondary age will soon be enrolled in secondary schools. To the degree that this is so, to like degree should all be as a rule "promoted" (if this old-fashioned term be still retained). At the end all will as a rule "graduate," with whatever recommendations for further work fit the conditions then obtaining.

Two reasons seem especially to support the plan outlined above. First, all pupils will (so I believe) profit by giving a good portion of their school time to such a life-process program as ignores subject divisions. Only thus can they learn to study and work as life requires. Second, many pupils, just as many adults, have no need to specialize in the way and along the lines set out by existing school subjects. In fact, it probably hurts most of such pupils to spend time on such logically organized subject matter. In the years gone by these pupils have usually dropped out of school. Now they continue to the embarrassment of all concerned. Such pupils need help with the problems of life itself and less of the formal school work. The plan proposed allows adjustment to meet each particular case, and thus allows the more intellectually inclined and the more specifically interested to pursue their work under conditions more favorable to them.

A word now about the more practical side of the problem. This plan is here proposed for study and experimentation. So far as is known it has never been tried. It would appear to be feasible both for small and for large high schools. Just what changes actual trial would require in the plan we can, of course, tell only upon such trial. Two things would seem necessary for a beginning: first, that there be a will to try the plan, and second, that teachers be found who can carry on the activity program on the high-school level. In 6–3–3 school systems that already have the "activity" program in the elementary school there could easily be found sixth-grade teachers who would like to carry on like work on seventh- and eighth-grade levels. And similarly in many 8–4 school systems, there can be found seventh- and eighth-grade teachers already carrying on "activity" programs who would like to go forward into the ninth grade. It would be comparatively easy for the larger institutions that prepare both elementary and secondary teachers to take on the new work of preparing activity home-room teachers for the high school. This need involve no heartburning, since the present specialized preparation for high school teachers could continue much as hitherto. However, teachers expecting to go to small high schools would have to prepare both along the "activity" line and in one or more subject-matter specialities.

That we need to change the secondary school rather drastically is admitted by an increasing number of American educators. The foregoing plan is proposed as both easy to try and promising of good returns.

Harold Benjamin

~~~~~~

The first great educational theorist and practitioner of whom my imagination has any record (began Dr. Peddiwell in his best professorial tone) was a man of Chellean times whose full name was *New-Fist-Hammer-Maker* but whom, for convenience, I shall hereafter call *New-Fist*.

New-Fist was a doer, in spite of the fact that there was little in his environment with which to do anything very complex. You have undoubtedly heard of the pear-shaped, chipped-stone tool which archeologists call the *coup-de-poing* or fist hammer. New-Fist gained his name and a considerable local prestige by producing one of these artifacts in a less rough and more useful form than any previously known to his tribe. His hunting clubs were generally superior weapons, moreover, and his fire-using techniques were patterns of simplicity and precision. He knew how to do things his community needed to have done, and he had the energy and will to go ahead and do them. By virtue of these characteristics he was an educated man.

New-Fist was also a thinker. Then, as now, there were few lengths to which men would not go to avoid the labor and pain of thought. More readily than his fellows, New-Fist pushed himself beyond those lengths to the point where cerebration was inevitable. The same quality of intelligence which led him into the socially approved activity of producing a superior artifact also led him to engage in the socially disapproved practice of thinking. When other men gorged themselves on the proceeds of a successful hunt and vegetated in dull stupor for many hours thereafter, New-Fist ate a little less heartily, slept a little less stupidly,

---

and arose a little earlier than his comrades to sit by the fire and think. He would stare moodily at the flickering flames and wonder about various parts of his environment until he finally got to the point where he became strongly dissatisfied with the accustomed ways of his tribe. He began to catch glimpses of ways in which life might be made better for himself, his family, and his group. By virtue of this development, he became a dangerous man.

This was the background that made this doer and thinker hit upon the concept of a conscious, systematic education. The immediate stimulus which put him directly into the practice of education came from watching his children at play.

"If I could only get these children to do the things that will give more and better food, shelter, clothing, and security," thought New-Fist, "I would be helping this tribe to have a better life."

Having set up an educational goal, New-Fist proceeded to construct a curriculum for reaching that goal. "What things must we tribesmen know how to do in order to live with full bellies, warm backs, and minds free from fear?" he asked himself.

To answer this question, he ran various activities over in his mind. "We have to catch fish with our bare hands in the pool far up the creek beyond that big bend," he said to himself.

Thus New-Fist discovered the first subject of the first curriculum—fish-grabbing-with-the-bare-hands.

"Also we club the little woolly horses," he continued with his analysis.

So woolly-horse-clubbing was seen to be the second main subject in the curriculum.

"And finally, we drive away the saber-tooth tigers with fire," New-Fist went on in his thinking.

Thus was discovered the third subject—saber-tooth-tiger-scaring-with-fire.

For a long time, however, there were certain more conservative members of the tribe who resisted the new, formal educational system on religious grounds. "The Great Mystery who speaks in thunder and moves in lightning," they announced impressively, "the Great Mystery who gives men life and takes it from them as he wills—if that Great Mystery had wanted children to practice fish-grabbing, horse-clubbing, and tiger-scaring before they were grown up, he would have taught them these activities himself by implanting in their natures instincts for fish-grabbing, horse-clubbing, and tiger-scaring. New-Fist is not only impious to attempt something the Great Mystery never intended to have done; he is also a damned fool for trying to change human nature."

To the human-nature-cannot-be-changed shouters, New-Fist pointed out the fact that paleolithic culture had attained its high level by changes in human nature and that it seemed almost unpatriotic to deny the very process which had made the community great.

By this appeal the forces of conservatism were won over to the side of the new school, and in due time everybody who was anybody in the community knew that the heart of good education lay in the three subjects of fish-grabbing, horse-clubbing, and tiger-scaring. New-Fist and his contemporaries grew old and were gathered by the Great Mystery to the Land of the Sunset far down the creek. Other men followed their educational ways more and more, until at last all the children of the tribe were practiced systematically in the three fundamentals. Thus the tribe prospered and was happy in the possession of adequate meat, skins, and security.

It is to be supposed that all would have gone well forever with this good educational system if conditions of life in that community had remained forever the same. But conditions changed, and life which had once been so safe and happy in the cave-realm valley became insecure and disturbing.

A new ice age was approaching in that part of the world. A great glacier came down from the neighboring mountain range to the north. Year after year it crept closer and closer to the headwaters of the creek which ran through the tribe's valley, until at length it reached the stream and began to melt into the water. Dirt and gravel which the glacier had collected on its long journey were dropped into the creek. The water grew muddy. What had once been a crystal-clear stream in which one could see easily to the bottom was now a milky stream into which one could not see at all.

Fortunately for the tribe, however, there were men in it of the old New-Fist breed, men who had the ability to do and the daring to think. One of them stood by the muddy stream, his stomach contracting with hunger pains, longing for some way to get a fish to eat. Again and again he had tried the old fish-grabbing technique that day, hoping desperately that at last it might work, but now in black despair he finally rejected all that he had learned in the schools and looked about him for some new way to get fish from that stream. There were stout but slender vines hanging from trees along the bank. He pulled them down and began to fasten them together more or less aimlessly. As he worked, the vision of what he might do to satisfy his hunger and that of his crying children back in the cave grew clearer. His black despair lightened a little. He worked more rapidly and intelligently. At last he had it—a net, a crude seine. He called a companion and explained the device. The two men took the net into the water, into pool after pool, and in one hour they caught more fish—intelligent fish in muddy water—than the whole tribe could have caught in a day under the best fish-grabbing conditions.

Another intelligent member of the tribe wandered hungrily through the woods where once the stupid little horses had abounded but where now only the elusive antelope could be seen. He had tried the horse-clubbing technique on the antelope until he was fully convinced of its futility. He knew that one would starve who relied on school learning to get him meat in those woods. Thus it was that he too, like the fish-net inventor, was finally impelled by hunger to new ways. He bent a strong, springy young tree over an antelope trail, hung a noosed vine therefrom, and fastened the whole device in so ingenious a fashion that the passing animal would release a trigger and be snared neatly when the tree jerked upright. By setting a line of these snares, he was able in one night to secure more meat and skins than a dozen horse-clubbers in the old days had secured in a week.

A third tribesman, determined to meet the problem of the ferocious bears, also forgot what he had been taught in school and began to think in direct and radical fashion. Finally, as a result of this thinking, he dug a deep pit in a bear trail, covered it with branches in such a way that a bear would walk out on it unsuspectingly, fall through to the bottom, and remain trapped until the tribesmen could come up and dispatch him with sticks and stones at their leisure. The inventor showed his friends how to dig and camouflage other pits until all the trails around the community were furnished with them. Thus the tribe had even more security than before and in addition had the great additional store of meat and skins which they secured from captured bears.

As the knowledge of these new inventions spread, all the members of the tribe were engaged in familiarizing themselves with the new ways of living. Men worked hard at making fish nets, setting antelope snares, and digging bear pits. The tribe was busy and prosperous.

There were a few thoughtful men who asked questions as they worked. Some of them even criticized the schools.

"These new activities of net-making and operating, snare-setting, and pit-digging are indispensable to modern existence," they said. "Why can't they be taught in school?"

The safe and sober majority had a quick reply to this naive question. "School!" they snorted derisively. "You aren't in school now. You are out here in the dirt working to preserve the life and happiness of the tribe. What have these practical activities got to do with schools? You're not saying lessons now. You'd better forget your lessons and your academic ideals of fish-grabbing, horse-clubbing, and tiger-scaring if you want to eat, keep warm, and have some measure of security from sudden death."

The radicals persisted a little in their questioning. "Fishnet-making and using, antelope-snare construction and operation, and bear-catching and killing," they pointed out, "require intelligence and skills—things we claim to develop in schools. They are also activities we need to know. Why can't the schools teach them?"

But most of the tribe, and particularly the wise old men who controlled the school, smiled indulgently at this suggestion. "That wouldn't be *education*," they said gently.

"But why wouldn't it be?" asked the radicals.

"Because it would be mere training," explained the old men patiently. "With all the intricate details of fish-grabbing, horse-clubbing, and tiger-scaring—the standard cultural subjects—the school curriculum is too crowded now. We can't add these fads and frills of net-making, antelope-snaring, and—of all things—bear-killing. Why, at the very thought, the body of the great New-Fist, founder of our paleolithic educational system, would turn over in its burial cairn. What we need to do is to give our young people a more thorough grounding in the fundamentals. Even the graduates of the secondary schools don't know the art of fish-grabbing in any complete sense nowadays, they swing their horse clubs awkwardly too, and as for the old science of tiger-scaring—well, even the teachers seem to lack the real flair for the subject which we oldsters got in our teens and never forgot."

"But, damn it," exploded one of the radicals, "how can any person with good sense be interested in such useless activities? What is the point of trying to catch fish with the bare hands when it just can't be done any more? How can a boy learn to club horses when there are no horses left to club? And why in hell should children try to scare tigers with fire when the tigers are dead and gone?"

"Don't be foolish," said the wise old men, smiling most kindly smiles. "We don't teach fish-grabbing to grab fish; we teach it to develop a generalized agility which can never be developed by mere training. We don't teach horse-clubbing to club horses; we teach it to develop a generalized strength in the learner which he can never get from so prosaic and specialized a thing as antelope-snare-setting. We don't teach tiger-scaring to scare tigers; we teach it for the purpose of giving that noble courage which carries over into all the affairs of life and which can never come from so base an activity as bear-killing."

All the radicals were silenced by this statement, all except the one who was most radical of all. He felt abashed, it is true, but he was so radical that he made one last protest.

"But—but anyway," he suggested, "you will have to admit that times have changed. Couldn't you please *try* these other more up-to-date activities? Maybe they have *some* educational value after all?"

Even the man's fellow radicals felt that this was going a little too far.

The wise old men were indignant. Their kindly smiles faded. "If you had any education yourself," they said severely, "you would know that the essence of true education is timelessness. It is something that endures through changing conditions like a solid rock standing squarely and firmly in the middle of a raging torrent. You must know that there are some eternal verities, and the saber-tooth curriculum is one of them!"

A PROPOSAL FOR BETTER CO-ORDINATION OF SCHOOL AND COLLEGE WORK—MAY, 1932

Wilford M. Aikin

~~~~~~

Students of education in America know that the elementary school has changed fundamentally in organization, curriculum, and procedure within the last decade, and that profound changes are taking place in our universities and colleges. But similar reconstruction in the secondary schools is difficult, if not impossible, under present conditions. Recognizing the need of improvement in secondary education and realizing that any significant change involves the co-operation of the colleges, the Progressive Education Association appointed, almost two years ago, a Commission on the Relation of School and College. Last December, a generous grant of funds for the work was provided by the Carnegie Corporation of New York.

UNDERLYING IDEAS

The educational emphasis in this Plan is based upon a conviction that the secondary schools must become more effective in helping young people to develop the insight, the powers and

SOURCE: Reprinted with permission from *The Story of the Eight-Year Study*, by Wilford M. Aikin. Copyright © 1942, by McGraw-Hill Book Company, Inc.

the self-direction necessary for resourceful and constructive living. We wish to work toward a type of secondary education which will be flexible, responsive to changing needs, and clearly based upon an understanding of young people as well as an understanding of the qualities needed in adult life.

We are trying to develop students who regard education as an enduring quest for meanings rather than credit accumulation; who desire to investigate, to follow the leadings of a subject, to explore new fields of thought; knowing how to budget time, to read well, to use sources of knowledge effectively and who are experienced in fulfilling obligations which come with membership in the school or college community.

To this end we should like to provide, more fully than the present organization of secondary education permits, for changes such as are indicated under the following headings:

A. GREATER MASTERY IN LEARNING

A greater mastery in learning is achieved through the acquisition of such techniques as reading with speed and comprehension, observing accurately, organizing and summarizing information; ability to work with many kinds of materials; capacity to see facts in their relationships; ability to state ideas clearly; techniques essential as a foundation for later advanced study.

B. MORE CONTINUITY OF LEARNING

More continuity of learning can be achieved through the elimination, wherever advisable, of limited, brief assignments and courses; a more coherent development of fields of study; provision for more consecutive pursuit of a particular subject through several years; encouragement (including the devising of ways and means and the allowance of sufficient time in the school schedule) of the desire to investigate; development of the power and impetus to pursue a subject beyond the school requirement, and stimulation of the desire to put ideas to use.

There should be less emphasis on subjects and more on continuous, unified sequence of subject matter, planned on a four-year or six-year basis. English is the only course that at present even approximates this aim. Continuous courses in the sciences and social sciences would take the place of such fragments of subject matter as chemistry or modern European history. Chemistry has its biological, geological, or astronomical implications that should not be overlooked if the whole of science is to have significance. Similarly, such cultures as those of South America and Asia should have a place in history courses, for comparative study, as well as those of Europe and the United States. Mathematics and foreign languages also would be reorganized in a manner to enable the pupil to get a "long" view of these fields of subject matter.

C. RELEASE OF CREATIVE ENERGIES

The release of creative energies can be achieved through experience and training in various arts, including both practice and appreciation (ex: painting, modeling, writing, drama, music); through the encouragement, in all work, of independent, individual thinking and of fresh combining of thought; through providing opportunities, with guidance, for young people to exercise their desire to do something "on their own" (ex: tinkering, inventing, constructing, special pursuits in reading, instrumental music).

D. CLEARER UNDERSTANDING OF THE PROBLEMS OF OUR CIVILIZATION, AND THE DEVELOPMENT OF A SENSE OF SOCIAL RESPONSIBILITY

Clearer understanding of the problems of our civilization and the development of a sense of social responsibility can be attained through including, in the curriculum, studies bearing upon specific problems of American civilization and that of the modern world, and the outstanding individual and collective efforts to solve these problems; through using every opportunity to help students to realize the interdependence and inter-relationships of human lives; through helping students to develop social responsibility, in feeling and in practice as well as in appreciation of the issues involved, by means of such activities as participation in school community life with concern for the general welfare, discussion groups on social and economic problems, field trips to study industrial processes, housing conditions, or the machinery of government; a model league of nations, or assembly programs which require, as do all the foregoing activities, much reading and investigation in the broad fields of social relationships.

E. REVISION OF CURRICULUM MATERIALS AND THEIR ORGANIZATION

Revision of curriculum materials and their organization can be attained, aside from the changes in curriculum materials to be inferred from the above-mentioned changes in practice, by such other experiments as: reorganizing the sequence of material in different fields of knowledge, for secondary education (ex: mathematics, science, history, language); unifying the subjects of study and removing some of the boundaries now existing between closely related fields (ex: history in its relation to the facts of economics, geography, literature and fine arts); addition of new materials from fields of knowledge not hitherto included in typical secondary school curricula (ex: certain materials from the fields of economics, anthropology, geology).

F. GUIDANCE OF STUDENTS

The function of guidance in education needs much greater study and emphasis. While it is important that the student should have as much independence and responsibility as he can use wisely, counsel of the best sort should be available when he needs it. Some one should know him well and be able and ready to examine his problems with him and to help him solve them. He should be helped to see his career through school and college as a developing experience, with each phase in a definite relationship toward the whole.

Under the Directing Committee, plans will be worked out to achieve this purpose. The program will include: more thorough study of the needs of individuals, with corresponding adjustment of the school program to their needs; record-keeping for later analysis; more intelligent preparation of the student for the use of the opportunities provided by the colleges.

G. TEACHING

It is evident that the changes in secondary education suggested in this memorandum cannot occur without teaching of a very high quality. This would be true of any experimental work. We fully recognize the scarcity of teachers who are qualified in background, in training and in personality for this type of work. There are, however, some teachers now at work who could successfully carry through the suggested program. Some of these are already studying its possibilities. Others will be discovered as the work is begun.

Schools, colleges, and universities that are undertaking the training of teachers will be interested in helping select the most promising candidates and in training them in the best possible ways for this work. We fully realize that the discovery and training of better teachers must go hand in hand with wise experimentation, and that experiments must move slowly enough to keep within the limits of available good teaching.

THE STORY OF THE EIGHT-YEAR STUDY

Report by Herbert E. Hawkes

Some seven years ago the Commission of the Progressive Education Association on School and College Relations was organized under subventions from the Carnegie Corporation of New York and the General Education Board. One of the most important

SOURCE: Reprinted with permission from *The Story of the Eight-Year Study*, by Wilford M. Aikin. Copyright © 1942, by McGraw-Hill Book Company, Inc.

questions on which this Commission, which is usually referred to as the Eight-Year Study, wished to obtain reliable evidence was that of the relation between the pattern of the preparatory school program and college success. Thirty schools of various types were selected for participation in the Study, some of them known as very progressive, others as relatively conservative. Liberal arts colleges from every part of the country were almost unanimous in expressing their willingness to admit from these schools, during the eight-year period of the Study, students who seemed competent to carry the work of the college successfully, without reference to specific requirements for admission.

Seven of the eight years have passed, and many students who entered the Thirty Schools when the Study started have now completed three years of college work. Students in the following years have completed two and one year, respectively, of college residence. There is now available a wealth of information as to the college success of these students who received their preparation in the Thirty Schools. Many predictions were ventured at the beginning of the Study, but only recently do we have a real ground for conviction.

It should be stated that many of the Thirty Schools modified their curriculum radically after entering the Study; others have made only slight changes. So far as I know, none of the colleges which these students have entered have modified their curriculum or requirements for their degrees for these students as a group. That is, we have light on the question as to whether the work of these schools which most of us would classify as progressive schools, and the character of the teaching and general experience in these schools, fits or misfits students for college work.

About 2,000 students from the Thirty Schools entered college in September of each year from 1936 to 1939 inclusive. Of these students, 1,475 were enrolled in about 30 colleges in sufficiently large groups to justify a detailed following of their success during their college residence. It should be mentioned that the Thirty School graduates score distinctly higher on aptitude or intelligence tests than the average entering student. So far as one can judge, their mean is in about the 65th percentile. It was therefore necessary in determining the college success of these students, to set up a control or comparison group in each college in which each Thirty Schools student is matched as exactly as is humanly possible in terms of age, sex, race, aptitude, interests, size and type of home community, and family background. It goes without saying that such a comparison group does not furnish a perfect statistical control, but it is probably as nearly perfect as the measurement of college success in terms of instructors' grades.

The earliest basis for comparison appears when these students present themselves for placement tests in order to determine whether they ought to be promoted above or demoted below the point that their raw entrance records would indicate. Results on this point are only fragmentary and from three liberal arts colleges in state universities. In these three institutions, 41 Thirty School graduates were exempt from the usual freshman courses in English, foreign languages, history, or chemistry, as against 26 in the comparison group. Six Thirty Schools students were required to repeat courses on the basis of the placements, while two of the comparison group were so required. This is not a complete or a surprising result, since the Thirty Schools graduates might be expected to have concentrated more intensely during their preparatory school course on the subjects of their greatest interest.

In order to obtain a comparison between the Thirty Schools graduates and their mates in the control group, members of the staff of the Eight-Year Study have visited the institutions where any considerable number of the students were registered in order to become personally acquainted with them and with their controls, so that they might reach as well considered opinions as possible regarding their adjustment to the work of the college, and the measure of success that they attained, both in their studies and in their social relations. Comparisons in each of the major fields of study between the Thirty Schools graduates and their control mates have been made with scrupulous care. I will not go into the statistical results at this time. Sufficient to say that a comparison of the 1,475 students from the Thirty Schools, which were about evenly divided between the sexes, indicates very little difference in college grades between them and their controls. On the whole, the students from the Thirty Schools were superior to the control group. Those who have been in college for three years excelled slightly in the humanities, the social sciences, and the physical sciences. The grades were almost exactly even in English and the biological sciences. They were distinctly inferior in the foreign languages, but distinctly superior in such subjects as fine arts, music and the like. I will not attempt to analyze the results for those who have had only two or one year of college experience, except to say that the students from the Thirty Schools who entered in 1938, and whose college records for only one year are available, excel their controls from the other type of school in every field of study, notably in English, humanities, physical sciences, and mathematics. This may reflect the careful job that the faculties of the Thirty Schools have done during the past three years in improving their curriculum, and affording a more adequate intellectual training for their students.

One further observation is interesting. A report on the college success of the graduates of the six of the Thirty Schools whose programs differ most from the conventional pattern is compared with that of their comparison groups. A complementary report has been made on the college success of the graduates of the six of the Thirty Schools which differ least from the conventional pattern as compared with their matched pairs. There were 361 students from the least conventional six schools, and 417 from the most conventional schools. It turns out that the students from the least conventional schools excelled their controls by a score that may roughly be expressed as 27 to 7, while the students from the most conventional schools of the Thirty were excelled by their control group by a score that may roughly be expressed as 14 to 16. That is, so far as these data are significant, the students from the schools whose pattern of program differed most from the conventional were very distinctly superior to those from the more conventional type of school.

I should add that in extra curricula interests non-athletic in character, the graduates of the Thirty Schools were markedly more alert than their comparison group.

The results of this Study seem to indicate that the pattern of preparatory school program which concentrates on a preparation for a fixed set of entrance examinations is not the only satisfactory means of fitting a boy or girl for making the most out of the college experience. It looks as if the stimulus and the initiative which the less conventional approach to secondary school education affords sends on to college better human material than we have obtained in the past.

I may add that this report to you has been approved by a Committee of the Commission on School and College Relations consisting of the following membership: President Barrows of Lawrence College, President Park of Bryn Mawr, Dr. Gummere of Harvard, Dean Speight of Swarthmore, Dean Brumbaugh of Chicago, and myself.

THE EIGHT-YEAR STUDY . . . AFTER EIGHT YEARS

Frederick L. Redefer

Did the Eight-Year Study produce a permanent change in education and did it aid further improvements? What has happened to the Eight-Year Study eight years after?

The reports from those who represented the schools at this conference were far from encouraging. A few schools reported that among the faculty there was still a considerable element with a liberal educational viewpoint, that subject matter divisions were sometimes forgotten, that civic and community education was emphasized, that guidance and the needs of adolescents were at times the focal point in thinking about and planning an education. Only one school reported that it continued the work of developing a core curriculum. No school reported that it was

SOURCE: Frederick L. Redefer, "The Eight-Year Study . . . After Eight Years, *Progressive Education*, November, 1950. Reprinted by permission.

engaged in the development of a program of general education. While a few schools were still using the materials in the field of human relations, no school reported that the needs of adolescents were paramount in its thinking. Two of the fifteen schools reporting attested that some of the "spirit" of the Eight-Year Study remained. Others confessed frankly that "the patter persists but the spirit is no longer there." Several representatives stated that their schools had retreated to the traditional college preparatory program. One headmaster said, "The strong breeze of the Eight-Year Study has passed and now we are getting back to fundamentals. Our students write fewer articles in English and social science but they are better spellers." These were some of the residues of the Eight-Year Study.

It was the general consensus of opinion of the conference that the most important residue of the Eight-Year Study was the cooperative method of work that developed during the eight years. Teachers became active participants in education.

Representatives from the schools reported that there was a challenge that came from being a part of a national experiment and that with the end of the Study, teachers missed meetings, conferences with other teachers and the visits of consultants. Such is to be expected as students of group dynamics will report. Others reported that teachers were exhausted by the demands made on them, that challenges came too thick and fast for the faculty to digest them. But now that the Eight-Year Study is no more, there is a vital something missing in the present educational picture.

WHY WAS THE STUDY NOT A CONTINUING FORCE?

One of the conference participants confessed that "the schools after the experiment did not live up to expectations." Why did the Eight-Year Study tend to disintegrate when it was over in 1942? Various replies were made to this question although no statement was thoroughly explored. Several suggested that education during World War II and the postwar period belonged to a time when everything connected with "progressive education" was under fire. Many at the conference felt this pressure so strongly that they suggested that the name itself be dropped from any future activities. One or two wrote or reported that some administrators of school systems, for political or personal reasons, successfully scuttled the changes made during the Eight-Year Study. Others suggested that teachers in schools that had been pushed or led into the Study at too fast a rate dropped the changes when the War added new responsibilities. One headmaster queried whether the current social, economic and international situation would permit schools to experiment in education, whether our concern for security tended to strengthen conservatism and authoritarianism. He asked whether schools were losing the interest and respect of students because of the unreality of our educational concerns.

One member of the original directing Commission said that thirty schools should not have been chosen. "Thirty" was too large a number particularly when some of the schools were not truly experimental or even committed to the objectives of the Study. Another member summed up his reactions somewhat as follows. The Eight-Year Study and the Thirty Schools were too intramural. They did not view what they proposed to do in the social context in which they had to work. They were reluctant to face the nature and the sources of the resistance they would meet. They did not involve the parents, the Boards of Education or Trustees to any great degree. They did not involve the faculty of the cooperating colleges with the result that the academic civil servants resisted the experiment. They did not plan adequately for the orientation and induction of new faculty members. They allowed reaction to take the initiative with the result that they were constantly on the defensive.

Others entered the discussion at various points. There seemed to be general agreement that in future educational experiments, parents, Boards of Education and Trustees and school administrators should be involved to a greater degree. Plans should be made for the induction of new teachers for, as one conference member pointed out, 70 per cent of the faculty in his school have been appointed since the Eight-Year Study was over. Most agreed that teacher education institutions ought to be involved so that they could prepare teachers for new curricula and to continue the progress made. But if these weaknesses had been corrected in the

Eight-Year Study would the results have been more lasting? Would the postwar period have permitted a genuine education of young people for their world?

GENERAL EDUCATION IN A FREE SOCIETY

Harvard Report

~~~~~~

The fact that an educational institution grants a diploma on the basis of the completion of courses and the passing of examinations does not imply that its aim is wholly to impart learning. . . . Learning is also for the sake of cultivating basic mental abilities; in short, to foster the powers of reason in man. The ability to think in accordance with the facts and with the laws of inference, to choose wisely, to feel with discrimination is what distinguishes man from the animals and endows him with intrinsic worth. Yet reason, while an end, is a means as well—a means to the mastery of life. The union of knowledge and reason in the integrated personality—this is the final test of education. We are not now denying the central position of reason or of knowledge as ministering to reason; we are only urging that reason is or must strive to become a master of a highly complex inner kingdom consisting of many and diverse members, all of which go into the making of a complete man. To put the matter bluntly, the educational process has somewhat failed of its purpose if it has produced the merely bookish youth who lacks spirit and is all light without

SOURCE: Reprinted by permission of the publishers from *General Education in a Free Society: Report of the Harvard Committee*, Cambridge, Mass.: Harvard University Press, Copyright 1945, by the President and Fellows of Harvard College.

warmth. But to leave the matter in these terms is to make for dangerous confusion; we must safeguard our statement from the misunderstandings to which it is exposed. What are some of the important qualities, over and above intellectual ability, which are necessary for an integrated and sound human being?

The school will be concerned with the health of its pupils, both physical and mental. The human body must be healthy, fit for work, able to carry out the purposes of the mind. Mental health has two forms. The first is social adjustment, an understanding of other people and a responsiveness to their needs with its counterpart of good manners. The second is personal adjustment, the individual's understanding of himself, his poise and adequacy in coping with real situations. Obviously the two are inseparable.

While traditionally man has been viewed as primarily a rational animal, recent thinking has called attention to his unconscious desires and sentiments which becloud and sometimes sway his reason. To be sure, classical philosophers recognized the existence of the passions, but they tended to regard the latter as alien intrusions, and an unwanted complication. Yet passions, although dangerous because primitive and even savage, are a source of strength if properly guided; they supply the driving forces for achievement.

In the complete man we look for initiative, zest and interest, strength of resolution, driving power. In a free society much of improvement, in or outside government, comes from the initiative and the dogged perseverance of private citizens; and the clash of ambitions in the struggle for the rewards of life, when regulated by the rules of fair play and a concern for the common good, is a source of social progress.

So far we have been dealing with general objectives. But teachers naturally ask what should be done in the school to implement these aims. We wish to make it clear that to adopt the above list of the human powers is not at all to be committed to a comparable list of courses, as a part of formal instruction. There may or may not be courses in subjects such as health or manners, depending on the circumstances. Our point is that in a proper scheme of general education the mind will acquire the capacity to meet various particular and concrete problems in matters of health, human relationships, and the like. In this view the education of the mind leads to a maturing of the whole person. On any other view, the obvious danger is that schools will set for themselves so inclusive an objective, or perhaps one should say so many objectives, that their central and essential contribution will be neglected. The schools cannot do everything. When they attempt too many tasks, they sometimes fail to do any of them well. Other social institutions are concerned with helping the individual develop personal competence, while the schools have the special and major responsibility of furthering the growth of intellectual abilities. Our discussion of the qualities which go to make up the complete man is based upon the assumption that though these qualities are of the utmost importance, though they are, indeed, vital to the future well-being of our society, they are not the sole responsibility of the schools, and their cultivation must not stand in the way of developing those qualities for which the school bears the primary burden of responsibility.

However, the emotions and the will cannot be trained by theoretical instruction alone. Doubtless the three areas of knowledge, each in its own fashion, raise and discuss problems of human value. Yet values cannot be learned solely from books. Consider the case of social adjustment. Thinking is a solitary process, and in so far as education cultivates intellectual skills it is producing individualists. To be sure, thinking is stimulated by discussion with other people, but in the last resort one has to make up one's mind by oneself. Yet living is a cooperative process. Social adjustment is not something that just happens in the individual with the passing of years. One must learn to get along with other people just as one learns to use complex sentences. But the task of learning to get along with people is infinitely more difficult. Little children do not know how to get along with each other; a teacher or some other adult must constantly control the situation. If adults lived with each other after the fashion of children and regulated their disputes as children do, we should never have had a free society. The child has much to learn before he can behave as an equal among equals or cooperate with strangers for a common purpose. While the family and the neighborhood teach many of the preliminary lessons, the main task is really tackled in the training ground of actual situations, especially those of adolescence and adult living.

But while we admit that general instruction is not enough for our purpose, we also call attention to the fact that the school as it stands is equipped to exercise an influence over its pupils through media other than formal teaching. The school is an organization in which a certain way of life is practiced. The pupil acquires a habit by the process of unconscious absorption; no sermon need be preached. A word of ridicule uttered by another pupil may produce the desired effect. Furthermore, the teacher can and does exert an influence on the student by his example as well as by what he says on the platform. In our specialized society the teacher may think it enough to teach a subject. But impressionable young people get from a teacher much more than subject matter. They judge every action. In some respects the young are exceedingly intolerant; they expect in their teachers perfection to which they themselves do not aspire but which they want to see exemplified in all those in authority over them. Teachers should be more aware of their influence in matters unrelated to their subject.

Finally, in the school the pupil takes part in the various activities. No one who has examined the early histories of schools and colleges with the tales of "cows in the chapel" and "rioting on the common" can have much regret that students now have more legitimate outlets for their exuberance. Nonetheless, it is true that we may pursue a good thing too far and encourage a tone of anti-intellectualism. Or we may, particularly in urban schools, provide insufficient activities, inducing mere bookishness.

Ideally, as the name implies, activities should mean putting into practice the theory of the classroom. Activities provide a means by which the abstract skills imparted in the classroom are made relevant to concrete choices and actions. The educational value of activities, such as it is, comes from the fact that habituation and experience are necessary for the development of any skill, including intellectual skills. Student government, within limits, is valuable in shaping the quality of later citizenship. It is only when the student faces the actual difficulties of governing by democracy that he begins to appreciate the complexity of a free society. To learn to resist pressure, to discover the power of a minority, to have free speech used against one, to prescribe rules and then to abide by them, is training of the first order for democratic living. The connection of the activities with the curriculum is easy to show in the case of the French Club, the Debating Society, the Glee Club, and the Forum. It is harder to illustrate when we come to managerial offices and to athletics. Yet there is no doubt that decisiveness, initiative, and cooperativeness can be stimulated in the student who has to cope with problems encountered in the running of an organization or in team play.

The atmosphere of the school, the informal role of the teacher and the activities—these are all media by which practice and habituation supplement the work of formal instruction in the school. We must emphasize that rational explanation should accompany or follow habituation; that, in short, mere habituation is not enough, as the case of language may show. On the one hand, it is true that one does not know a language adequately if one knows its grammar and vocabulary only; one must be able to use the language and speak it with something of its peculiar idiom. On the other hand, it is also true that a street Arab who can speak his native tongue fluently is not because of that fact to be regarded as educated in language; and linguistic proficiency will become firmer when accompanied by an understanding of the formal structure of the language. Nor is social adjustment only the habitual facility of getting along with other people; it is also and essentially the understanding of other persons—of their desires, capacities, and valuations. Poise comes from an inner reserve, from a clarity and conviction as to purpose. Without these, personal force is apt to degenerate into that flashy and indeterminate quality miscalled "personality."

Have we exhausted all the potentialities of the school in the preceding account? No, not wholly. When the curriculum, the pervasive atmosphere of the school, and the activities, having done their best, still fall short of expected results, then the school must have recourse to types of instruction in specific subject matters. There is a difference between implicit and explicit instruction. By the former we mean indirect instruction, as when a student acquires skills of thought and communication from courses in general education, or acquires initiative and resourcefulness from his participation in sports. The normally intelligent youth will be able to draw his own conclusions, carrying over

into particular cases the spirit of his whole training. But there
are those who must be told specifically and explicitly. For instance, while many pupils will be able to absorb relevant knowledge about health from the general course in biology and other
allied courses, others will need explicit instruction in personal
hygiene. Again, while some will learn manners by contagion
from the established practices of the school, there will be others
who will have to be told the rules of polite behavior in so many
words. A school serving a community of first-generation immigrants may have to introduce courses on the American way
and on American standards of living. However, such explicit
instruction should be regarded as remedial and as peripheral to
the curriculum. Because the circumstances vary, no uniform list
of such special courses can be given, but some suggestions may
be made.

Education is not complete without moral guidance; and moral
wisdom may be obtained from our religious heritage. By law
and by custom little sectarianism is now to be found in the great
body of American schools and colleges. However, much of the
best tradition of the West is to be found in the distillations of
the prophets, in the homilies and allegories of an earlier age,
and in Biblical injunctions. These are not the property of a sect
or even of Christians; they constitute the embodiment of experience on the ethical plane which is, or should be, the heritage
of all. . . .

But the role of the school in the development of health may be
decisive. Although the first responsibility in this matter rests
with the family and the community, in some places the schools
must assume the task of giving direct instruction in health, personal or civic. For many young people the elementary facts about
diet, rest, exercise, drugs, and disease will have to be learned
away from home if they are to be learned at all. Such instruction
may make the difference between a debilitated and a healthy
community. The subject may take time from other pursuits of
more central intellectual importance. But no educational or social
system is sound unless it rests on solid physical foundations.

In an earlier section we spoke of the importance of shop training for students who intend to go into scientific or technological
work. Such experience is important for the general education

of all. Most students who expect to go to college are now offered an almost wholly verbal type of preparatory training, while hand training and the direct manipulation of objects are mainly reserved for the vocational fields. This is a serious mistake. The bookish student needs to know how to do things and make things as much as do those students who do not plan to take further intellectual training. The direct contact with materials, the manipulation of simple tools, the capacity to create by hand from a concept in the mind—all these are indispensable aspects of the general education of everyone. In some schools pupils receive such training in the elementary grades. Other students gain such experience outside of school; but for those who have had no experience in the use of tools, a high school course may offer the only possibility.

In modern society, where few children automatically follow their fathers' vocations, the school must inevitably give some help in choosing a career. Any treatment of American society should acquaint students with many sides of the conditions which they will have to face. Yet some students will need more detailed information about the requirements and possibilities of various kinds of work. Formal course instruction is of doubtful value for this purpose, which can be better served by individual guidance and by the provision of suitable reading in the school library.

Beyond the knowledge of future work, the student needs an experience in actual work. Clearly the school itself cannot be expected to provide this experience in any formal way. Yet it is beneficial for all, even more so for those who expect to enter business or one of the professions than for those who will engage in some form of manual or craft work. It is important that this experience be of such a kind as to contribute to the total productivity of society, although it need not be manual labor. In other words, it is desirable that it be genuine, rather than made, work. We repeat that we are thinking here not of any formal school requirement but of what is necessary for the maturing of a young person.

It is obvious that our account of education in its bearing on the entire human being presupposes a general theory of human nature and of human values. It is equally obvious that in the nature of the case such a theory had to be assumed rather than explicitly formulated in this report. A contrast with current tendencies may help clarify our views. In a natural reaction against the inherited type of formal and bookish learning, educational practice has tended to swing to the opposite extreme and to replace the traditional courses of the curriculum with highly specific and practical courses. The danger here is that training is being substituted for education. More recently a reaction to the reaction has appeared, which would place great books in a central, even monopolistic, position and which tends to identify education exclusively with cultivating the ability to think. We have taken a position somewhere between these two. We have stated that education looks to the whole man and not to his reason alone; yet we have maintained that the whole man is integrated only in so far as his life is presided over by his reason. While we thus regard the cultivation of the mind as the chief function of the school, we view reason as a means to the mastery of life; and we define wisdom as the art of living. We have stressed the importance of the trait of relevance; and we have urged that, while in school, the pupil should be helped to see beyond conceptual frameworks and make concrete applications. Yet since the school by its nature cannot reproduce the complexity of actual life, a merely functional approach to teaching is inadequate also.

An extreme and one-sided view easily calls attention to itself and gains fervent adherents; but a balanced view is apt to be less immediately striking. Reasonableness does not lead to exciting conclusions because it aims to do justice to the whole truth in all its shadings. By the same token, reasonableness may legitimately hope to attain at least to part of the truth.

A SOUND CORE PROGRAM—WHAT IT IS AND WHAT IT ISN'T

Harold B. Alberty

In recent years, many attempts have been made to clarify the concept of the core, as that term is applied to the high school curriculum. Yet probably no other term in the field of education is surrounded by so much confusion and so many misconceptions. It is literally true that there is no commonly accepted meaning of the term which makes it possible for administrators, teachers, and laymen to communicate intelligently concerning it.

Some of the fairly common definitions are: a group of required subjects, a combination of two or more subjects, a large block of time in which learning activities are planned cooperatively, any course taught by "progressive" methods.

Added to this confusion is the fact that many terms such as the following are used synonymously with core: common learnings, general education, unified studies, self-contained classrooms, basic courses, fused courses, and English–social-studies.

As a consequence, when one is told that a certain school has a core, it is unsafe to draw any conclusions whatever concerning the nature of the program.

In my opinion, the conception of core most likely to transform and improve general education in the high school is this: a group of structured problem areas, based upon the common problems, needs, and interests of adolescents, from which are developed teacher-student planned learning units or activities.

Following are some of the principal characteristics of an effective adolescent-problems core program based on this conception.

SOURCE: *Harold B. Alberty*, "A Sound Core Program—What It Is and What It Isn't," *NEA Journal*, January, 1956, pp. 20–22. Reprinted by special permission.

1. It deals with the area of general education and hence is directed primarily toward the development of the common values, understandings, and skills needed for effective democratic citizenship.

2. Since it provides for general education, it is required of all students at any given level.

3. It utilizes a block of time sufficiently large to deal with a broad, comprehensive unit of work, with homeroom and guidance activities, and with individualized instruction.

4. It is based upon the common problems, needs, and interests of youth as ascertained by the teaching staff and the core teacher in cooperation with his students. It draws freely upon all pertinent resources, including logically organized subjects or fields of knowledge.

5. It has a clearly defined but flexible scope and sequence based on preplanned problem areas derived from the major values of democratic living and the common problems, needs, and interests of students.

6. Instruction is based upon learning units derived principally from the established problem areas, which are planned, carried forward, and evaluated by the teacher and the students.

7. It is supported and reinforced by a rich offering of special-interest activities—both formal and informal—designed to meet the particular needs of students and to develop their unique capacities, interests, and talents.

The foregoing presentation is intended as a frame of reference for discussing what I believe to be certain misconceptions concerning a sound core program. . . .

Misconception No. 1. The core concept is new and has had very limited application; hence, programs based upon it should be regarded as highly experimental, if not radical and dangerous.

As a matter of fact, the various elements of the adolescent-problems core as defined above have been in successful use for many years.

(*a*) The practice of setting aside a significant portion of the school day for general education is commonplace, as attested by the practices of most high schools and colleges.

(*b*) The problem approach and the utilization of direct, first-hand experience as starting points for learning have proved their effectiveness over a period of at least half a century—even before Dewey established his famous laboratory school in 1896. It was the very heart of the revolution in agricultural education which began about 1910. In 1923, Ellsworth Collings documented experimentally the desirability of a complete break with the subject-centered curriculum. Good elementary schools have used effectively the problem and direct-experience approach to learning for many years.

(*c*) The value of utilizing the broad unit-of-work approach was documented by the early followers of Herbart and later by Morrison, Miller, Thayer, and others. By 1930, the techniques of unit teaching were well known and practiced by many high school teachers.

(*d*) The use of student-teacher planning grew out of the success of the socialized recitation, which had its beginning in the early decades of the century. Its value have been well documented by studies in group dynamics in both education and industry.

(*e*) The success of teaching the so-called fundamentals through broad comprehensive units of experience has been documented over and over. Collings could again be cited as a pioneer in this field. His results have been verified in scores of experimental studies.

Thus it is evident that the features of a sound core program have long since passed the experimental stage.

Misconception No. 2. The core program is progressive or modern while the subject-centered special-interest program is conventional or even traditional.

This misconception gets us into great difficulties because it tends to create a cleavage between teachers working in the core program and those in the special-interest areas when they need to work together more effectively.

There is no valid basis for this misconception because the techniques of curriculum development and instruction open to the core teacher are, for the most part, equally applicable to the special-interest teacher. For example, the science teacher may base his course on problems, needs, and interests of students. The program will, of course, have a narrower scope than the core, since he is dealing with a restricted field of knowledge.

He may organize the course in terms of comprehensive units of work, using the logic of his field only as a way of determining scope and sequence. He may emphasize teacher-student planning if he regards the logical system of knowledge of his field as a guidepost rather than as a mandate to "cover ground." He may also perform a highly important specialized guidance function.

The difference between the two types of program is to be found in the fact that the core program deals with the area of general education, and hence finds its scope and sequence in the broad areas of living, while the special-interest areas deal with a content determined by the *particular field*. Both types of learning experience are essential to a well-rounded education.

Actually a good core program cannot be developed without the help of the subject specialist: in planning resource units or guides, in core classroom teaching at points of need, and in teaching his special field with constant reference to what goes on in the core so as to reinforce and enrich the core program.

Misconception No. 3. The core has no definable content. It is largely process, or methodology. Its values lie in the way the students learn. Almost any content is satisfactory, so long as the students share in planning, and are achieving certain democratic values held by the teacher.

This view is held by many teachers and some authorities who find their orientation in the more radical theories of the "left-wing progressives" in education and who hold that any attempt to define scope and sequence in advance of classroom teacher-student planning is a violation of the creative process. It places too much emphasis upon the utilization of the immediate felt and expressed wishes, wants, and desires of the students in the group.

Programs designed around this misconception have done much to bring the adolescent-problems core into disrepute because it is difficult, if not impossible, to explain to inquiring parents just what Johnny is learning because the teacher himself won't know until *after* the year's work is finished. It is likewise difficult if not impossible for special interest area teachers to plan their own programs or their participation in the core because of the highly tentative nature of the program. And it is difficult for administrators and supervisors to anticipate resources which will be needed.

It is my contention that the core program, based on a more realistic approach to education for effective citizenship, should have a content as capable of definition as that of a field of knowledge. The content can be derived: (*a*) from careful studies of problems of youth which grow out of their own basic drives and from the pressures and tensions of the environment which impinge upon them; and (*b*) from the democratic values to which we as a people are committed.

Such a definition of scope might well eventuate in a series of problem areas in the basic aspects of living from which cooperatively planned learning units would be developed. The sequence of learning would be determined largely by each individual core teacher and his students.

Misconception No. 4. The core is merely a better way of teaching the required subjects.

Clearly this misconception has some kinship with the one explained immediately above. There is, however, an important distinction. Proponents of this point of view hold that the core is a *method of teaching* which has for its aim the mastery of the conventional subjects—usually English and the social studies. To the other group, the principal aim is the attainment of the values which inhere in the process of living democratically.

The program which eventuates from this misconception is known as unified studies, English–social-studies, and multiple-period classes. It is taught by one teacher, in a block of time larger than one period.

Obviously there are certain advantages to such an arrangement. The teacher gets to know the students better and hence has the opportunity to develop a more effective homeroom guidance program. The student is likely to see interconnections among the subjects that are unified. However, it can be justified only as a transition from the conventional separate-subject program to the more vital adolescent-problems core.

Misconception No. 5. The core, once firmly established, will gradually absorb the entire curriculum and eventually result in the complete destruction of all subject fields.

This view is the result of a lack of understanding of the fundamental differences between education directed toward the development of the ideals, understandings, and skills needed by all for effective citizenship and education directed toward the development of the unique interests, abilities, or talents of the individual. The former is the distinctive province of the core; the latter can best be accomplished by teacher specialists in appropriately equipped shops, laboratories, and studios. Each of the two aspects of education has its distinctive functions; each reinforces the other.

The prevalence of this misconception is probably accounted for by the fact that the adolescent-problems core draws upon all pertinent fields of knowledge in dealing with common problems of living and calls for the assistance of the specialist in determining the potential contributions of such fields of knowledge. What it neglects to take into account is the need for courses or experiences designed specifically to meet the special needs, problems, and interests of students.

Misconception No. 6. The core is more suitable for the below-average or dull student who has difficulty in mastering the conventional subjects than for the bright student who expects to go to college.

There is no evidence known to the writer that indicates that the adolescent-problems core is peculiarly adapted to any *one* class of students. Current practices reveal its successful use in schools with selective enrollments as well as in schools with more heterogeneous populations. As a matter of fact, the core, with its emphasis upon broad units of work, affords the opportunity to provide for individual differences *within* the unit, so that students of all levels of ability may find stimulating experiences.

Misconception No. 7. The core is better adapted to the junior high school than to the senior high school.

It is difficult to understand the logic back of this familiar misconception, for no one would seriously argue that the problem-solving approach becomes ineffective at the senior high level. The nature of the pertinent problems, of course, will change as the students develop, but that means only that the school should adapt instruction to the student's maturity level.

Surveys of core-program development indicate that 85 to 90 per cent of all the cores are to be found in the seventh and eighth grades. In only a small number of schools is the core extended to the senior high school level.

Probably many educators are convinced that the core program is actually better adapted to the junior high school, but the present situation is due to additional factors.

Traditionally, the seventh and eighth grades were regarded as part of the elementary school, where most or all of the instruction was given by one teacher. Consequently, many principals who reacted against the extreme specialization of the early junior high schools saw the core as a way out which would have the sanction of tradition.

On the other hand, the traditional requirement of sixteen Carnegie units for high school graduation has tended to be a barrier to the extension of the core to the senior high school.

Finally, the teacher-certification problem has added to the difficulty of extension.

It is far easier to state the misconceptions concerning a sound core program which serve as blocks to its development than to suggest ways to remove the blocks.

All that the writer hopes for is that this analysis may stimulate thinking about a conception of curriculum development which has the potentiality for improving our present programs of general education in the high school.

EVENTS LEADING TO THE NATIONAL CONFERENCE ON
LIFE ADJUSTMENT EDUCATION FOR EVERY YOUTH

Charles A. Prosser

ORIGIN AND NATURE OF THE RESOLUTION

In January, 1944, the Vocational Education Division of the U.S. Office of Education undertook a study of Vocational Education in the Years Ahead. This study covered a period of 1½ years. There was a working committee of 10 persons; this was supplemented by a reviewing committee and a consulting committee. More than 150 persons participated in the study.

On May 31 and June 1, 1945, a final conference was held at the Wardman Park Hotel in Washington, D.C. At that meeting many problems were presented relating to a life-adjustment program of education for that major group of youth of secondary-school age not being appropriately served by preparation for college or by training for a specific vocation. According to Dr. J. C. Wright, at that time Assistant Commissioner for Vocational Education, and chairman of the Conference on Vocational Education in the Years Ahead, but few solutions to the grave and persisting problems were offered by the group assembled.

Near the close of that meeting, the chairman named Dr. Charles A. Prosser, well-known leader in education and for many years director of Dunwoody Institute, Minneapolis, Minn., to summarize the conference. As a part of his summarization, Dr. Prosser presented what has now become an historic resolution. This resolution recognized the need for a more realistic

---

SOURCE: Charles A. Prosser, "Life Adjustment Education for Every Youth," U.S. Department of Health, Education, and Welfare, Bulletin No. 22, 1951. Reprinted, 1953.

and practical program of education for those youth of secondary-school age for whom neither college-preparatory offerings
nor vocational training for the skilled occupations is appropriate. It contained a request for the U.S. Commissioner of Education "to call at some early date a conference or a series of
regional conferences between an equal number of representatives of general education and of vocational education—to consider this problem and to take such initial steps as may be
found advisable for its solution." The resolution was unanimously adopted by the consulting committee.

The work of the regional conferences consisted primarily
of exploratory discussions of the problems inherent in the resolution and of possible ways of reaching solutions to them. Some
time was spent in considering the nature of the youth with
whom the resolution was concerned, the characteristics they
have in common, if any, and the means by which they can be
identified. In addition, attention was devoted to the question
of what would constitute a suitable program of education for
those particular youth and to the question of how the changes
in schools and school systems which are indicated thereby can
be accomplished.

It was the consensus of those participating in the regional conferences:

1. That secondary education today is failing to provide adequately and properly for the life adjustment of perhaps a major
fraction of the persons of secondary-school age.

2. That public opinion can be created to support the
movement to provide appropriate life-adjustment education for
youth.

3. That the solution is to be found in the provision of educational experiences based on the diverse individual needs of
youth of secondary-school age.

4. That a broadened viewpoint and a genuine desire to serve
all youth is needed on the part of teachers and of those who
plan the curriculums of teacher-training institutions.

5. That local resources must be utilized in every community
to a degree as yet achieved only in a few places.

6. That functional experiences in the areas of practical arts,
home and family life, health and physical fitness, and civic

competence are basic in any program designed to meet the needs of youth today.

7. That a supervised program of what experience is is a "must" for the youth with whom the resolution is concerned.

8. That one of the principal barriers to the achievement of the ideals of the resolution is the multiplicity of small, under-staffed, and underfinanced school districts in this Nation.

9. That an intimate, comprehensive, and continuous program of guidance and pupil personnel services must constitute the basis on which any efforts to provide life-adjustment education must rest.[1]

The regional conferences served their purposes well. It was the groundwork laid at these conferences which made possible the considerable accomplishments of the National Conference.

---

[1] Reworded form of Prosser Resolution: "It is the belief of this conference that, with the aid of this report schools will be able better to prepare for entrance upon desirable skilled occupations those youth who by interest and aptitude can profit from such training. We believe that the high school will continue to improve its offerings for those youth who are preparing to enter college. In the United States the people have adopted the ideal of secondary education for all youth. As this ideal is approached the high school is called upon to serve an increasing number of youth for whom college preparation or training for skilled occupations is neither feasible nor appropriate. The practical problems connected with the provision of a suitable educational program for this increasing number are so great and the schools to date have had comparatively little experience in this enterprise that the problems merited cooperative study and action by leaders in all aspects of secondary education. We believe that, secondary school administrators and teachers and vocational education leaders should work together to the end that the number of students being made in secondary schools to meet this need will be greatly increased and to the end that the pronouncements made in recent years by various educational groups which are suggestive of needed curriculum patterns will receive increased study and implementation."

POOR STUDENT OR POOR SCHOOL?

Stephen M. Corey

No, I'm not very good in school. This is my second year in the seventh grade, and I'm bigger and taller than the other kids. They like me alright though, even if I don't say much in the classroom, because outside I can tell them how to do a lot of things. They tag me around and that sort of makes up for what goes on in school.

I don't know why the teachers don't like me. They never have very much. Seems like they don't think you know anything unless they can name the book it comes out of. I've got a lot of books in my room at home—books like *Popular Science Mechanical Encyclopedia,* and the Sears' and Ward's catalogs —but I don't very often just sit down and read them through like they make us do in school. I use my books when I want to find something out, like whenever Mom buys anything sec- ondhand I look it up in Sears' and Ward's first and then tell her if she's getting stung or not. I can use the index in a hurry.

In school, though, we've got to learn whatever is in the book and I just can't memorize the stuff. Last year I stayed after school every night for two weeks trying to learn the names of the Presidents. Of course I knew some of them like Washington and Jefferson and Lincoln, but there must have been thirty altogether and I never did get them straight.

I'm not too sorry, though, because the kids who learned the Presidents had to turn right around and learn all the Vice- Presidents. I am taking the seventh grade over, but our teacher this year isn't so interested in the names of the Presidents. She

SOURCE: Reprinted by permission of the Association for Childhood Education International, 3615 Wisconsin Avenue, N.W., Washington 16, D.C. "The Poor Scholar's Soliloquy," by Stephen M. Corey. From *Childhood Education,* January 1944, Vol. 20, No. 5.

has us trying to learn the names of all the great American inventors.

I guess I just can't remember names in history. Anyway, this year I've been trying to learn about trucks because my uncle owns three and he says I can drive one when I'm sixteen. I already know the horsepower and number of forward and backward speeds of twenty-six American trucks, some of them Diesels, and I can spot each make a long way off. It's funny how that Diesel works. I started to tell my teacher about it last Wednesday in science class when the pump we were using to make a vacuum in a bell jar got hot, but she said she didn't see what a diesel engine had to do with our experiment of air pressure so I just kept still. The kids seemed interested, though. I took four of them around to my uncle's garage after school and we saw the mechanic, Gus, tear a big truck Diesel down. Boy, does he know his stuff!

I'm not very good in geography either. They call it economic geography this year. We've been studying the imports and exports of Chile all week, but I couldn't tell you what they are. Maybe the reason is I had to miss school yesterday because my uncle took me and his big trailer truck down state about 200 miles, and we brought almost 10 tons of stock to the Chicago market.

He had told me where we were going, and I had to figure out the highways to take and also the mileage. He didn't do anything but drive and turn where I told him to. Was that fun! I sat with a map in my lap and told him to turn south, or southeast, or some other direction. We made seven stops, and drove over 500 miles round trip. I'm figuring out what his oil cost, and also the wear and tear on the truck—he calls it depreciation—so we'll know how much we made.

I even write out all the bills and send letters to the farmers about what their pigs and beef cattle brought at the stockyards. I only made three mistakes in 17 letters last time, my aunt said—all commas. She's been through high school and reads them over. I wish I could write school themes that way. The last one I had to write was on "What a Daffodil Thinks of Spring," and I just couldn't get going.

I don't do very well in school arithmetic, either. Seems I

just can't keep my mind on the problems. We had one the other day like this: "If a 57-foot telephone pole falls across a cement highway so that $17\frac{3}{6}$ feet extend from one side and $14\frac{9}{17}$ feet from the other, how wide is the highway?"

That seemed to me like an awfully silly way to get the width of a highway. I didn't even try to answer it because it didn't say whether the pole had fallen straight across or not.

Civics is hard for me too. I've been staying after school trying to learn the "Articles of Confederation" for almost a week, because the teacher said we couldn't be good citizens unless we did. I really tried, because I want to be a good citizen. I did hate to stay after school, though, because a bunch of us boys from the south end of town have been cleaning up the old lot across from Taylor's Machine Shop to make a playground out of it for the little kids from the Methodist Home. I made the jungle gym from old pipe, and the guys made me Grand Mogul to keep the playground going. We raised enough money collecting scrap this month to build a wire fence clear around the lot.

Dad says I can quit school when I am fifteen, and I am sort of anxious to because there are a lot of things I want to learn how to do and as my uncle says, I'm not getting any younger.

EMPHASIZE TASKS APPROPRIATE FOR THE SCHOOL

Ralph W. Tyler

~~~~~~

In identifying the tasks which are particularly appropriate for the school, its special characteristics need to be carefully considered. One major feature of the high school is the fact that its teachers have been educated in the arts and sciences. Frequently this characteristic is played down or overlooked because subject matter has often been viewed as dead material —a collection of items to be remembered but not a vital ingredient in life itself. Too frequently we have failed to identify the constructive role of the arts and sciences in education. Properly understood, the subject matter of these fields is not dead but can be the source of a variety of understandings, values, abilities, and the like which aid the student in living more effectively and more happily. The school should be drawing upon these resources to enrich the lives of the students. Our effort should not be to make the classroom more like life outside the school but to make life outside the school more in harmony with the values, purposes, and knowledge gained from the classroom.

This viewpoint emphasizes college and university education in the arts and sciences as a primary resource for the high school to use, but this is a valid position only insofar as the contributions of the arts and sciences are used as vital means of learning and not as dead items to recall. This can be done and often is. All of us can think of illustrations of the way in which each of the major fields of science and scholarship can provide things that open up avenues for living. In science, for example, the kinds of problems with which the scientist deals

SOURCE: Ralph W. Tyler, "Emphasize Tasks Appropriate for the School," *Phi Delta Kappan*, November, 1958, pp. 72–74. Reprinted by permission.

in seeking to understand natural phenomena and to gain some control over them, the methods that scientists use for studying problems, the concepts they have developed for helping to understand the phenomena with which they deal, the data they are obtaining about various natural phenomena and the generalizations which they have developed for relating factors and for explaining phenomena, all give us tools for understanding our natural world and for seeking to gain more control over it. They also give us a basis for continuing our own study and learning about natural phenomena long after high school.

The other subject fields can furnish similar examples of problems, methods, concepts, and generalizations so important in finding meaning and effectiveness in life. When we build the high-school curriculum, the arts and sciences need to be treated as vital means of learning. They must be examined carefully for their possible contributions rather than viewed as matters of rote memorization. Furthermore, the education of teachers in these fields should be effectively utilized. All too often we have employed teachers in jobs that do not draw upon their education. The task of the school is partly defined by this important characteristic: the employment by the high school of teachers who are educated in the arts and sciences.

THE SCHOOL'S UNIQUE RESOURCES

A second significant characteristic is the skill of the high-school staff in facilitating the learning of students. By and large, teachers are effective in teaching. Their training and experience have been largely focused on it. In addition to these characteristics of the teaching staff, there are three other features of the high school to be considered in selecting appropriate educational tasks. The school has special types of equipment and facilities, such as libraries and laboratories. The arrangements of enrollment and attendance in the high school permit the organization of learning experiences over a considerable period of time. The high school has built a tradition commonly recognized and respected in the community. This tradition includes such elements as impartiality, objectivity, and concern for human values. These are very important characteristics not possessed in equal degree by other social institutions. The kinds of jobs the school undertakes should primarily be those which depend upon these characteristics, since they provide for unique contributions.

Considering these features of the school, several kinds of educational tasks are recognized as particularly appropriate. One of these has already been mentioned, namely, learning, which is based substantially upon the arts and sciences. A second is the learning of complex and difficult things that require organization of experience and distribution of practice over considerable periods of time. A number of illustrations will quickly come to mind. Probably reading and mathematics are most commonly recognized as fields in which the basic concepts and skills require careful organization, beginning with simple materials and moving gradually to more complex matters over the years of elementary and secondary school. Clearly, this kind of learning is uniquely possible in the school rather than in the less well-organized conditions of other agencies.

A third kind of educational task appropriate for the school is to provide learning where the essential factors are not obvious to one observing the phenomenon and where the principles, concepts, and meanings must be brought specially to the attention of the learner. Thus the scientific concepts and principles which explain the growth and development of plants are not obvious to the observer of plants or even to an uneducated farm hand. The school can more effectively provide for this learning than can the home or the job.

PROVIDING OUT-OF-ORDINARY EXPERIENCE

A fourth kind of learning appropriate for the school is where the experiences required cannot be provided directly in the ordinary activities of daily life. Geography and history are excellent illustrations of fields where daily life experience alone is not likely to provide sufficient insight into historic matters and matters relating to places far removed. If young people are to develop an understanding of history, it will require the attention of a specialized agency able to provide materials serving to give vicarious experiences and to organize them effectively. The same is true for geography. We cannot depend entirely upon the informal experiences of daily life to provide these kinds of learning.

A fifth kind of learning particularly appropriate for the school is that which requires more "purified experience" than is commonly available in life outside the school. Students may learn something of art, music, literature, or human relations from the examples commonly found in the community, but where these fall far short of the best, the students have no chance to set high standards for themselves. The school can provide examples for study and enjoyment which represent the best available.

A sixth kind of learning particularly appropriate to the school is that in which reexamination and interpretation of experience are very essential. Our basic ethical values are commonly involved in the daily experiences of youth. Questions of justice, fairness, goodness arise again and again on the playground, in the marketplace, and elsewhere. It is not likely, however, that sheer contact with these ideas will be enough to help the individual youth to develop values that are clearly understood and effectively utilized. The school can provide opportunity from time to time to recall these experiences, to examine them, and seek to interpret them, thus clarifying the meaning of values as well as helping youth to appreciate them more adequately. In the realm of ethical values this type of responsibility will be shared by the home, the Church, and youth organizations, but in the realm of esthetic values it is probably true that only the school is likely to provide the opportunity systematically.

These six kinds of learning which are peculiarly appropriate for the high school ought to be strongly emphasized in its program in contrast to other learnings which can be provided by other agencies. There are, of course, educational jobs which are good in themselves but do not require the particular conditions that the school provides. When the school undertakes these tasks, it must either neglect other important things or attempt more than it can do well, spreading itself too thin, and not achieving as effective educational results as it should. Concentrating its efforts upon the educational job which the high school is uniquely fitted to undertake and encouraging other community agencies in their responsibilities will greatly raise the educational level of the nation.

HOW THE JUNIOR–HIGH SCHOOL CAME TO BE

John H. Lounsbury

The movement to reorganize secondary education has come a long way since Charles W. Eliot made the suggestion in 1888. From that date until 1909–1910, the reorganization movement remained at the talking stage. Indianola Junior-High School of Columbus, Ohio, opened in September, 1909, became the first school specifically called a junior-high school. Today, there are 5,000 junior-high schools. The reorganized schools, that is those that deviate from a four-year high school following an eight-year elementary school, now make up 76 percent of the 24,000 secondary schools and enroll 82 percent of the 11 million secondary pupils.

The movement involving the development of the junior-high school, though already quite successful, is relatively young. Yet the institution's existence is long enough so that the history of the junior-high-school movement can be viewed with reasonable objectivity. Our understanding of the present and our vision for the future are incomplete without a knowledge of how and why the junior-high school came to be.

During the 1920's, the junior-high school and its partners in

SOURCE: John H. Lounsbury, "How the Junior-High School Came to Be," *Educational Leadership*, Vol. 18, December, 1960. Reprinted by permission.

the reorganization movement were rapidly growing educational innovations. In the 1930's the junior-high school, the senior-high school, and the combination junior-senior high school became accepted members of the American school family. By the close of the 1950's, the separate junior-high school followed by the separate senior-high school had become the predominant pattern of secondary-school organization in the United States. Together these institutions enrolled 50 percent of the secondary-school population.

The history of the junior-high school parallels the social, economic, and political developments of the half-century which encompasses its life. It was initiated, developed, and grew because a variety of factors, all related to the times and existing educational theory and practice, supported it in one way or another.

Among the factors functioning to aid the growth and development of the junior-high school were: In the 1890's, college officials wanted secondary schools to speed up and improve college preparation; several national committees issued influential reports supporting reorganization proposals in the period 1892 to 1918; educators were seeking a solution to the appallingly high rate of drop-outs and retardations as revealed by the pioneer studies of Ayers, Strayer, and Thorndike; numerous psychologists, including G. Stanley Hall, supported special institutions as being better for coping with adolescents.

MANY FACTORS

The junior-high school did not develop and grow because of any *one* factor; it grew because of many. It grew because educators aspired to practice new understandings of individual differences which the psychologists were clarifying. It grew because the growing masses of immigrants and urban dwellers required an extensive type of citizenship education. And it grew because it provided a partial solution to the school building shortage caused by World War I and again by World War II.

Nor can the credit for the junior-high school be given to any one individual; not to Eliot, not to Thorndike, not to Hall.

Many individuals contributed to the development. In some instances, the champions came from different philosophical camps. Public-school leaders were concerned with meeting immediate needs and viewed the junior high as a means, board of education members may have seen reorganization as an economy move, while teachers may have supported reorganization for the new and improved special facilities it would bring.

Over the long haul, however, a dominant factor undergirding the successful development of the junior-high school has been the desire of educators to provide an appropriate educational program for early adolescence. This desire was both an original impetus and a continuing concern. Without denying the assistance of other factors in the development of the junior-high school, it can be noted that the support of some of these factors has not been sustained.

The movement's first fatality, for instance, was the economy of time, the original reason for reorganization. The drop-out problem, which motivated many early efforts to reorganize, has largely been resolved at the junior-high-school level. The assistance which the junior-high school received from the guidance movement is now given to other schools as well. But the attempt to provide an effective educational program based on the nature of young adolescents remains as the basic theme of the junior-high-school movement.

Junior-high-school growth seems also to have been assisted by many chronological coincidences. The way a variety of developments worked together to the advantage of the reorganization movement is at least a partial explanation for the notable success which the movement has enjoyed.

There is the coincidence of G. Stanley Hall publishing his volumes on adolescence in 1905. What if he had published his works in 1925? What if the school building shortage caused by World War I had come *before* the series of committee reports dealing with reorganization rather than *after?* What if the drop-out studies had been made in the 1880's rather than in 1907–1911? What if the movement to chart individual differences had come about before any mention of reorganization had been made?

A number of similar questions might be posed, and probably would be equally difficult to answer. They are, perhaps, purely academic, yet they serve to point up how important the chronological convergence of numerous factors was to the growth and development of the junior-high school.

In summary, many factors worked together to cause the inauguration and early success of the crusade to reorganize secondary education. The original impetus for reorganization came from the colleges and was concerned with economy of time and with college preparation. Discussions about reorganization then began to broaden their base and proposals became linked with other school problems, such as the high rate of elimination and retardation. Psychology furnished studies offering further justification. The culture provided fertile soil for the seeds of reorganization whether planted by college presidents, by public-school administrators, by psychologists, or by professional educators. So the movement to reorganize secondary education, coming at a propitious time, prospered.

The junior-high school may not have been all that many hoped it would be. It may never have proved itself on some counts, yet it has achieved marked success in its relatively brief history. Many new educational practices and ideas have been tested in the junior-high school. More experimentation is in the offing, as glimpses of the future are beginning to come into clearer focus. The junior-high-school story is unfinished; its success to date augurs well for the future.

REPORT OF THE COMMITTEE FOR THE WHITE HOUSE CONFERENCE ON EDUCATION

A Report to The President

~~~~~~

RECOMMENDATIONS

1. As the duties of the schools expand, the establishment of priorities in education should be studied by every board of education. This Committee believes that the development of the intellectual powers of young people, each to the limit of his capacity, is the first responsibility of schools.

2. Overspecialization of vocational education should be avoided. There are almost 50,000 trades in this country, and specialized instruction for all of them cannot be provided. Broadly conceived programs of vocational education must be maintained which are not likely to be outmoded rapidly by technological change and which offer basic instruction that can be useful in many jobs.

3. The school system must be flexible within itself. Pupils should be able to shift from one program to another as they grow and change in interests and abilities. This Committee thinks that for every child to have, throughout his school career, the chance to change to the kind of education found best for him is more important than the time saved by choosing a few pupils early in their lives for accelerated, specialized programs, as is often done in Europe. The American people have time as well as the physical resources to allow this kind of flexibility.

4. Educational programs which fully exercise and develop the abilities of especially brilliant students must be maintained. A

SOURCE: *A Report to The President, the Committee for the White House Conference on Education, Full Report, April 1956* (Washington, D.C.: U.S. Department of Health, Education, and Welfare, 1956), pp. 4–5, 8–13.

system which wastes the talents of those who have the most to offer has no part in the new American ideal for the schools. Social equality can be maintained by the schools without hampering the intellectual progress of the unusually able. Increased stress must be placed on meeting the challenge of those students who have the capacity for the greatest intellectual growth . . .

Consequently, the identification and careful handling of talented youth are urgent and commanding requirements.

5. School leaders should *help* foster all desirable characteristics in children, but they should not be tempted to consider themselves the only agency in the field. The major influence upon children is their home and the whole community in which they are raised. We must never lose sight of the insistent need to increase the excellence of our schools while increasing their scope; the two goals are not incompatible except under conditions of bad management or inadequate resources. The problems of the schools are great, but they never should be allowed to obscure the worthiness of their goals. In the judgment of this Committee, the people will probably continue to insist that all needs of all children be met, one way or another. The attempt to provide schools capable of playing their full part in making that ideal a reality may well prove to be one of the wisest decisions ever made by the American people.

RECOMMENDATIONS FOR IMPROVING PUBLIC SECONDARY EDUCATION

James B. Conant

~~~~~~

THE REQUIRED PROGRAM FOR ALL

A high school program contains general and elective courses. The general courses are GENERAL EDUCATION. They should be *required,* as follows: Four years of English; three or four years of social studies, including two years of history (one, American), and a senior course in American Problems or American Government; one year of mathematics (algebra or general mathematics); and at least one year of science, which might well be biology or general physical science.

General Education includes nine or ten courses requiring homework and takes about half the pupil's time. The other requirements should be *elective courses,* with a significant sequence of courses as their central core.

ABILITY GROUPING

In the required subjects (with the exception of the course in American Problems) and in subjects elected by students with a wide range of ability, pupils should be grouped according to ability, subject by subject. Three groups usually are enough: one for the more able in the subject, one for the middle group, and one for the slow learners who really need special attention. In this arrangement, a pupil might be in a top section in English, but in

SOURCE: James B. Conant, *The American High School Today* (New York: McGraw-Hill Book Company, 1958), pp. 44–76. Reprinted by permission.

a middle section in mathematics. There should be no hard and fast lines.

DIVERSIFIED TALENTS REQUIRE DIVERSIFIED ELECTIVE PROGRAMS

High school pupils cannot be neatly divided into categories according to academic ability. However, it is useful to think in terms of groups, if it be remembered that assignment to these groups must remain flexible.

1. The highly gifted are some 3 percent of the pupil population, nationally. In some schools they are too few for special classes. In this case, a special counselor should be assigned to the group as a tutor to see to it that the pupils take challenging courses and develop their special interests. Where numbers are adequate, these pupils should be in class under the Advanced Placement Program of the College Entrance Examination Board. This program begins advanced work early and culminates in actual college courses in the twelfth grade.

2. The academically talented are the top 15 to 20 percent nationally. For them the following minimum program is strongly recommended: Four years of mathematics, three years of science, four years of one foreign language, and the required courses in English and social studies.

This is not to say that the pupils below the top 15 to 20 percent should not take academic electives in addition to the required academic courses. But they may not be able to handle so full a program as can the academically talented, and the electives should be chosen carefully each year with the aid of the counselor.

3. Pupils interested in developing skills which are marketable directly on graduation should be enrolled in the regular English, social studies, and other courses required for graduation, and should not be isolated from the other pupils.

For boys there should be industrial arts courses made available first. Then mechanical drawing, shop work, and other vocational courses should follow. Federal aid through the Smith–Hughes Act is available for these vocational programs.

The nature and extent of these programs should depend on the employment opportunities in the area. In each specialized trade there should be an advisory committee from labor and management in the community.

For girls and some boys there should be the range of business education courses.

In communities suited to them programs in distributive education and diversified occupations should be offered.

4. Pupils whose reading skill is markedly low—say, sixth-grade ability in the ninth grade—should receive special instruction under teachers who are interested in working with this group and who are sympathetic with its problems. Remedial reading should be part of the work, and special text books should be provided. The elective courses should include simple vocational work but should not be part of the regular vocational programs. This group should not be confused with the mentally retarded pupils, whose education in some states is provided in the regular high schools through special teachers and with the help of special state funds.

INDIVIDUALIZED PROGRAMS

It should be the school policy that every pupil has an individualized program. There should be no classification by tracks, as academic, vocational, etc. However, in advising pupils, counselors should recommend sequences established by school board policy as suggested previously under item 2 of the Diversified Talents recommendation. Consideration should always be given to sensible program changes requested by pupils.

THE COUNSELING SYSTEM

In a comprehensive high school of adequate size there must be counseling. It should start in the elementary school and be articulated with the secondary school. There should be one full-time counselor for every 250 to 300 students in the high school. Counselors should have had teaching experience and should have professional training for counseling. They should be sympathetic with the entire school program and should counsel students on the basis of ability and worthy goals.

ENGLISH COMPOSITION

To insure the development of ability to write English, half of the time devoted to English should be given to composition. Pupils should average one theme a week, and themes should be corrected by the teacher and discussed with the pupils. To allow time for these themes, English teachers should teach no more than one hundred pupils. A school-wide composition test should be given annually, and in the ninth and eleventh grades those tests should be corrected by both a pupil's teacher and a test committee. Pupils who do not obtain grades in the eleventh-grade test commensurate with their ability should take a special composition course in the twelfth grade.

FOREIGN LANGUAGES

A school board should offer the third and fourth years of a foreign language no matter how few enroll. Counselors should urge pupils to complete four years of a foreign language if the pupils show ability in the foreign language field. Competence does not come from two years of foreign language study in a high school. School policy should recommend the study of a foreign language for at least three years, and preferably for four.

THE ACADEMIC INVENTORY

The academic inventory is a device for examining the program elected by the students during their four years. It should be requested of the principal by the board of education each year for the graduating class.

If the distribution of academic ability in the school corresponds to the national norm, the academic inventory form should be completed for each pupil in the top 15 percent of the graduating class.

With name omitted, the form should state the sex of the pupil, ability level, courses taken during the four years, and the grades obtained. Examination of the summary of the inventory will show to what extent the academically talented pupils have studied the subjects they should have studied, and will roughly measure the efficacy of the counseling system. If ability distribution in the school is abnormal, the percent of pupils included should be increased or decreased accordingly.

RANK IN CLASS

The school board should stop the practice of designating rank in class by marks received and the practice of naming a valedictorian. Since class rank is calculated by averaging the grades in all subjects, bright pupils often elect easy courses in order to insure high grades and high class standing. This fact was brought out in an examination of the programs sent us by a number of schools.

ACADEMIC HONORS LIST

Each year a list should be published of the graduates who elected the recommended sequence for the academically talented and made an honors average in these courses. This achievement might be indicated by a seal or notation on the diplomas of those pupils. There should also be suitable recognition of pupils with outstanding achievement in other sequences in the program of studies.

SUPPLEMENT TO THE DIPLOMA

In addition to the diploma, each graduate should receive a durable record of all courses studied and the grades obtained. The existence of this record should be so well publicized that employers ask to see the record of courses rather than the diploma when questioning a job applicant about his education.

DR. CONANT'S RECOMMENDATIONS TO THE CITIZENS

1. At the Local Level—Selecting a Good School Board

If the citizen's first obligation to the public schools is to support them, then the second obligation in many districts is to select an able, devoted board of education. Board of education members should be selected not because they represent elements or factions in the district, but because they understand the importance of the public schools and are competent to help establish policy for the operation of the schools. They should be persons who realize that the business of the board of education is with policy, and not with details on school operation, which should be handled by the professional staff.

2. At the State Level—High Schools of Sufficient Size

Unless a high school has a graduating class of at least 100, that school is too small to offer a sufficiently diversified curriculum to meet the needs of all its pupils and the needs of our nation.

More than half of our 21,000 high schools do not meet the minimum criterion of a graduating class of 100.

In fact, 30 percent of our high school pupils attend high schools too small to do an adequate job.

Citizens should face this situation realistically and resolutely. The small high school should be eliminated by district reorganization. When persons say that geography will not allow consolidation of high schools, we should be sure that it is not human nature that is the prohibiting agent.

THE CONANT REPORT: A PRELIMINARY APPRAISAL

William M. Alexander

Even before the report appeared, questions and criticisms were voiced by some educators as to the procedures of the Conant study. Some objected to describing as a "study" a series of first-hand school observations even by such an intelligent observer as the former Harvard president and U.S. high commissioner to Germany. Others objected to limiting the observations to "comprehensive" high schools. Neither of these objections is likely to be lessened very much by the report itself.

Indeed, other limitations may now be noted. Dr. Conant visited fifty-five schools in eighteen states. He was concerned only with grades 9–12 (although he expects, according to our recent conversation, to study grades 7 and 8 now). He gave scant attention to the big cities and to suburban schools. By his own statement . . . "this report is in no sense a survey of the comprehensive high school," and "the study has made no attempt to answer such questions as 'How satisfactory is the typical American high school?'" His evaluation of the schools to determine their comprehensiveness was based on his own criteria, developed after some preliminary school visits, and reviewed by a number of experienced school administrators. The recommendations resulting from the study are closely related to the criteria, and perhaps some could have been made without the intervening school visits.

This reviewer hopes that such criticisms of the procedures employed by the Conant study will not interfere with discussion of the report itself. In the first place, despite the somewhat misleading title, this study was not intended to be an all-inclusive one. In the second place, the recommendations are specific, and

SOURCE: William M. Alexander, "The Conant Report: A Preliminary Appraisal," *Phi Delta Kappan*, March, 1959, pp. 247–249. Reprinted by permission.

their careful discussion should be beneficial even if further data need to be collected on some of them. In the third place, useful data were gathered in the study and made available in the report, especially in the appendixes. Finally, and more significant, this eminent American, unlike several self-appointed and outspokenly vitriolic critics of education, *has* visited the schools, talked to school people, and made determined and positive efforts to test, and even reconstruct his own ideas against present school practice. . . .

Other recommendations appear highly controversial. Grouping by ability in each required subject and some electives is recommended (No. 4) with little data to resolve existing controversies in this regard. Reducing the English teacher's load to 100 pupils (No. 6) may not be accepted by other teachers as the way to assure better English composition. The recommended program for academically talented students (No. 9) leaves little room for electives unless the school day is reorganized into more than six periods, as is proposed in another recommendation (No. 12) and is sure to provoke disagreement.

Three recommendations seem somewhat inconsistent with Conant's emphasis on individualization and flexibility in programming: prerequisites to be completed with a grade of "C" before admission to certain further courses in mathematics, science, and foreign languages (No. 13); academic honors list for the academically talented but some unspecified "special recognition" for students in nonacademic sequences (No. 15); "practical" courses in chemistry and physics with standards "such that students with less than average ability will have difficulty passing the course" (No. 19). One wonders if parents and others may not shy away from practices which appear to relegate the below-average achiever to a second-rate program. Although fully accepting the desirability of a "stiff" program for the academically talented students, the reviewer believes some of these will continue to be "late bloomers" who need opportunity for challenge throughout high school. And might not even the below-average but hard-working student benefit from really "practical" chemistry and physics?

His study of the American high school should add to James B. Conant's niche in American educational history. His great prestige will make the report read and talked about in many homes and organizations heretofore interested only in local school issues or perhaps momentarily in some less constructive and authoritative but more sensational article or book. This report is decidedly timely, and it will be heard respectfully. Undoubtedly, it will be cited to support many school improvement programs and proposals during the next few years.

It will be unfortunate if the full use of the report is dissipated by violent disagreement with specific recommendations. Yet there is this danger. Secondary school educators who wish it used by local study groups, faculties, and boards of education should make certain that Sections I and II are studied and discussed before futile controversies are fed by specific recommendations in Section III.

In summary, my considered appraisal leads to these predictions:

1. That this report will be widely read and even more widely cited.

2. That it will be used effectively to resist movements toward establishing selective academic high schools.

3. That it may aid proponents of school consolidation efforts, but not enough to create any sharp reductions in the number of small schools unless the financial and social difficulties in consolidation are generally aided by other sources.

4. That the twenty-one specific recommendations will be used to support and refute many local proposals, with the final decisions being based on such varied factors as to make impossible any evaluation of the Conant report's influence on these decisions.

5. Most important, that this report may mark the completion of an already significant turn in the public press and in public discussions away from attacks on secondary education and toward realistic appraisal of the financial and personnel problems involved in improving secondary education in the United States.

Instructional Practices

~~~~~~

Instructional practices vary with each teacher. Just as no one philosophy of education prevails in this country, neither is there a singular teaching procedure in effect throughout the nation's schools. The schoolmasters of colonial times were harsh and authoritarian, or they were understanding and democratic, according to their personal feelings, because none of them was trained directly for the teaching profession. It is imperative that the student of secondary education understand the evolution of these practices or what is commonly called teaching method.

Not until the establishment of the first Normal School at Lawrence, Massachusetts, in 1837, was professional attention given to the art of teaching. From the exhortations of Pestalozzi and Rousseau, educators drew inspiration, but this was not at all widespread; rather, the admonitions of the faculty psychology of John Locke prevailed. Even though the latter was misinterpreted, the emphasis on rigorous training to develop the compartments of the mind was the accepted mode of teaching. "As the strength of the body lies chiefly in being able to endure hardship, so also does that of the mind." [1]

[1] John Locke, *Some Thoughts on Education* (Boston: 1830), in the Library of Education, Vol. I.

Interest and motivation were not considered essential in the classrooms of nineteenth-century United States. Lessons were frequently moralistic, disconnected, and difficult for difficulty's sake. Memorization, rote learning, and the authoritarian approach were closely wedded to the concept of mental training, whereas terms such as *reflective thinking, conceptualization, individual differences,* and *democratic values* were unknown to the teachers of this era.

Herbart's promulgation of the Five Formal Steps—Preparation, Presentation, Comparison, Generalization, and Application—captivated the teachers of America as *the* method in the 1890's. For the first time, the teachers had a pattern to emulate that was basically sound, but their interpretation of the process as a mechanical outline led to a stultification of the teaching process.

Herbert Morrison amplified the Herbartian method by adding the Unit concept, which extended the teaching process by pointing out that merely covering subject matter is not necessarily the most desirable educational objective. Morrison's emphasis on adaptation as the basic learning product is closely allied to current thinking on the development of generalizations. In his effort to select and organize learning activities into units, he offered escape from the daily recitation method of earlier centuries.

Dewey, Herbart, and Morrison held the doctrine of interest in common. From this point of agreement, however, Dewey moved to an emphasis upon interaction with an evolving society rather than adaptation to this society. His method was shaped by numerous forces: the industrial revolution, the scientific movement, the concept of evolutionary democracy, and modern psychology. The resulting methodology made its impact felt in the John Dewey Experimental School at the University of Chicago in the 1890's. The process of learning now became as important as that which was to be learned. In the words of Dewey, "To teach not so much things as the meanings of things"[2] became the battle cry of the Progressives. One of the implications of this point of view for the secondary school was that the teacher's authority could no longer be imposed on all students. The teacher's role was transformed from the image of an authoritarian figure to that of a person functioning as a guide and counselor in the learning process. According to this methodology, which is based on the philosophy of experimentalism, subjects are included in the curriculum not because of their esteemed traditional value, but rather because of the worth they have in assisting the student's adjustment to the present society. Life adjustment education was the natural derivative of this approach, and programs developed that included subjects such as driver education, social studies, and senior problems along with the traditional subjects of English, history, and mathematics. Extracurricular activities were now considered equally important in the curriculum. Further, the method to be employed in the classroom was that of problem solving.

Manifestations of the experimentalist's methodology were to be found in Dewey's writings as well as those of his most articulate disciple, William Heard Kilpatrick. The latter's project method found wide acceptance in the elementary school and to a certain extent in the junior high school. The various stages in Kilpatrick's procedure consisted of purposing, planning, executing, and judging; these steps corresponded closely to Dewey's "complete act of thought." Of particular significance here is that the entire Kilpatrick process, which is applicable to the class, at the same time recognizes the individual within the group.

Individualized instruction has played an interesting role in the history of instructional practices, not so much because of its extensive acceptance or practice but because it called attention to the inadequacy of the daily recitation approach.

[2] John Dewey, *How We Think* (Boston: D. C. Heath & Company, 1933), p. 236.

A pioneer in the area of classroom practices, Frederick Burk of San Francisco State College, in 1913 established a series of lessons for individual students that might be followed and executed at their own rate of speed, to be graded and checked by the teacher. If the student mastered the lesson, he proceeded to the next series of lessons—precursor of the teaching machine! Two disciples of Burk, Helen Parkhurst in Dalton, Massachusetts, and Carleton Washburne of Winnetka, Illinois, were able to put the idea of individual instruction into practice at their respective schools. Although certain successes were apparent and attracted considerable attention, neither the Dalton Plan, nor the Winnetka Plan exerted a major influence on the main stream of American secondary education. The major objections, even on the part of the Progressives or experimentalists were that these plans were much too mechanistic and denied what they considered to be the purpose of learning.

Theory and practice have never been completely reconciled in American education. Although most teachers were exposed to the methodology of the experimentalists in the 1930's and were further encouraged by the findings of the Eight-Year Study, researchers were unable to find that the newer methods advocated were being widely practiced. In the classrooms of the nation slavish adherence to textbooks and "ground to be covered" persisted along with unconscious attachment to Herbartian procedures, which precluded any advancement in the teaching process.

With the advent of Sputnik there has been a renaissance of thinking in respect to methodology or instructional practices. Attention is being focused on such terms as *discovery, conceptualization, critical thinking, inquiry,* and *creativity.* Much of the writing in this area today is reminiscent of the works of Dewey and Kilpatrick in the late twenties. The major question still remains, Will these "new procedures" be accepted? More important, will they be practiced in the high schools of tomorrow?

SOME THOUGHTS ON EDUCATION

John Locke

~~~~~~

As the father's example must teach the child respect for his tutor, so the tutor's example must lead the child into those actions he would have him do. His practice must by no means cross his precepts, unless he intend to set him wrong. It will be to no purpose for the tutor to talk of the restraint of the passions whilst any of his own are let loose; and he will in vain endeavour to reform any vice or indecency in his pupil, which he allows in himself. Ill patterns are sure to be follow'd more than good rules. . . .

SOURCE: John Locke, *Some Thoughts on Education*. Reprinted by permission of the publishers from Robert Ulich, editor, *Three Thousand Years of Educational Wisdom: Selections from Great Documents*, Cambridge, Mass.: Harvard University Press, Copyright 1947, 1954, by the President and Fellows of Harvard College.

In all the whole business of education, there is nothing like to
be less hearken'd to, or harder to be well observ'd, than what I
am now going to say; and that is, that children should, from their
first beginning to talk, have some *discreet, sober,* nay, *wise* person
about them, whose care it should be to fashion them aright, and
keep them from all ill, especially the infection of bad company.
I think this province requires great *sobriety, temperance, tender-
ness, diligence,* and *discretion;* qualities hardly to be found united
in persons that are to be had for ordinary Salaries, nor easily to
be found anywhere. . . .

The consideration of charge ought not to deter those who are
able. The great difficulty will be where to find a *proper* person:
for those of small age, parts, and virtue are unfit for this employment, and those that have greater, will hardly be got to undertake such a charge. You must therefore look out early, and en-
quire everywhere; for the world has people of all sorts. . . .

. . . one fit to educate and form the mind of a young gentleman is not everywhere to be found, and more than ordinary care
is to be taken in the choice of him, or else you may fail of your
end.

The character of a sober man and a scholar is, as I have above
observed, what every one expects in a tutor. This generally is
thought enough, and is all that parents commonly look for; but
when such an one has emptied out into his pupil all the latin and
logic he has brought from the university, will that furniture make
him a fine gentleman? Or can it be expected, that he should be
better bred, better skilled in the world, better principled in the
grounds and foundations of true virtue and generosity, than his
young *tutor* is?

To form a young gentleman as he should be, 'tis fit his *governor*
should himself be well-bred, understanding the ways of carriage
and measures of civility in all the variety of persons, times, and
places; and keep his pupil, as much as his age requires, constantly
to the observation of them. This is an art not to be learned nor
taught by books. Nothing can give it but good company and
observation joined together. The tailor may make his clothes
modish, and the dancing-master give fashion to his motions; yet
neither of these, though they set off well, make a well-bred gentleman: No, though he have learning, to boot, which, if not well

managed, makes him more impertinent and intolerable in conversation. Breeding is that which sets a gloss upon all his other good qualities, and renders them useful to him, in procuring him the esteem and good-will of all that he comes near. Without good breeding his other accomplishments make him pass but for proud, conceited, vain, or foolish.

Courage in an ill-bred man has the air and escape not the opinion of brutality: learning becomes pedantry; wit, buffoonry, plainness, rusticity; good nature, fawning. And there cannot be a good quality in him, which want of breeding will not warp and disfigure to his disadvantage.

* * *

Besides being well-bred, the *tutor* should know the world well; the ways, the humours, the follies, the cheats, the faults of the age he is fallen into, and particularly of the country he lives in. These he should be able to shew to his pupil, as he finds him capable; teach him skill in men, and their manners; pull off the mask which their several callings and pretences cover them with, and make his pupil discern what lies at the bottom under such appearances . . . that when he comes to launch into the deep himself, he may not be like one at sea without a line, compass, or sea-chart, but may have some notice beforehand of the rocks and shoals, the currents and quick-sands, and know a little how to steer, that he sink not before he get experience. . . .

A great part of the learning now in fashion in the schools of *Europe*, and that goes ordinarily into the round of education, a gentleman may in a good measure be unfurnish'd with, without any great disparagement to himself or prejudice to his affairs. But prudence and good breeding are in all the stations and occurrences of life necessary; and most young men suffer in want of them, and come rawer and more awkward into the world than they should, for this very reason, because these qualities, which are of all other the most necessary to be taught, and stand most in need of the assistance and help of a teacher, are generally neglected and thought but a slight or no part of a *tutor's* business. Latin and learning make all the noise; and the main stress is laid upon his proficiency in things a great part whereof belong not to a gentleman's calling; which is to have the knowledge of a man of business, a carriage suitable to his rank, and be eminent and useful in his country, according to his station. . . .

The great work of a *governor*, is to fashion the carriage, and form the mind; to settle in his pupil good habits and the principles of virtue and wisdom; to give him by little and little a view of mankind, and to work him into a love and imitation of what is excellent and praiseworthy; and, in the prosecution of it, to give him vigour, activity, and industry. The studies which he sets him upon, are but as it were the exercises of his faculties, and employment of his time, to keep him from sauntering and idleness, to teach him application, and accustom him to take pains, and to give him some little taste of what his own industry must perfect. For who expects, that under a *tutor* a young gentleman should be an accomplish'd critic, orator, or logician? go to the bottom of metaphysics, natural philosophy, or mathematics? or be a master in history or chronology? though something of each of these is to be taught him. But it is only to open the door, that he may look in, and as it were begin an acquaintance, but not to dwell there. And a governor would be much blamed that should keep his pupil too long, and lead him too far in most of them. But of good breeding, knowledge of the world, virtue, industry, and a love of reputation, he cannot have too much: And if he have these, he will not long want what he needs or desires of the other.

*   *   *

. . . We learn not to live, but to dispute; and our education fits us rather for the university than the world. But 'tis no wonder if those who make the fashion suit it to what they have, and not to what their pupils want. The fashion being once establish'd, who can think it strange, that in this, as well as in all other things, it should prevail? . . . Reason, if consulted with, would advise, that their children's time should be spent in acquiring what might be useful to them when they come to be men, rather than to have their heads stuffed with a deal of trash, a great part whereof they usually never do ('tis certain they never need to) think on again as long as they live; and so much of it as does stick by them they are only the worse for. This is so well known that I appeal to parents themselves, who have been at cost to have their young heirs taught it, whether it be not ridiculous for their sons to have any tincture of that sort of learning when they come abroad into the world? whether any appearance of it would not lessen and disgrace them in company? And that certainly must be an admirable acquisition, and deserves well to make a part in education, which men are asham'd of where they are most concern'd to shew their parts and breeding.

AN ACCOUNT OF SCHOOL LIFE AT

PHILLIPS ANDOVER ACADEMY, 1780

A Letter from the First Principal

School begins at eight o'clock with devotional exercises; a psalm is read and sung. Then a class consisting of four scholars repeat memoriter two pages in Greek Grammar, after which a class of thirty persons repeats a page and a half of Latin Grammar; then follows the "Accidence tribe," who repeat two, three, four, five and ten pages each. To this may be added three who are studying arithmetic; one is in the Rule of Three, another in Fellowship, and the third is in Practice. School is closed at night by reading Dr. Doddridge's Family Expositor, accompanied by rehearsals, questions, remarks and reflections, and by the singing of a hymn and a prayer.

SOURCE: A letter from the first principal, Eliphalet Pearson, to the Trustees in 1780. "An Account of School Life at Phillips Andover Academy, 1780," given in M. E. Brown and H. G. Brown, *The Story of John Adams, A New England Schoolmaster* (New York: Charles Scribner's Sons, 1900), pp, 47, 48.

GERTRUDE'S METHOD OF INSTRUCTION

Johann Heinrich Pestalozzi

. . . It was quite early in the morning when Arner, Glülphi and the pastor went to the mason's cottage. The room was not in order when they entered, for the family had just finished breakfast, and the dirty plates and spoons still lay upon the table. Gertrude was at first somewhat disconcerted, but the visitors reassured her, saying kindly: "This is as it should be; it is impossible to clear the table before breakfast is eaten!"

The children all helped wash the dishes, and then seated themselves in their customary places before their work. The gentlemen begged Gertrude to let everything go on as usual, and after the first half hour, during which she was a little embarrassed, all proceeded as if no stranger were present. First the children sang their morning hymns, and then Gertrude read a chapter of the Bible aloud, which they repeated after her while they were spinning, rehearsing the most instructive passages until they knew them by heart. In the mean time, the oldest girl had been making the children's beds in the adjoining room, and the visitors noticed through the open door that she silently repeated what the others were reciting. When this task was completed, she went into the garden and returned with vegetables for dinner, which she cleaned while repeating Bible-verses with the rest.

It was something new for the children to see three gentlemen in the room, and they often looked up from their spinning toward the corner where the strangers sat. Gertrude noticed this, and said to them: "Seems to me you look more at these gentlemen

SOURCE: Reprinted by permission from Robert Ulich, editor, *Three Thousand Years of Educational Wisdom: Selections from Great Documents,* Cambridge, Mass.: Harvard University Press, Copyright 1947, 1954, by the President and Fellows of Harvard College.

than at your yarn." But Harry answered: "No, indeed! We are working hard, and you'll have finer yarn to-day than usual."

Whenever Gertrude saw that anything was amiss with the wheels or cotton, she rose from her work, and put it in order. The smallest children, who were not old enough to spin, picked over the cotton for carding, with a skill which excited the admiration of the visitors.

Although Gertrude thus exerted herself to develop very early the manual dexterity of her children, she was in no haste for them to learn to read and write. But she took pains to teach them early how to speak; for, as she said, "Of what use is it for a person to be able to read and write, if he cannot speak?—since reading and writing are only an artificial sort of speech." To this end she used to make the children pronounce syllables after her in regular succession, taking them from an old A-B-C book she had. This exercise in correct and distinct articulation was, however, only a subordinate object in her whole scheme of education, which embraced a true comprehension of life itself. Yet she never adopted the tone of instructor toward her children; she did not say to them: "Child, this is your head, your nose, your hand, your finger"; or: "Where is your eye, your ear?"—but instead, she would say: "Come here, child, I will wash your little hands," "I will comb your hair," or: "I will cut your finger-nails." Her verbal instruction seemed to vanish in the spirit of her real activity, in which it always had its source. The result of her system was that each child was skilful, intelligent and active to the full extent that its age and development allowed.

The instruction she gave them in the rudiments of arithmetic was intimately connected with the realities of life. She taught them to count the number of steps from one end of the room to the other, and two of the rows of five panes each, in one of the windows, gave her an opportunity to unfold the decimal relations of numbers. She also made them count their threads while spinning, and the number of turns on the reel, when they wound the yarn into skeins. Above all, in every occupation of life she taught them an accurate and intelligent observation of common objects and the forces of nature.

All that Gertrude's children knew, they knew so thoroughly that they were able to teach it to the younger ones; and this they often begged permission to do. On this day, while the visitors were present, Jonas sat with each arm around the neck of a smaller child, and made the little ones pronounce the syllables of the A-B-C book after him; while Lizzie placed herself with her wheel between two of the others, and while all three spun, taught them the words of a hymn with the utmost patience.

When the guests took their departure, they told Gertrude they would come again on the morrow. "Why?" she returned; "You will only see the same thing over again." But Glülphi said: "That is the best praise you could possibly give yourself." Gertrude blushed at this compliment, and stood confused when the gentlemen kindly pressed her hand in taking leave.

The three could not sufficiently admire what they had seen at the mason's house, and Glülphi was so overcome by the powerful impression made upon him, that he longed to be alone and seek counsel of his own thoughts. He hastened to his room, and as he crossed the threshold, the words broke from his lips: "*I must be schoolmaster in Bonnal!*" All night visions of Gertrude's school-room floated through his mind, and he only fell asleep toward morning. Before his eyes were fairly open, he murmured: "I will be schoolmaster!"—and hastened to Arner to acquaint him with his resolution.

Prospectus of the Rev. Mr. Peers's School

In this department, the younger students will have the foundation laid, by constant and appropriate *practice,* of valuable habits such as *observation, analysis, induction,* etc. For the attainment of this, the most important of the two great ends of education, the principles laid down by that revered philanthropist, with whose name we have honoured this branch of our school, are admirably calculated. The following are some of them.

I. "The instruction given should be adapted to the age and capacity of the pupil, so that he will comprehend it easily and perfectly.

II. "A regular and easy progression should be observed, beginning with that which is simple and plain, and proceeding by easy and gradual steps, to that which is complicated and difficult.

III. "In this progress, nothing should be passed, till it is perfectly understood and familiarized, so that it will be retained, both as a useful acquisition in itself, and as a facility to the acquisition of other matters connected with and depending upon it.

SOURCE: "Pestalozzian Department in a Kentucky School, 1830," *Prospectus of the Rev. Mr. Peers's School* . . . (Lexington, Kentucky, printed by Joseph G. Norwood, 1830), p. 15. The four principles given above are practically identical with those set out by Dr. Joseph Buchanan in *Western Spy and Literary Cadet,* March 3, 1821, and given in N. H. Sonne's *Liberal Kentucky, 1780–1828* (New York: Columbia University Press, 1939), p. 96. Buchanan was born in Virginia, was a graduate of Transylvania University, a physician, educator, and writer and exponent of liberalism. He studied with Joseph Neef at the latter's school near Philadelphia and was an energetic advocate of the Pestalozzian methods of teaching. Rev. Mr. Peers may have taken the principles from the source indicated above.

IV. "A plan of discipline and excitement should be employed which will produce great ardor and industry of pursuit, and supersede the necessity of coercion by an appeal to force or fear."

Among other things in which our pupils will be *practiced* in conformity with these principles, are elementary Mathematical exercises relating both to number and form, *exact copies of which as used in Pestalozzi's school* we have been fortunate enough to obtain (together with many valuable directions), from a Swiss gentleman who aided in organizing his institution.

SCHOOLS FROM THE BOSTON ERA

Otis W. Caldwell and Stuart A. Courtis

. . . The careful observer will learn, by looking over our tables, the general system of instruction pursued in our schools; namely, that of verbal or book knowledge; and by comparing one School with another, he will see what masters vary most from the usual routine, and teach most thoroughly. Generally speaking, the questions which would be asked by one who teaches from books, as the names of the principal lakes, rivers, etc., are answered correctly; but take such a question as this: Do the waters of Lake Erie run into Lake Ontario, or those of Ontario into Erie? —and 287 answer correctly, while 130 answer incorrectly. Now, if we take into consideration what is unquestionably true, that many of those who did not know answered by guess, and that

SOURCE: Otis W. Caldwell and Stuart A. Courtis, *Then and Now in Education* (Yonkers, N.Y.: World Book Company, 1923). Reprinted by permission.

they were just as likely to guess right as wrong, much the largest
proportion of our best scholars could not tell which way the
waters run, in spite of all the fame of Niagara!

To the question: What is the general course of rivers in North
and South Carolina; and in Tennessee and Kentucky?—pretty
correct answers were given; but to the next question: What is
the reason that the waters of these four contiguous states run in
opposite directions?—only 128 showed by their answers that they
had ever thought of the reason; 308 did not answer at all; and
of the 51 incorrect answers, most were as vague as the reply of
one scholar, who said, that these waters run in opposite directions
because it was the will of God!

To the question: What is meant by the line of perpetual snow?
—only 5 percent of correct answers was given; and to the question: Upon which range of mountains is the line of snow most
elevated above the ocean, the Rocky Mountains of North America, or the Cordilleras of Mexico?—only 19 percent answered
correctly, notwithstanding it is a question with which guessers
were as likely to go right as to go wrong.

The verbal examination which followed in geography con-
firmed the opinion which would be drawn from the answers
to the printed questions. In a few schools, the children seem to
have been taught orally, and upon correct principles; but generally they were lost when taken out of the common routine of
questions. They could bound states and countries; name capitals,
capes, and mountains; enumerate rivers, lakes, and bays; and
answer a series of questions put by the master of half an hour's
duration; but, questioned as to the drainage of countries, their
capacities for commerce, the causes which direct streams and
determine the force of water—their want of comprehension of
these and similar subjects, showed plainly, in almost every school,
that they had learned geography as if it were only a catalogue
of names of all the divisions of water, from ponds up to oceans;
of land, from towns to empires.

THE USE OF THE PURPOSEFUL ACT
IN THE EDUCATIVE PROCESS

William Heard Kilpatrick

～～～～～～～～～～～～～～～～～～～～～～～～～～～～～

The word *project* is perhaps the latest arrival to knock for admittance at the door of educational terminology. Shall we admit the stranger? Not wisely unless two preliminary questions have first been answered in the affirmative: First, is there behind the proposed term and waiting even now to be christened a valid notion or concept which promises to render appreciable service in educational thinking? Second, if we grant the foregoing, does the term *project* fitly designate the waiting concept? Because the question as to the concept and its worth is so much more significant than any matter of mere names, this discussion will deal almost exclusively with the first of the two inquiries. It is indeed entirely possible that some other term, as *purposeful act,* for example, would call attention to a more important element in the concept, and, if so, might prove superior as a term to the word *project.* At the outset it is probably wise to caution the reader against expecting any great amount of novelty in the idea here presented. The metaphor of christening is not to be taken too seriously: the concept to be considered is not in fact newly born. Not a few readers will be disappointed that after all so little new is presented.

It may be well to come closer to the customary subject matter of the school. Let us consider the classification of the different types of projects: Type 1, where the purpose is to embody some idea or plan in external form, as building a boat, writing a letter, presenting a play; type 2, where the purpose is to enjoy some

---

SOURCE: Willliam Heard Kilpatrick, *The Project Method* (New York: Teachers College, Columbia University, 1918), pp. 16, 17, 18. Reprinted by permission.

(esthetic) experience, as listening to a story, hearing a symphony, appreciating a picture; type 3, where the purpose is to straighten out some intellectual difficulty, to solve some problem, as to find out whether or not dew falls, to ascertain how New York outgrew Philadelphia; type 4, where the purpose is to obtain some item or degree of skill or knowledge, as learning to write grade 14 on the Thorndike Scale, learning the irregular verbs in French. It is at once evident that these groupings more or less overlap and that one type may be used as means to another as end. It may be of interest to note that with these definitions the project method logically includes the problem method as a special case. The value of such a classification as that here given seems to me to lie in the light it should throw on the kind of projects teachers may expect and on the procedure that normally prevails in the several types. For type 1 the following steps have been suggested: purposing, planning, executing, and judging. It is in accord with the general theory here advocated that the child as far as possible take each step himself. Total failure, however, may hurt more than assistance. The opposed dangers seem to be on the one hand that the child may not come out master of the process, on the other, that he may waste time. The teacher must steer the child through these narrows, taking care meanwhile to avoid the other dangers previously discussed. The function of the purpose and the place of thinking in the process need but be mentioned. Attention may be called to the fourth step, that the child as he grows older may increasingly judge the result in terms of the aim and with increasing care and success draw from the process its lessons for the future.

Type 2, enjoying an esthetic experience, may seem to some hardly to belong in the list of projects. But the factor of purpose undoubtedly guides the process and—I must think—influences the growth of appreciation. I have, however, as yet no definite procedure steps to point out.

Type 3, that of the problem, is of all the best known, owing to the work of Professors Dewey and McMurry. The steps that have been used are those of the Dewey analysis of thought.[1] The type lends itself, next to type 4, best of all to our ordinary

[1] Dewey, *How We Think* (Boston: D. C. Heath & Company, 1933), Chap. 6.

schoolroom work. For this reason I have myself feared its over-emphasis. Our schools—at least in my judgment—do emphatically need a great increase in the social activity possible in type 1. Type 4, where the purpose has to do with specific items of knowledge or skill, would seem to call for the same steps as type 1—purposing, planning, executing, and judging. Only here, the planning had perhaps best come from the psychologist. In this type also there is danger of over-emphasis. Some teachers indeed may not closely discriminate between drill as a project and a drill as a set task, although the results will be markedly different.

The limits of the article forbid a discussion of other important aspects of the topic: the changes necessitated by this plan in room furniture and equipment, perhaps in school architecture, the new type of text-book; the new kind of curriculum and program, possibly new plans of grading and promotion, most of all a changed attitude as to what to wish for in the way of achievement. Nor can we consider what this type of procedure means for democracy in furnishing us better citizens, alert, able to think and act, too intelligently critical to be easily hoodwinked either by politicians or by patent-medicines, self-reliant, ready of adaptation to the new social conditions that impend. The question of difficulties would itself require a separate article: opposition of tradition, of taxpayers; unprepared and incompetent teachers, the absence of a worked out procedure; problems of administration and supervision. All these and more would suffice to destroy the movement were it not deeply grounded.

In conclusion, then, we may say that the child is naturally active, especially along social lines. Heretofore a regime of coercion has only too often reduced our schools to aimless dawdling and our pupils to selfish individualists. Some in reaction have resorted to foolish humoring of childish whims. The contention of this paper is that wholehearted purposeful activity in a social situation as the typical unit of school procedure is the best guarantee of the utilization of the child's native capacities now too frequently wasted. Under proper guidance purpose means efficiency, not only in reaching the projected end of the activity immediately at hand, but even more in securing from the activity the learning which it potentially contains. Learning of all

kinds and in its all desirable ramification best proceeds in proportion as wholeheartedness of purpose is present. With the child
naturally social and with the skillful teacher to stimulate and
guide his purposing, we can especially expect that kind of learning we call character building. The necessary reconstruction
consequent upon these considerations offers a most daring "project" to the teacher who but dares to purpose.

THE DALTON PLAN

Helen Parkhurst

The Dalton Laboratory Plan is not a system or a method,
which through ages of use has petrified into a monotonous and
uniform shape, to be branded on to succeeding generations of
pupils as sheep are branded on going into a fold. It is not a
curriculum, which, all too often, is simply the machine by means
of which the brand is stamped upon the individuals caught in
the meshes of the system. Practically speaking, it is a scheme
of educational reorganization which reconciles the twin activities
of teaching and learning. When intelligently applied it creates
conditions which enable the teacher to teach and the learner
to learn.

In order to apply the scheme it is not necessary or even desirable to abolish classes or forms as units of organization in the
school, nor the curriculum as such. The Dalton Laboratory Plan
preserves both. Each pupil is classified as a member of a form,

SOURCE: From the book *Education on the Dalton Plan* by Helen Parkhurst. Copyright, 1922, by E. P. Dutton & Co., Inc. Renewal, 1950, by
Helen Parkhurst. Reprinted by permission of the publishers.

and for each form a maximum and a minimum curriculum is drawn up. But at its inception it lays the whole work proposition before the pupils in the shape of a contract job. The curriculum is divided up into jobs, and the pupil accepts the work assigned for his class as a contract. Though dispensed with above middle school, the younger children may sign a definite contract, which is returned to each individual as soon as his job is completed.

I _____, pupil of _____ standard form, contract to do the _____ assignment.
Date and signature _____.

As every month of the year has its own assigned work, a contract-job for any one form comprises a whole month's work. For convenience we arrange the different parts of the curriculum under the heading of major and minor subjects:

Major Subjects	Minor Subjects
Mathematics	Music
History	Art
Science	Handiwork
English	Domestic Science
Geography	Manual Training
Foreign Languages, etc.	Gymnastics, etc.

The first category of subjects is not more important than the other, but they are classified as "major" because they are used as the basis of promotion in most schools, and college entrance examinations thus necessitate that more time should be given to them. The value of the minor subjects lies in their expansive influence upon the student. The study of them creates a response to beauty and also an increased power of expression. But if in the lower school, which includes children ranging from eight to twelve years, foreign languages are not required as a basis for promotion, they should be classified as minor subjects for lower-school pupils.

For the purpose of simplifying the initial application of the Dalton Laboratory Plan, I recommend that it should be applied firstly to major subjects alone. As the new scheme becomes familiar it can gradually be extended to the minor subjects. Take, for example, a school wherein the major subjects for Form II are Mathematics, Science, History, Geography, English, and

French. The first contract-job for a pupil belonging to that form would be a block of the year's curriculum comprising a month's work in each of these major subjects. In the United States we reckon a school month as twenty days. The contract would therefore cover the ground divided as below:

TWENTY DAYS

FORM II CONTRACT JOB

1 month of French	1 month of English	1 month of Science	1 month of Mathematics	1 month of Geography	1 month of History

This diagram represents a required standard of work for the performance of which each pupil in Form II would contract. Though the standard is the same, the pupils are not. As their mental legs must be of different lengths, their rate of speed in study must vary also. Some may not even need the twenty days for their contracted work; others may not be able to get it done in that time. It is of the essence of the Dalton Laboratory Plan that pupils should progress each at his own rate, for only so can the work be assimilated thoroughly. Thus each pupil must be allowed to organize his method of working as he thinks best. Unfortunately at the outset we cannot assume that these pupils know how to work, though as the new plan is put into operation they will gradually learn to organize both their time and work to better and better advantage. But efficiency means speed, and speed will only be attained when good habits of work are established. It takes time to counteract the habit of dependence bred in the pupil by constantly telling him what to do, when and how to do it. This system made him a servant, occasionally an efficient servant, but always dependent on orders. And though the reorganization of school machinery is quickly effected the response of the pupil to the changed conditions is not always as rapid. It is the business of the teacher to see that the adjustment proceeds, however, slowly. The process can be helped by making the divided curriculum clear, and by seeing that the pupil grasps the whole scope and nature of the work he contracts to accomplish. Unless he understands what is required of him his organization of his time will be defective.

By giving his task in the form of a contract for whose execution he feels himself responsible, we give the work dignity and him the consciousness of a definite purpose. This feeling is increased if we make him aware of our confidence in his desire and in his power to execute it. A pupil must not, however, be permitted to continue the study of any major subject beyond the limits of the month's assignment unless he has completed his contract in every subject. He must not be allowed to work up to a higher standard than his form average in one or two subjects and fall below it in the rest of them. This would merely give him an opportunity of evading progress in those studies in which he is weak and lose to him the value of correlated and vitalized subjects. Uniformity of standard insures that he will so organize his time that most of it will be devoted to overcome his individual weaknesses and difficulties. The plan teaches him to *budget his time* so that it is sufficient to his needs and to have him go slowly and thoroughly. In this way he will be well prepared for each succeeding step. His subject diet will be well balanced and his culture will be well rounded.

The amount of any monthly assignment is a part and a very vital part of the teacher's problem. A good curriculum should be so balanced and co-related that neither too much nor too little is included in the contract-job. In the lower school not more should be required than the pupils can easily accomplish by a wise division of their time. That a ten-year-old child should learn all that a normal child of his age can learn is the ideal to set before us. A study of child psychology is necessary if we are to reorganize the machinery of education so that it corresponds to his powers and satisfies his needs at every age.

Turning from the pupil to the school building, it is evident that the Dalton Laboratory Plan exacts the establishment of laboratories, one for each subject in the curriculum, though with a small teaching staff two subjects may be studied in a single laboratory. A specialist in that particular subject, or subjects, should be in charge of each laboratory whose relation to the scheme I will deal with later on. For the moment I want to emphasize the point that these laboratories are the places where the children experiment—where they are free to work on their jobs, not places where they are experimented upon.

The text-book library of the school must be distributed among these laboratories according to subject. It is of course essential that the necessary books should be always accessible to every student—a supply of scientific books in the science laboratory, history books in the history laboratory, and so on. With regard to these books, it is well to have a few standard text-books and to increase as far as possible the number of reference books. Do not be afraid of including in the school library books that are designed for adult readers, the kind of books which have hitherto been found rather on home, than on school, bookshelves. Remember that no book can be too well written to interest a child. The dry terseness of the ordinary school manual, devoid of any literary quality, is responsible for half the distaste of learning so characteristic of the average school boy or girl. It is at school that our future men and women should become acquainted with those literary treasures which are the common heritage of humanity. And regarded merely as a mine of information, nothing could be more valuable in the development of the pupil's intelligence than the opportunity thus given him of comparing the different views of different authors on the subject he is studying.

Among the impediments to true education which is ruthlessly abolished by the Dalton Laboratory Plan is the time-table. Even to the teacher the time-table is a bugbear. How often have I heard head masters and mistresses complain of the difficulty of dividing time so that no member of the teaching staff should feel his special subjects slighted! As a result the time-table is usually compiled rather in the interest of the instructors than of the pupils. To the latter the time-table is nothing less than a curse. Its banishment is in fact the first step towards his liberation.

Let us assume that in a given school laboratory time for all classes or forms extends from 9 to 12 o'clock every morning. Under the Dalton Plan this three-hour period is devoted to the study of the major subjects—Geography, History, Mathematics, Science, English, and French. Before setting out to organize their time themselves each pupil consults his teacher, who, under the new plan, has become a subject specialist, or adviser. Together they go over the pupil's contract work, classifying his subjects as strong and weak. Those subjects which a child loves and enjoys studying will usually be found among his strong subjects. The subjects he is weak in are almost invariably those which he finds difficult to understand and assimilate, chiefly because he has not hitherto been able to give enough time to them.

It is also essential to [Mary] that she should realize exactly what progress she is making in the subject of her choice. For this purpose I invented the graph device before alluded to. As it merits a chapter to itself I will now refer to it only casually as a part of the laboratory equipment and procedure. There are three sets of graphs. The first provides each special teacher and adviser with the means of following the individual progress of each pupil, and of comparing it with that of the other members of the class. It also enables the pupil himself to compare his progress with that of his classmates. But [Mary] has also her own contract-job graph, on which she records her daily progress. The third graph pictures the progress of the class or form as a whole, as well as the individual progress.

So that the pupil should never lose sight of the job in its entirety, progress is measured in weeks of work accomplished. [Mary] has six major subjects with four weeks of work on each of them. Her contract thus entails twenty-four weeks of work. On the weekly graph she is therefore marked, not in each separate subject, but in the number of weeks' work done out of the total required, week by week.

In this manner a pupil advances steadily, job by job, through the curriculum of his class. If in a school year of nine or ten months he only finishes eight jobs on account of absence or illness, he begins the ninth job in the following year. The clever child may, on the contrary, accomplish in one year the work mapped out to cover eighteen months. Often the slow, apparently less intelligent, child gains in rapidity, and in any case he builds well and soundly at his own natural rate.

Henry C. Morrison

~~~~~~

The primary consideration, then, in any teaching enterprise, whether it be a book course or the development of conduct or the care of the pupil's physical well-being, is the identification of the learning units.

THE MASTERY FORMULA. The units having been identified, the next problem is the technique of pedagogical attack. Here we apply what we shall call the "mastery formula": Pre-test, teach, test the result, adapt procedure, teach and test again to the point of actual learning. It will be noted that this is precisely the procedure adopted by other practitioners who work in the field of organic changes. The physician, for instance, who undertakes the cure of a patient, first makes his diagnosis, then formulates and applies a treatment, then tests the results of his treatment, modifies treatment in accordance with his test results, and so on to success or failure. Even if he fails, the physician is eager to know why he failed. He does not merely dismiss the case with the verdict, "Failed to recover," or, in performance terminology, "Failed to pass." Again, the agriculturist, in handling a crop, first analyzes the market and the soil which he has available, formulates a procedure, applies his cultivation, tests growth, applies correctives, and so on to the harvest. The scientific teacher compares with the agriculturist, the lesson-hearer with the peasant farmer. We refrain from drawing the parallel in the case of the physician. The most important difference between the teacher and these other practitioners is to be found in the fact that the latter enjoy the resources of well-developed sciences, while the teacher's science is still in its infancy.

SOURCE: Reprinted from *The Practice of Teaching in Secondary Schools* by Henry C. Morrison by permission of The University of Chicago Press. Copyright 1931 by The University of Chicago Press.

PRE-TEST. There are few units, indeed, in the secondary school in the approach to which the pre-test can wisely be omitted. It serves two important purposes: first, it orients the teacher and gives him ground for intelligent approach to the particular problem before him; and, second, it tends to establish in the minds of the pupils a connection between prospective learning and present attainments. It may, in rare instances, disclose the fact that one or more pupils may be excused from presence in class during the learning process as applied to the particular unit, on the ground that they have already attained the learning for which the unit stands. Now and then a pupil may be found on the pre-test of the first unit, if there are several units, who reveals evidence that he need not take the course at all. This is likely to be the case in courses in English written expression especially and is often the case in elementary science.

In practice, the orientation of the teacher is perhaps the matter of most importance. Teachers are prone to take specific preparation for a given unit or course for granted. It thus often happens that, while the section is in general ready for the unit, there are details which, if left untaught, will create wasteful and perhaps fatal inhibitions. This is particularly true of the technical vocabulary of a science. It is perhaps unnecessary to emphasize the principle that the result of the pre-test is no part of the system of appraising pupil progress. Its office is purely to throw light on the teaching process, and to include its results in any average of marks, if such still exist, is of course pedagogically absurd.

TESTING AND RETEACHING. Nor is there needed extended comment on the teaching test. Suffice it to emphasize the principle that the results of the testing member of the mastery formula are purely for the purpose of deciding: first, whether or not the teaching has in fact registered and the teacher can now go on to the next step or the next unit; or, second, what modification of procedure is needed, assuming that the test discloses that the teaching has not fully registered. The results are no part of the final appraisal of the pupil's progress. To include them would be as absurd as it would be for the physician to submit an average of pulse, respiration, blood count, urine content, throughout the history of treatment, as his final evaluation of the extent of the patient's recovery. In the case of both patient and pupil, it is the final condition alone which is significant. The test results may be way-marks as well as guides on the road to recovery or to mastery, but they are not themselves any part of recovery or of mastery.

When the result of the teaching discloses non-learning in the class as a whole or in any significant number of pupils, there is first indicated due study of the meaning of the test results. Mere scoring a test will not suffice. Every set of such results is a body of phenomena which arose in some sequence of cause and effect. As such they have meaning, and the meaning can usually be found by the teacher who is actuated and guided by scientific motives. Putting the test results and the teacher's recollection of the teaching procedure together, there should emerge an hypothesis touching the character and location of the fault in the teaching. The teaching is then redirected and the element is retaught. Lest the term *teaching* should mislead the reader, we note that reteaching may very well at certain stages take the form of redirection of study or other forms of pupil activity.

Now, it is exceedingly important that the teacher give to the results of teaching tests this serious study before reteaching. The routinist falls into the error of testing, scoring the result, and reteaching without surveying the ground. He may well repeat this process indefinitely before he makes his point register, with great waste of time, energy, and pupil interest, or may fail altogether and hastily conclude that a great share of the pupils are non-learners, and were predestined to be such from the foundation of the world, or else that the "method" is a failure. Before reteaching at all, every effort should be made to find out what the trouble is.

Such is direct teaching of the learning unit, or, on our principles, teaching as distinguished from lesson-hearing in any of its forms. The essence of the matter is application of the mastery formula, and the root of the latter is the teaching, test, and reteaching. From the pupil's point of view, the issue is, "I do not catch the idea, please repeat"; or perhaps, "Tell me wherein I am wrong, in order that I may correct myself." The teacher who fails to heed this aspect of the pupil's attitude, grades, performance and passes him on seems to me to be guilty of a peculiarly contemptible piece of malpractice.

Reteaching is often misconceived as mere tutoring. The euphemistic term is *helping the pupil*. As such, the process rapidly degenerate into mere doing the pupil's learning for him, or at least attempting such an impossible task. "After-school classes" are very prone indeed to become routine tutoring periods, though not necessarily such. When teacher and administration work together in an intelligent handling of the whole teaching problem, no such devices are called for.

Reteaching is sometimes formalized as doing tasks over again with the result that there is built up in the pupil the attitude "Oh well, I shall have another chance." Of course this is the get-by attitude in another form. It has been a troublesome obstacle in the laboratory, and doubtless other schools have encountered it.

Testing and reteaching is a continuous process. Testing is not only applied to the issue "Has the pupil learned?" but also to the issue "Is the pupil learning?" Some units may require several weeks in their learning, and some of them several years. The reading unit in foreign language, for instance, usually implies a growth period extending over many months. Some of the conduct attitudes are developing throughout the whole period of general education. Hence, to leave reteaching to the point at which it is estimated that mastery of the unit ought to be present is practically to confine the whole educational period to a single unit, or else to leave every unit unlearned.

EXTENT OF RETEACHING. Two questions are now naturally suggested: How many times should reteaching be done? For what proportion of pupil failures on a teaching test should the whole section be retaught?

In general, reteaching should be done until mastery takes place. There is a pedagogical problem to be solved, and it is the teacher's business to find the solution. The number of reteachings required is a measure of the teacher's professional equipment and skill. Ordinarily, the teacher who is willing to study the problem will find that the number of reteachings required steadily diminishes as the course goes on. The teacher becomes better adjusted to the class and the pupils become better learners. Nevertheless, the reteachings may keep tediously up, and after a time the problem becomes critical. There is then indicated a broader study of the whole situation. The teacher may well find it necessary to call into consultation one of his associates and the supervisory help of the principal's office. A fault hitherto unnoticed by the teacher may be discovered. It may be found that the course has been unwisely placed in the program of study. It may be found that the class is, in fact, so heterogeneous that it cannot be taught as a single section—a situation, by the way, which is almost certain to be encountered periodically in the graded system under the lesson-learning and passing-grade teaching procedure, for the simple reason that a section is bound to include numerous non-mastery promotions, that is, pupils who have not acquired earlier essential learnings. Whatever is found should be found as matter of fact on evidential grounds and not as matter of mere guesswork.

Theoretically and ideally, whenever a pupil has learned, he should go on with his learning even though he be the only one in the section to do so. Practically, it does not altogether work out that way. Assuming that the section is reasonably homogeneous, that the pre-test has been properly administered and followed up, and that the teacher's control of attention is adequate, the early teaching in a course is apt to disclose something like the following situation.

On the teaching test, perhaps one-third of the class shows evidence of learning. On the retest, another third shows that teaching is registering. On a second retest, all but two or three in a class section of thirty respond. Now, shall the first third submit to reteaching twice and the second third once after they have responded to the test? The teacher's best judgment will have to settle the matter, and we trust that subsequent chapters will more and more give ground for judgment. When as large a proportion as two-thirds fail to respond, it is worth while to verify the learning of the first third by reteaching and retest, and even a second round of reteaching. It not infrequently happens that some of those who responded on the first test do not respond on the second retest. Either the first test was not conclusive as a test or they made simply a fortunate response. Further, when the test gives room for qualitative differences in the response itself, the response of some of the last third is often better than that of the first third on any of the tests, that is, it is better evidence of the presence of learning. The fast learner is not always a sound learner, nor is the slow learner always a poor learner.

The small remainder of the pupils are indicated for special individual treatment. On the next unit, one or more of them may pass out of this group and others may join it. Ordinarily, however, something like 5 to 10 percent, it may be, will segregate as non-learners and linger farther and farther behind the body of the class group as a whole. These soon become registered as "problem cases" and perhaps as "remedial cases." They form an important subject of discussion. . . . It is essential to note here that they are positively identified as non-learners, instead of being simply cast to one side as people who failed to make a passing grade and are futilely required to repeat the course. The teacher knows that they are not learning, and forms a tentative hypothesis of the reason why they do not learn. They differ from the "corrective cases" who are for a time in and out of the lagging group but who eventually catch the stride and go on with the progressing group. Since we shall have occasion frequently to use the terms which have been quoted, let us adopt them into our terminology and find for each a definite meaning in the following manner.

VOLUNTARY PROJECT. In the majority of cases, however, the supplementary project is the most useful recourse. For each unit, an ample series of such projects is kept before the class and each pupil is allowed to select. Some may not select at all, and this has an important significance. Some work at a single supplementary project during a large part of the year. Some work out several such during the year. Thus the superior pupil validates his superiority, not by rank in class, but by the acquisition of additional masteries. It is sometimes objected that this is not "fair" to the superior pupil, since it requires him to do more than others do. The objection is of course purely an instance of the performance stereotype at work and the commercial view of education. If education is a matter of contract between pupil and school in which the pupil does certain work in consideration of credits and an ultimate diploma which the school covenants to award, then the objection holds. If education is conceived as a process of superior adjustment, then the supplementary project is a rare opportunity to the superior pupil, on the one hand, and evidence to the teacher of growth toward intellectual self-dependence, on the other.

Now, the whole theory of systematic teaching rests upon the mastery formula and its application. It does not guarantee success to all teachers nor to any teacher for all pupils; but it does furnish a method by which such progress as is made can be real progress, and it furnishes a method by which the individual pupil can be duly given that consideration to which he is entitled by a society which brought him into the world without his will or wish. More than that even, it gives us a theory of teaching, on the basis of which may be developed actual individual self-dependence, in brief, citizens who are capable of thinking for themselves in the place of citizens who merely assert the right to think for themselves. Finally, it makes teaching, as a systematic procedure, a soluble problem, whereas it is otherwise merely a routine with no problem conception about it.

CORE STUDIES

Evanston Township High School

The Evanston Township High School has been widely known for many years. It was an early pioneer in the development of the general education concept. . . . The most helpful brief description of its program is found in a leaflet published by the school itself.

Core Studies Is the Name of a Course. Core studies have been offered by the Evanston High School since 1937. The name *Core* comes from the objectives of the course, which is to give each pupil who elects it a *core* of

---

SOURCE: Evanston Township High School, *Core Studies* (Evanston, Ill., n.d.). Reprinted by permission.

1. basic subject matter fundamentals that should be a part of the education of every American child;
2. experiences in democratic living that will develop the skills and attitudes appropriate for citizenship in our American democracy.

Core Studies Is a Personal Approach to Education.   Whatever the subject matter considered, emphasis is placed on the development of each pupil in terms of his own needs, abilities, and aspirations. The Core method emphasizes maturity in behavior and the growth of self-discipline. It develops those personal, social, and academic skills that will contribute to further education and successful living with others. As counselor, the Core teacher is always available for help and guidance.

Core Is a Daily Two-Period Class.   Core receives the two credits of English and Social Studies and replaces these subjects in the program of the pupils who elect it. The remaining six periods of the pupil's school day are spent in the regular science, mathematics, language, and physical education classes of the high school.

Core Is Reading, Writing, Speaking, and Listening.   Core is subject matter as well as varied activities. Core involves theme assignments, book reports, class discussions, functional grammar, and examinations. Pupils in Core learn to give individual and group reports, to participate in panels and group discussions, and to use various techniques of presenting materials, such as the tape recorder, board drawings, and the opaque projector. They learn to work on committees, to plan and organize subject matter units and social activities, and to do research and present their findings in oral or documented form.

Core Is a Program of General Education.   Core is English and Social Studies plus phases of art, music, science, and other subject areas when they contribute to a better understanding of the topic being studied. Special periods are organized and committees established to encourage appreciation and participation in these fields.

Core Offers to Its Pupils a Well-Rounded Program.   For instance, in the course of a week a pupil in Core will have

1. reporting and discussions on the chosen unit;

2. time devoted to reading, writing, and English skills;
3. individual reports or panel discussions on current news;
4. some experience with literature and the fine arts; and
5. a Core business meeting, perhaps a speaker or field trip.

The Subject Matter of Core Is Very Similar to the English and Social Studies Courses It Replaces. However, there is a difference in the manner of planning and presenting the materials of study and in the objectives sought. For illustration, in four years of Core a pupil would have a sequence similar to the following:

Freshman—Orientation
Our High School and
  Community
Choosing a Career
New Horizons in Literature
The U.S. and World Affairs

Sophomore—World Mindedness
Drama Through the Ages
War and Peace
The Atomic Age
The Development of Law and
  Justice

Junior—U.S. Life and Culture
America in Literature
Our Economic System
The American People
Our Government; Its Structure and Development

Senior—Life Adjustment
Marriage and Family Living
Our Literary Heritage
College and Careers
Consumer Education

Core Is a Program of Life Adjustment. In Core, consideration is given to the real-life situations which pupils now face and which will continue to confront them, such as problems of personality adjustment, group relations, and the personal factors in success and progress. Since the Core teacher is the counselor to the pupils in his Core, counseling is an integral part of the program. The use of the *Personalized Evaluation* helps each pupil to understand himself and others. Known and latent interests are developed in the process of the pupil-teacher planning. Pupil committees such as the Planning or News Committees help determine the nature and type of units to be studied.

Core Is a Program of Citizenship Education. In Core, the pupils not only study our democratic tradition, they also participate in it. To this end each Core is organized upon democratic principles with officers, committees, and organization to enable it to function effectively. Each pupil, therefore, has many opportunities to be a member of a working committee, to assume leadership roles, to develop initiative and responsibility, and, together with the help of the teacher, to plan, organize, and present the materials they select for study. This co-operative planning combined with the problem-solving technique of the "scientific method" helps pupils develop poise and self-reliance. Each Core class has representation in the homeroom student council.

The Core Program at ETHS Includes a Homeroom as Well as a Classroom Program. All pupils taking Core share in common social and educational experiences. Each Core class has a Core mother who helps coordinate each class with the total program. Core meetings are held to help teachers and parents understand and improve the program. A *Parent Planning Committee,* a *Newsletter,* and a *PTA Board* help maintain balance and continuity. By working together for the four years of high school, pupils, parents, and teachers know each other very well and co-operate effectively for personal, college, and career planning.

The Core Approach Is Not New. It has been in operation at ETHS since 1937 and much longer elsewhere. The ETHS Core Program is well known throughout the United States.

Parents Say. . . . The Core Program encourages independent thinking, develops leadership qualities, teaches individual responsibility and initiative, and through the double period, fosters favorable teacher and pupil relationships.

Insight into the functioning of the general education class at Evanston can be gained from the following description of a specific unit, provided by the teacher of a ninth-grade class:

CANDIDATES AND CAMPAIGNS

The pressure was on—a national election was in the offing and the air waves and the press were saturated with highly charged political comment. So many questions were being raised, so many new words and historical incidents were being discussed—the whole subject was not only interesting but vital to pupils and voters-to-be.

Having completed its orientation unit, one freshman core was ready to select a topic for study. After considerable discussion it was agreed that "Campaigns and Candidates" met all the requirements of the criteria that had been developed by the class. The core had already studied the "problem-solving" technique as a possible procedure for many types of situations. The new unit presented the problem, we had studied the technique—now to put them together.

After more discussion and preliminary research, the following working outline and assignment of reports was made. It was recognized that in the work leading up to the selection of the topic and the development of the outline that some elements of steps 1 and 2 in the problem-solving technique had been covered. However, a great deal of data still had to be collected by individuals now that some overview of the purpose and scope of the unit had been achieved.

REPORT OUTLINE

I. Political Parties
    A. Historical Beginning: Republican, Democratic, { Bill C.
        and Third Parties   { Dave S.
    B. Founders: First and Great Leaders   Bill S.
    C. Present Status and Strength: Traditions, etc. { Jay / Chuck
    D. Party Platforms: Background to Stand { Phil / Sandy
    E. Present Organization: State, Local, National { Helen
        Committees, etc.   { Dave C.
II. Election System
    A. Electoral College { Gerry / DeWitt
    B. Primary and Voting qualifications, etc. { Boyce / Tom B.
    C. Conventions, "Political Machines," etc., and { Ronnie
        Actual Voting   { Carlton
III. Candidates (President and Vice-President)
    A. Qualifications—Constitutional Provisions { Roland
    B. Record, Previous Experience   { Bill M.
    C. Personal Life   Andrea
    D. Campaign Routes—Procedures   Carolee
    E. View of Candidates on Platforms, Other Issues   Ken
    F. Supporters { Lucille / Box S.

A PROPOSED CURRICULUM BASED

ON RECONSTRUCTIONISM

Theodore Brameld

~~~~~~

THE FIRST YEAR HAS TWO CHIEF OBJECTIVES:

1. to provide the student with motivation and orientation and to build in him a sense of the importance of the entire secondary program; and

2. to examine the need for goals in the sphere of economic-political reconstruction and to determine their character.

Neither objective can, of course, be attained in a single year; these objectives, perhaps even more than those of the three remaining years, are constantly given further consideration as the student moves forward.

Nevertheless, the necessity of beginning with political-economic objectives should be made clear. However excellent his earlier schooling has been, the young person approaching adulthood may still need to perceive *why* it is important that secondary education be devoted to the governing task of goal-seeking. It is equally important for him to perceive that the crucial ontological realities of that task center in economic-political experience; hence, it is essential for him to understand that these realities must be discerned, analyzed, and refashioned constructively as early as possible in his secondary schooling if other areas are to receive proper consideration.

SOURCE: Theodore Brameld, *Toward a Reconstructed Philosophy of Education.* Copyright © 1956, Holt, Rinehart and Winston, Inc. Reprinted by permission.

MOTIVATION AND ORIENTATION

Beginning with the Student.   Movement toward the first objective can begin through cooperative examination of contemporary
culture and of the empirical relations of individuals—in this case,
students—to it. We tap John's well springs of interest by detecting
his uncertainties, tensions, instabilities, and confusions as they
are related to those of his family and to Centerville, where he
lives. We then relate these difficulties to whatever certainties,
stabilities, and clarities constitute, by contrast, the positive aims
of John, his family, and Centerville.

Establishing motivation in this way requires that the school
foster a spirit of mutual respect and insist upon honesty of expression. Teachers speak of their uncertainties as well as their certainties, and the class seeks to enlist the interest of parents and other
townspeople in its problems. Students make a concerted effort to
estimate in a preliminary way how secure or insecure the local
community is; how much agreement or disagreement there is
about its own problems, practices, and plans. Meanwhile the reconstructionist teacher, governed though he is by his utopian
values and therefore critical of many such existing practices and
future plans, will not impose his convictions upon any one. He
directs this initiating period of study chiefly by making sure that
students penetrate deeply enough to discover the actual, rather
than the merely ideological, picture of the community. He lets
the picture speak for itself.

Moving Outward.   The student's understanding increases as
the status of Centerville is seen to be dependent upon the status
of other Centervilles and of the state, region, nation, and world.
The aim is to widen the analysis, both geographically and historically; to see, for example, how the prosperity or poverty of
Centerville depends upon the state of the economy of the entire
nation and indeed the world, and how this dependence emerges
directly from the forces of contraction and expansion in recent
history. There is, accordingly, a need to study the past in order
to foster concern for both present and future—indeed, history is
indispensable throughout the four years.

From consideration of the best evidence obtainable both

through firsthand observation and through books, students begin to feel the impact of the crisis-culture on themselves and their community. They recognize the achievements of capitalism, of liberal democracy, of the arts, and in human relations, and they assess them as dispassionately as possible. But they weigh these achievements against such stubborn realities as depression, insecurity, and war—in short, they begin to discover group conflicts, group allegiances, and group conditioners, and therefore begin to sense the power of the unrational that underlies those realities. The whole tone of the study, indeed, is indicated by our earlier interpretation of the reconstructionist ontology; the examples cited there are illustrative of the approach to cultural reality that is needed here.

Beginning the Quest for the Normative. As more and more motivation is established, students are ready to consider the question of what *would be* better by comparison with what now *is*. Technically speaking, ontological investigation soon gives rise to axiological study. With John, his family, and his community still in the forefront of attention, the final process in this introductory period is the attainment of a crude, preliminary consensus about common values.

The temptation to jump quickly from the concrete and graphic level on which study has thus far proceeded to a high and nebulous level of generalization is to be strictly avoided. But once the insecurities that students discover in their own environment are grasped, it should not be difficult to move to defining the simple and specific meanings of such a value as security. It should be possible to analyze its meaning to John and his family first in its immediate economic sense of adequate income, and then to go on to define security in its more complex psychological senses—as it is understood by psychologists, for example, when they speak of the need of children for parental security or of adults for a sense of belongingness and recognition.

These discussions should also begin to develop the student's awareness of the palpable inconsistencies in the value patterns of modern culture—inconsistencies that reflect a basic cultural disequilibrium. The cultural conflicts . . . should be articulated in terms which are in keeping with the experience of students; for example, it will be recognized by students that acceptance of the belief that "honesty is the best policy" is very often associated in the same person with the belief that, in a competitive society, sharp dealing is necessary to economic success and therefore desirable. Because the search for values is a thoroughly inductive process, any imposition by the teacher of his own value system is unnecessary and undesirable. The value of social-self-realization, or some verbal equivalent, although it is more than likely to emerge as a generalized ideal from our methods of learning, need not necessarily be understood in exactly the same way by any two groups. It is a value too rich, too complex, too dynamic to be subjected to rigid definition.

In this connection students should become aware of one question that is particularly important to the entire curriculum: Is it, or is it not, reasonable to expect that people in sharply different environments (assuming that sufficient schooling is available) could be expected to reach a consensus about their values that will provide a common basis for the worldwide reconstruction of culture? Or, to put the issue in another way: If they could have access to dependable evidence and could communicate freely, would a majority of the people in such widely separated and different regions as our deep South, the far West, New England, China, India, Finland, and Liberia be likely to agree upon a definition of such a single goal as security? Would they be able to agree, also, that "security" means not only adequate food, shelter, and clothing—although these are basic—but group protectiveness and other satisfactions as well? And so with the other goals we named earlier as essential to our reconstructed civilization: Can it be expected that these, too, will be agreed upon by a majority (two thirds, shall we say?) of people of all races, nationalities, and classes?

The reconstructionist teacher believes . . . that such, a consensus *can* be won as his kind of education reaches more and more people. The extent to which students will agree with him will vary, of course, according to their own socio-economic position (upper-class and upper-status students are less likely to agree than others), upon the thoroughness of their study, upon their experience with people belonging to different races and classes and to other groups in their own community. Given, however, widespread and conscientious participation, plus general meetings that pool the partial consensuses of smaller groups, there is a reasonably good expectation of achieving positive agreements among people in general and students in particular.

AN ANALYSIS OF REFLECTIVE THINKING

John Dewey

~~~~~~

We now have before us the material for the analysis of a complete act of reflective activity. In the preceding chapter we saw that the two limits of every unit of thinking are a perplexed, troubled, or confused situation at the beginning and a cleared-up, unified, resolved situation at the close. The first of these situations may be called *pre*-reflective. It sets the problem to be solved; out of it grows the question that reflection has to answer. In the final situation the doubt has been dispelled; the situation is *post*-reflective; there results a direct experience of mastery, satisfaction, enjoyment. Here, then, are the limits within which reflection falls.

Five Phases, or Aspects, of Reflective Thought. In between, as states of thinking, are (1) *suggestions*, in which the mind leaps forward to a possible solution; (2) an intellectualization of the difficulty or perplexity that has been *felt* (directly experienced) into a *problem* to be solved, a question for which the answer must be sought; (3) the use of one suggestion after another as a leading idea, or *hypothesis*, to initiate and guide observation and other operations in collection of factual material; (4) the mental elaboration of the idea or supposition as an idea

---

SOURCE: John Dewey, *How We Think* (Boston: D. C. Heath & Company, 1933), pp. 106–118. Reprinted by permission.

or supposition (*reasoning*, in the sense in which reasoning is a part, not the whole, of inference); and (5) testing the hypothesis by overt or imaginative action.

We shall now take up the five phases, or functions, one by one.

The First Phase, Suggestion. The most "natural" thing for anyone to do is to go ahead; that is to say, to *act* overtly. The disturbed and perplexed situation arrests such direct activity temporarily. The tendency to continue *acting* nevertheless persists. It is diverted and takes the form of an idea or a suggestion. The *idea* of what to do when we find ourselves "in a hole" is a substitute for direct action. It is a vicarious, anticipatory way of acting, a kind of dramatic rehearsal. Were there only one suggestion popping up, we should undoubtedly adopt it at once. But where there are two or more, they collide with one another, maintain the state of suspense, and produce further inquiry. The first suggestion in the instance recently cited was to jump the ditch but the perception of conditions inhibited that suggestion and led to the occurrence of other ideas.

Some inhibition of *direct* action is necessary to the condition of hesitation and delay that is essential to thinking. Thought is, as it were, conduct turned in upon itself and examining its purpose and its conditions, its resources, aids, and difficulties and obstacles.

The Second Phase, Intellectualization. We have already noted that it is artificial, so far as thinking is concerned, to start with a ready-made problem, a problem made out of whole cloth or arising out of a vacuum. In reality such a 'problem' is simply an assigned *task*. There is not at first a situation *and* a problem, much less just a problem and no situation. There is a troubled, perplexed, trying situation, where the difficulty is, as it were, spread throughout the entire situation, infecting it as a whole. If we knew just what the difficulty was and where it lay, the job of reflection would be much easier than it is. As the saying truly goes, a question well put is half answered. In fact, we know what the problem *exactly* is simultaneously with finding a way out and getting it resolved. Problem and solution stand out *completely* at the same time. Up to that point, our grasp of the problem has been more or less vague and tentative.

A blocked suggestion leads us to reinspect the conditions that confront us. Then our uneasiness, the shock of disturbed activity, gets stated in some degree on the basis of observed conditions, of objects. The width of the ditch, the slipperiness of the banks, not the mere presence of a ditch, is the trouble. The difficulty is getting located and defined; it is becoming a true problem, something intellectual, not just an annoyance at being held up in what we are doing. The person who is suddenly blocked and troubled in what he is doing by the thought of an engagement to keep at a time that is near and a place that is distant has the suggestion of getting there at once. But in order to carry this suggestion into effect, he has to find means of transportation. In order to find them he has to note his present position and its distance from the station, the present time, and the interval at his disposal. Thus the perplexity is more precisely located: just so much ground to cover, so much time to do it in.

The word *problem* often seems too elaborate and dignified to denote what happens in minor cases of reflection. But in every case where reflective activity ensues, there is a process of *intellectualizing* what at first is merely an *emotional* quality of the whole situation. This conversion is effected by noting more definitely the conditions that constitute the trouble and cause the stoppage of action.

The Third Phase, the Guiding Idea, Hypothesis. The first suggestion occurs spontaneously; it comes to mind automatically; it *springs* up; it "pops," as we have said, "into the mind"; it flashes upon us. There is no direct control of its occurrence; the idea just comes or it does not come; that is all that can be said. There is nothing *intellectual* about its occurrence. The intellectual element consists in *what we do with it,* how we use it, *after* its sudden occurrence as an idea. A controlled use of it is made possible by the state of affairs just described. In the degree in which we define the difficulty (which is effected by stating it in terms of objects), we get a better idea of the kind of solution that is needed. The facts of data set the problem before us, and insight into the problem corrects, modifies, expands the suggestion that originally occurred. In this fashion the suggestion becomes a definite supposition or, stated more technically, a *hypothesis*.

Take the case of a physician examining a patient or a mechanic inspecting a piece of complicated machinery that does not behave properly. There is something wrong, so much is sure. But how to remedy it cannot be told until it is known *what* is wrong. An untrained person is likely to make a wild guess—the suggestion—and then proceed to act upon it in a random way, hoping that by good luck the right thing will be hit upon. So some medicine that appears to have worked before or that a neighbor has recommended is tried. Or the person fusses, monkeys, with the machine, poking here and hammering there on the chance of making the right move. The trained person proceeds in a very different fashion. He *observes* with unusual care, using the methods, the techniques, that the experience of physicians and expert mechanics in general, those familiar with the structure of the organism or the machine, have shown to be helpful in detecting trouble.

The idea of the solution is thus controlled by the diagnosis that has been made. But if the case is at all complicated, the physician or mechanic does not foreclose further thought by assuming that the suggested method of remedy is certainly right. He proceeds to act upon it tentatively rather than decisively. That is, he treats it as a guiding idea, a working hypothesis, and is led by it to make more observations, to collect more facts, so as to see if the *new* material is what the hypothesis calls for. He reasons that *if* the disease is typhoid, *then* certain phenomena will be found; and he looks particularly to see if *just* these conditions are present. Thus both the first and second operations are brought under control; the sense of the problem becomes more adequate and refined and the suggestion ceases to be a *mere* possibility, becoming a *tested* and, if possible, a *measured* probability.

The Fourth Phase, Reasoning (in the Narrower Sense). Observations pertain to what exists in nature. They constitute the facts, and these facts both regulate the formation of suggestions, ideas, hypotheses, and test their probable value as indications of solutions. The ideas, on the other hand, occur, as we say, in our heads, in our minds. They not only occur there, but are capable, as well, of great development there. Given a fertile suggestion occurring in an experienced, well-informed mind, that mind is capable of elaborating it until there results an idea that is quite different from the one with which the mind started.

For example, the idea of heat in the third instance in the earlier chapter was linked up with what the person already knew about heat—in his case, its expansive force—and this in turn with the contractive tendency of cold, so that the idea of expansion could be used as an explanatory idea, though the mere idea of heat would not have been of any avail. Heat was quite directly suggested by the observed conditions; water was felt to be hot. But only a mind with some prior information about heat would have reasoned that heat meant expansion, and then used the idea of expansion as a working hypothesis. In more complex cases, there are long trains of reasoning in which one idea leads up to another idea known by previous test to be related to it. The stretch of links brought to light by reasoning depends, of course, upon the store of knowledge that the mind is already in possession of. And this depends not only upon the prior experience and special education of the individual who is carrying on the inquiry, but also upon the state of culture and science of the age and place. Reasoning helps extend knowledge, while at the same time it depends upon what is already known and upon the facilities that exist for communicating knowledge and making it a public, open resource.

A physician to-day can develop, by reasoning from his knowledge, the implications of the disease that symptoms suggest to him as probable in a way that would have been impossible even a generation ago; just as, on the other hand, he can carry his observation of symptoms much farther because of improvement in clinical instruments and the technique of their use.

Reasoning has the same effect upon a suggested solution that more intimate and extensive observation has upon the original trouble. Acceptance of a suggestion in its first form is prevented by looking into it more thoroughly. Conjectures that seem plausible at first sight are often found unfit or even absurd when their full consequences are traced out. Even when reasoning out the bearings of a supposition does not lead to its rejection, it develops the idea into a form in which it is more apposite to the problem. Only when, for example, the conjecture that a pole was an index pole had been thought out in its implications could its particular applicability to the case in hand be judged. Suggestions at first seemingly remote and wild are frequently so transformed by being elaborated into what follows from them as to become apt and fruitful. The development of an idea through reasoning helps supply intervening or intermediate terms which link together into a consistent whole elements that at first seemingly conflict with each other, some leading the mind to one inference and others to an opposed one.

The Fifth Phase, Testing the Hypothesis by Action. The concluding phase is some kind of testing by overt action to give *experimental corroboration,* or *verification,* of the conjectural idea. Reasoning shows that *if* the *idea* be adopted, certain consequences follow. So far the conclusion is hypothetical or conditional. If when we look we find present all the conditions demanded by the theory, and if we find the characteristic traits called for by rival alternatives to be lacking, the tendency to believe, to accept, is almost irresistible. Sometimes direct observation furnishes corroboration, as in the case of the pole on the boat. In other cases, as in that of the bubbles, experiment is required; that is, *conditions are deliberately arranged in accord with the requirements of an idea or hypothesis to see whether the results theoretically indicated by the idea actually occur.* If it is found that the experimental results agree with the theoretical, or rationally deduced, results, and if there is reason to believe that *only* the conditions in question would yield such results, the confirmation is so strong as to induce a conclusion—at least until contrary facts shall indicate the advisability of its revision.

Of course, verification does not always follow. Sometimes consequences show failure to confirm instead of corroboration. The idea in question is refuted by the court of final appeal. But a great advantage of possession of the habit of reflective activity is that failure is not *mere* failure. It is instructive. The person who really thinks learns quite as much from his failures as from his successes. For a failure indicates to the person whose thinking has been involved in it, and who has not come to it by mere blind chance, what further observations should be made. It suggests to him what modifications should be introduced in the hypothesis upon which he has been operating. It either brings to light a new problem or helps to define and clarify the problem on which he has been engaged. Nothing shows the trained thinker better than the use he makes of his errors and mistakes. What merely annoys and discourages a person not accustomed to thinking, or what starts him out on a new course of aimless attack by mere cut-and-try methods, is a stimulus and a guide to the trained inquirer.

The Sequence of the Five Phases Is Not Fixed. The five

phases, terminals, or functions of thought, that we have noted do not follow one another in a set order. On the contrary, each step in genuine thinking does something to perfect the formation of a suggestion and promote its change into a leading idea or directive hypothesis. It does something to promote the location and definition of the problem. Each improvement in the idea leads to new observations that yield new facts or data and help the mind judge more accurately the relevancy of facts already at hand. The elaboration of the hypothesis does not wait until the problem has been defined and adequate hypothesis has been arrived at; it may come in at any intermediate time. And as we have just seen, any particular overt test need not be final; it may be introductory to new observations and new suggestions, according to what happens in consequence of it.

There is, however, an important difference between test by overt action in practical deliberations and in scientific investigations. In the former the practical commitment involved in overt action is much more serious than in the latter. An astronomer or a chemist performs overt actions, but they are for the sake of knowledge; they serve to test and develop his conceptions and theories. In practical matters, the main result desired lies outside of knowledge. One of the great values of thinking, accordingly, is that it defers the commitment to action that is irretrievable, that, once made, cannot be revoked. Even in moral and other practical matters, therefore, a thoughtful person treats his overt deeds as experimental so far as possible; that is to say, while he cannot call them back and must stand their consequences, he gives alert attention to what they teach him about his conduct as well as to the non-intellectual consequences. He makes a problem out of consequences of conduct, looking into the causes from which they probably resulted, especially the causes that lie in his own habits and desires.

In conclusion, we point out that the five phases of reflection that have been described represent only in outline the indispensable traits of reflective thinking. In practice, two of them may telescope, some of them may be passed over hurriedly, and the burden of reaching a conclusion may fall mainly on a single phase, which will then require a seemingly disproportionate development. No set rules can be laid down on such matters.

The way they are managed depends upon the intellectual tact and sensitiveness of the individual. When things have come out wrong, it is, however, a wise practice to review the methods by which the unwise decision was reached, and see where the misstep was made.

THE METHOD OF INQUIRY

Earl S. Johnson

~~~~~~

The Method of Inquiry Is Tentative. The method of inquiry has none of the lock step, certainty, or the cocksureness of the Herbartian or Morrison methods. It has a tentativeness which does not permit the teacher to know the exact order of steps to be taken respecting a given problem of inquiry. This is just the state of mind in which the scientist, bent on scientific research, finds himself. The absence of certainty as to the order of steps is, however, more than compensated for by the thrill which accompanies inquiry which takes its cue from whatever lies at hand.

An Ideal Order of the Steps in Inquiry. The method of inquiry is a *method;* hence it does not operate at haphazard. Each phase or step seems almost to suggest if not dictate the next step. This is true, wherever you start. I shall now show the ideal order of its steps or phases. I shall leave the area of study unnamed and I shall not give a name to the problem on which it is used. I wish to make it clear, however, that the method of inquiry is applicable to all *problems* in the area of human affairs—and which

SOURCE: Reprinted with permission of the publisher from *Theory and Practice of the Social Studies* by Earl S. Johnson. Copyright 1956 by The Macmillan Company.

are not necessarily *social* problems. They are all, however, problems of cause-and-effect. . . .

1. The identification or creation of a problem situation of some kind: "Who killed Cock Robin?"—or its social studies equivalent. Note that it is a problem situation, not a discrete problem. The *Gestalt* or form is not clear; there is a field of things which appear to belong together but the lines of relationship are obscure. The *Gestalt* has no clear center.

There is an "idea" in it, but do not worry if it cannot be stated at once. That is just why it is a problem situation rather than a problem. If the idea is readily apparent then you have nothing about which to invite a search. It is "too easy" and the task is over before it is begun. Even if the idea which is central to the problem situation were stated that would not, of itself, guarantee that its meaning is known. Only to "say it" is not to find it.

You try to excite the class: the response is variable. You are manipulating stimuli. All sorts of exploratory activities might be employed: a movie, a short talk, suggestions from the class, etc. These are to serve the purpose of putting the class in *a tension* to bring it to *attention*. This is an ever-so-slight frustration, not more than that. Or call it the creation of a block or a doubt. You want to get the class in a "slight jam"—from which you wish to help to rescue it. If there is nothing to overcome, if there is no tension to release, then there is no beginning. If no beginning, no middle; and if no middle, no end.

In short, in this phase—which may reappear in the course of the enterprise because the path of inquiry, like true love, seldom runs smoothly—you try to create such a state of concern and interest that every other object except the one at hand is banished from the minds of all. That takes some doing.

You and the class have but one objective at this time: to get a clue which will give insight into how the problem may be stated in explicit terms. The more the class shares in the planning of it, the greater interest you start with. If your students press you to teach about it, you may be sure that they have some views and opinions on it—whatever the "it" turns out to be. These will range from cocksure to cloudy ones.

But what is your aim or objective? Only this: to get a sharper picture of what makes something "tick," how something works, etc. You state your objectives only in a very general way: one or more hunches, clues or call them hypotheses if you wish, so that the act of inquiry may begin and go forward. You are simply "going hunting"—what explicit game will be bagged no one knows. Scouting for game is the first objective; the more specific objectives will follow when the game shows up—rabbits, quail, or maybe larger "animals."

2. Throughout this phase you are doing your best to suggest clues without giving the plot away. *You* know the answer but you are not going to take your students by the hand and lead them to it. You want a *hunt*—not a sure-fire *find*. Your attempt to stimulate interest takes the form of raising and planting questions. I say "raising questions" rather than "asking questions." The difference is this: to ask a question suggests a direct answer response; to raise a question connotes that some time must elapse before it is "lowered"; it is for consideration, not for immediate answer.

Many kinds of assignments, many enterprises or projects, may enter here; if questions are asked, facts will be needed, and facts suggest further questions. The problem situation is beginning to clear up—a problem is emerging. The questions tease it out of hiding. They might be such as these: to whom is this a problem? To whom not, and why in both cases? What facts seem to suggest this? How did the problem arise? How widely is it felt? What specific interest or stake do various groups have in it? What facts are known about it? What would happen if it were solved? Would new problems be created in the very solving of this one? What resources—machinery, finance, leadership—are needed to solve it? Are the causal factors simple or complex? How readily can they be seen by ordinary people? How deeply is the community affected by the problem? Who will be hurt if it is solved?

3. These questions help to narrow the field of your students' perceptions, and help to sharpen the *Gestalt* by putting things into place. They have their origin in wild, vague, or random hunches, but they are the raw materials for specific hypotheses. They give you the search leads. Research is quite as appropriate because there is always a trace of common-sense wisdom at work which needs to be reworked or researched. Assume that two

or more promising hypotheses (*née* hunches) come to light. That's right, come to light. They spring to the mind by the provocation which questions create. (Teaching is always more provoking than "telling.") These hypotheses suggest a division of labor which will be filled out in terms of the different interests and ideas that have been aroused and manifested. Some students will work alone—don't force people to co-operate; we want some lone wolves, the good kind! Committees may be formed: research committees who will dig and delve. Such activities as these may be tried out to see what they produce: interviews, "resource people" brought into class, bibliographies assembled, a map may be appropriate—it is better hand-made than "bought"—all learning has a kinesthetic aspect—biology is part of thinking; a movie, a filmstrip, may throw some light on the problem, a field trip, etc. At appropriate times, difficult if not impossible to plan with calendar precision, the findings will be pooled—discussion may ensue, even ought to.

4. In this net of experience, the "right" hypothesis is caught.

5. This "right" hypothesis has earned its place through competition. It is now put to work. It leads to the appropriate data. These data are the ground for a judgment or conclusion. Once the data confirm it, it is put to test in similar situations. This may require some changes in it and subsequent changes in a judgment or conclusion. But this depends on the size of the universe which is being examined as well as its complexity. Once these revisions have been made the inquiry is satisfied.

The Teacher's Role in Inquiry. This continuum of learning experiences applies to both you and your students. For them it should have a fresh and exciting character. For you it may be pretty routine, even "old stuff," because of your greater knowledge. You may, nevertheless, find a great reward in a new experience in *communication* rather than in the discovery of new truth. This suggests what your role is, as distinct from your students'. You have an idea (or more than one) in the back of your head. It is as clear and precise as you can state it to yourself. This is the bull's-eye of the enterprise, which may be a whole unit or a part of one. (For your students it is much less clear, even unknown.) If the matter at hand has to do with the provisions of the Constitution you have, in your head, the *idea* that learning them by heart will be well-nigh worthless *unless* they are seen as *means to insure justice* or whatever else you wish to emphasize. This *idea of justice* is your central and crystal-clear idea. You will, eventually, seek to make it as central and crystal-clear to your students. Suppose that the enterprise has to do with the importance of *distance in space* as a factor related to the ability of the people, in a country with such great land expanse as ours, to act in concert on some public issue. Many other factors are, of course, involved, but at this time you want to drive home the significance of "distance in space." That is *your* central idea. And so it goes. But, not until you are sure of *your* central idea, or sense one that the students seem to be trying to work out, can you know which stimuli to manipulate. Your selection and manipulation of them is guided by an idea.

Although, ideally, everything I have said involves the fullest participation of your students, the responsibility which you have inherited as *leader* cannot be minimized. This involves you in suggesting, correcting, demonstrating, asking questions, giving encouragement, praising, and the many things which no teacher can completely delegate to students. Nothing can escape *you*. You are all eyes and ears. You are the teacher and it is your business to *teach*. . . .

While I would not for a minute suggest that you arrogate to yourself the role of authoritarian, you have every right to think of yourself as an *authority* in both method and substance. This requires the balance of a sense of humility and genuine pride—in what proportions I cannot tell you.

A Classification of Aims. Although a later chapter will deal with aims, it is appropriate now to identify those which are basic to every unit of study: reliable knowledge, skill in inquiry, and attitudes. These will, we hope, defeat ignorance, muddle-headedness, and apathy. New methods of perceiving will be learned, new facts acquired and these, in turn, will engender new attitudes and patterns of conduct. Thus knowledge, policy, and action will be related. Doubts, dissatisfactions, and states of unrest will take the form of ideas, and these will be tested. The *activities* in which you and your students co-operatively engage will mediate the whole enterprise. In it all, the fallacy that the mind is first sharpened and then used will be exposed for what it is.

The mind will be sharpened by its *use*. Learning will be interpreted as problem solving. Interest will be the shaft which gives unity and continuity to the whole experience. Thus the course of productive thinking will run.[1]

LEARNING AND THINKING

Jerome S. Bruner

I should like to consider now some conditions in our schools today that promote and inhibit progress across the barrier from learning to thinking. I should point out in advance that I am not very cheerful on this subject.

The Passivity of Knowledge-Getting. I have been struck during the past year or so, sitting in classrooms as an observer, by the passivity of the process we call education. The emphasis is upon gaining and storing information, gaining it and storing it in the form in which it is presented. We carry the remainder in long division so, peaches are grown in Georgia, transportation is vital to cities, New York is our largest port, and so on. Can the facts or the methods presented be mimicked? If so, the unit

[1] An account of the dynamics and logic of productive thinking is to be found in Max Wertheimer, *Productive Thinking* (New York: Harper & Row, 1945). See especially "Introduction," pp. 1–13, in which Tables I, Ia, and II set forth the course of thinking under the rules of deductive and inductive logic, and the association theory, respectively. Read "Conclusion," pp. 189–215, in which these theories are examined and compared with the logic of the method of inquiry which I have used.

SOURCE: Jerome S. Bruner, "Learning and Thinking," *Harvard Educational Review*, Vol. 29, No. 3, Summer 1959, pp. 184–186. Reprinted by permission.

is at an end. There is little effort indeed which goes into the process of putting the information together, finding out what is generic about it. Long division is a skill, like threading a needle. The excitement of it as a method of partitioning things that relates it to such matters as subtraction is rarely stressed. One of the great inventions of man—elementary number theory—is presented as a cookbook. I have yet to see a teacher present one way of doing division and then put it squarely to the class to suggest six other ways of doing it—for there are at least six other ways of doing it than any one that might be taught in a school. So too with algebra. 'Algebra is not a set of rules for manipulating numbers and letters except in a trivial sense. It is a way of thinking, a way of coping with the drama of the unknown. Lincoln Steffens, in his *Autobiography*, complains upon his graduation from the University of California that his teachers had taught him only of the known, how to commit it to mind, and had done little to instruct him in the art of approaching the unknown, the art of posing questions. How does one ask questions about the unknown? Well, algebra is one technique, the technique for arranging the known in such a way that one is enabled to discern the value of an unknown quantity. It is an enriching strategy, algebra, but only if it is grasped as an extended instance of common sense.

Once I did see a teacher specifically encourage a class to organize and use minimal information to draw a maximum number of inferences. The teacher modeled his technique, I suppose, on the tried method of the story-teller. He presented the beginnings of the Whiskey Rebellion and said to his pupils, much in the manner of Ellery Queen speaking to his readers, "You now have enough to reconstruct the rest of the story. Let's see if we can do it." He was urging them to cross the barrier from learning into thinking. It is unhappily true that this is a rare exception in our schools.

So knowledge-getting becomes passive. Thinking is the reward for learning, and we may be systematically depriving our students of this reward as far as school learning is concerned.

One experiment which I can report provides encouragement. It was devised and carried out by the research group with which I am associated at Harvard in collaboration with teachers in the fifth grade of a good public school. It is on the unpromising topic of the geography of the North Central States and is currently in progress so that I cannot give all of the results. We hit upon the happy idea of presenting this chunk of geography not as a set of knowns, but as a set of unknowns. One class was presented blank maps, containing only tracings of the rivers and lakes of the area as well as the natural resources. They were asked as a first exercise to indicate where the principal cities would be located, where the railroads, and where the main highways. Books and maps were not permitted and "looking up the facts" was cast in a sinful light. Upon completing this exercise, a class discussion was begun in which the children attempted to justify why the major city would be here, a large city there, a railroad on this line, etc.

The discussion was a hot one. After an hour, and much pleading, permission was given to consult the rolled-up wall map. I will never forget one young student, as he pointed his finger at the foot of Lake Michigan, shouting, "Yipee, *Chicago* is at the end of the pointing-down lake." And another replying, "Well, O.K.: but Chicago's no good for the rivers and it should be here where there is a big city [St. Louis]." These children were thinking, and learning was an instrument for checking and improving the process. To at least a half dozen children in the class it is not a matter of indifference that no big city is to be found at the junction of Lake Huron, Lack Michigan, and Lake Ontario. They were slightly shaken up transportation theorists when the facts were in.

The children in another class, taught conventionally, got their facts all right, sitting down, benchbound. And that was that. We will see in six months which group remembers more. But whichever does, one thing I will predict. One group learned geography as a set of rational acts of induction—that cities spring up where there is water, where there are natural resources, where there are things to be processed and shipped. The other group learned passively that there were arbitrary cities at arbitrary places by arbitrary bodies of water and arbitrary sources of supply. One learned geography as a form of activity. The other stored some names and positions as a passive form of registration.

The Episodic Curriculum. In a social studies class of an elementary school in a well-to-do suburb of one of our great eastern cities, I saw groups of twelve-year-old children doing a "project" on the southeastern states. Each team was gathering facts that might eventually end up on a map or a chart or some other graphic device. The fact-gathering was atomized and episodic. Here were the industrial products of North Carolina. There was the list of the five principal cities of Georgia. I asked the children of one team what life would be like and what people would worry about in a place where the principal products were peanuts, cotton, and peaches. The question was greeted as "unfair." They were gathering facts.

It is not just the schools. The informational environment of America seems increasingly to be going through such an atomization. Entertainment is in fifteen-minute episodes on TV, to be taken while sitting down. The school curriculum is built of episodic units, each a task to itself: "We have now finished addition. Let us now move to multiplication." Even in our humor the "gag" threatens to replace the shrewd observer of the human comedy. I have seen an elementary school play fashioned entirely on a parody of radio commercials. It was a brave effort to tie the 10-second atoms together.

I do not wish to make it seem as if our present state of education is a decline from some previous Golden Age. For I do not think there has ever been a Golden Age in American public education. The difference now is that we can afford dross less well than ever before. The volume of positive knowledge increases at a rapid rate. Atomizing it into facts-to-be-filed is not likely to produce the kind of broad grasp that will be needed in the world of the next quarter century. And it is certainly no training for the higher education that more and more of our children will be getting.

I have not meant the above as a plea for the "central subject" or the "project" method of teaching. It is, rather, a plea for the recognition of the continuity of knowledge. One hears professional educators speak of "coverage," that certain topics must be covered. There are indeed many things that must be covered, but they are not unconnected things. The object of learning is to gain facts in a context of connectivity that permits the facts to be used generatively. The larger the number of isolated facts, the more staggering the number of connections between them —unless one can reduce them to some deeper order. Not all of them can. Yet it is an ideal worth striving for, be it in the fifth grade or in graduate school. As Robert Oppenheimer put it in a recent address before the American Academy, "Everything cannot be connected with everything in the world we live in. Everything can be connected with anything."

RELATIONSHIP OF SOME TEACHING METHODS TO SOME PRINCIPLES OF LEARNING

Norman E. Wallen and Robert M. W. Travers

PRINCIPLE 1: Behavior which represents the achievement or partial achievement of an educational objective should be reinforced.

Significance of the Principle for Classroom Learning. This principle means that there are known events which, if they occur subsequent to a response, facilitate the learning of the response, at least for some learners. The principle has great potential importance for education, because many of the common reinforcers are at least partially under the control of the teacher. Beginnings have been made in research on the identification of reinforcers. That such research is likely to be fruitful is evident from the studies that have been undertaken on the effects of praise and blame (Forlano & Axelrod, 1937; G. G. Thompson & C. W.

SOURCE: Norman E. Wallen and Robert M. W. Travers in *Handbook of Research in Teaching* (Champaign, Ill.: American Educational Research Association, 1962), pp. 494–499. Reprinted by permission.

Hunnicutt, 1944), a simple classification of potential reinforcers. These studies suggest that although praise may, in most cases, be a better reinforcer, blame is better for some students, and that the efficiency of each type can be predicted with some accuracy even with a fairly crude questionnaire measure of student personality. It is also known that certain kinds of information may serve as reinforcers, at least under some conditions.

A special class of reinforcers is described by the phrase *knowledge of results*. Whenever the learner has a clearly defined goal toward which he is striving, and when the attainment of the goal depends upon the comparison of the learner's behavior with some kind of standard, such comparisons may function as reinforcers. This aspect of reinforcement, easily demonstrated in the laboratory, has also been demonstrated in educational settings.

Despite the excellent beginnings that have been made in research in this area, little is known about the reinforcing effect of the following practices which are frequently observed in schools:

1. Public display of the accomplishments of the student.
2. Providing new problems to be solved after the student has shown some skill in solving a particular class of problem.
3. Physical contact with the teacher.
4. Praising a child for good behavior but with an implied reprimand for the other children.
5. The smiles or laughter of the teacher.
6. Gestures of approval from fellow students.
7. Meeting standards set by the pupil himself.
8. Disagreement of the teacher with the student.

Utilization of the Principle by Different Teaching Methods. Teaching methods show substantial differences in the presumed reinforcers which they introduce and also in the extent to which they recognize and utilize reinforcement at all. For example, what is commonly referred to as the lecture method of teaching assumes that information can be communicated without making any provision for reinforcement. The transmission is strictly an intellectual process. Other traditional forms of teaching rely upon grades, release from the learning situation ("You may go as soon as you have the right answers"), reduction in anxiety, or the promise that the results of learning will be appreciated later in life. Recitation methods appear to rely either on direct approval as a reinforcer or on silence, as when the teacher indicates only when a pupil is wrong and moves on to the next question when he is right. Newer methods rely more upon "intrinsic" reinforcers which are assumed to derive from the learning activity or the response itself. Group approval, teacher approval, and self approval are also mentioned as reinforcers in some descriptions of modern teaching methods. Skinner (1958) used a concept similar to that of "intrinsic" reinforcers when he stated that some activities are self-reinforcing. Discussion methods of conducting classes, in which the pupils interact with one another, would appear to rely upon social conditions such as approval of another's response.

Since we do not know which set of reinforcers or which combination is most effective, differences in method must represent differences in personal preferences. Perhaps a person is likely to recommend the use of those reinforcers which are effective for him.

PRINCIPLE 2: The introduction of cues which arouse motivation toward the achievement of an educational objective will increase the effectiveness with which that objective is achieved.

Utilization of the Principle and Its Corollaries by Different Teaching Methods. The state of knowledge in this area is unsatisfactory. The fact that the most significant work is of recent origin is reflected in the vague and confused thinking about motivation which characterizes most teaching methods. The methods which derive from the Rousseau tradition are based on the assumptions that the world surrounding the child is full of cues adequate to arouse motivation and that the teacher must take great care not to remove these cues or inhibit their effect. The progressive education movement after World War I followed this tradition and attempted to fill the classroom with objects and materials which would raise the level of arousal. Individual differences in the arousal produced by different classes of cues were taken into account by the variety provided. Visitors to such classrooms generally agreed that they witnessed a high level of activity among the pupils, though some would question whether it was directed toward desirable goals.

Traditional education has tended to adopt the reverse policy of avoiding distracting elements in the classroom so that the pupil would devote more attention to either the teacher or his books. Where the moving-about of the pupils was restricted, as it was in such classrooms, a rich range of materials would have little value. In this situation great reliance was placed on the arousal value of the teacher and the printed materials. In some cases the teacher was able to perform this arousal function with great success, but in others the teacher had to fall back on the utilization of anxiety as a motive. To some extent, the policies of the progressive education movement represented a revolt against the use of anxiety as a motive manipulated by the teacher.

Other teaching methods disregard to a great degree the operation of motivational variables. The typical lecture method assumes that a lecturer can transmit information and that whatever motivation is necessary has to be inherent in the student. Still, even the most ardent protagonist of the lecture method would agree that some lecturers are much more capable than others of "arousing interest." How a lecturer is to do this is not generally specified. Advocates of self-selection teaching methods (Olson, 1959 [1]) assume that a rich environment will provide cues which arouse a pupil in such a way that worth-while long-term goals are eventually achieved.

Undoubtedly, the designer of a teaching method may have considerable choice concerning what motives to invoke. The same educational goal may be achieved through the operation of many different motivational variables. Choice may depend also on factors other than the efficiency of the learning process. Objections to the use of anxiety as a motive are based more on ethical than on psychological issues.

Utilization of the Principle by Different Teaching Methods. Long before current knowledge of methods of teaching problem-solving, the protagonists of particular teaching methods adopted policies for teaching problem-solving skills. Some of these prac-

[1] W. C. Olson, *Child Development* (2nd ed.; Boston: D. C. Heath & Company, 1959).—Eds.

tices were based on practical experience and have subsequently been justified by research. For example, teachers of mathematics in a traditional framework of education commonly gave their students large numbers of problems to solve related to each principle that was studied. Physics teachers have done likewise. Experience in teaching in these areas seems to justify this practice, and it is also largely in accordance with recent research on problem-solving. In contrast, the project method of Kilpatrick assumed that the kind of problem-solving involved in working on large projects would develop the required problem-solving skills. Furthermore, lecture and demonstration methods of teaching problem-solving assume that the process can be learned efficiently by vicarious experience, though in fairness one must state that lecture methods have often been coupled with problem-solving assignments given as homework. In recent years, those who have proposed that teaching be centered around the use of teaching machines have seen the possibility of exposing the pupil to carefully planned programs of problems. Mechanized teaching equipment offers the possibility of developing learning sets much more systematically than is possible with the typical recitation method. Indeed, they are ideally suited to making use of the operation of this particular principle.

PRINCIPLE 4: Since learners differ in their capacity to make the responses to be acquired, learning will be most efficient if it is planned so that each learner embarks on a program commensurate with his capacity to acquire new responses.

Utilization of the Principle by Different Teaching Methods. Emphasis on individual differences and on differences within the same individual over a period of time has been largely responsible for the development of many of the "methods" mentioned previously, such as the activity, progressive, and laboratory approaches. Carried even further, it has lead to the propagation by Olson (1959) of an interesting approach to teaching method called "self-selection." In essence, the child is allowed a great deal of freedom in structuring his learning situation whether it be in terms of books to read, arithmetic workbooks, or presumably the broader areas of what responses are to be learned. This approach places great reliance on the child's seeking those experiences which will develop desired responses. Thus, the role of the teacher, according to Olson (1959, p. 404), is to "guarantee that every classroom situation, or its immediate surroundings, will have in it tasks which are interesting in terms of the intrinsic content, and which also cover a range of difficulty as great as the variability in the human material with which he deals." Research with this technique is virtually nonexistent, though Olson does mention a study in arithmetic at the third- and fourth-grade level which, he believed, indicated that on the whole the children were sound in the judgment of their abilities and that the gains under a considered self-selection plan seemed somewhat better than under a more laissez-faire procedure maintained in previous years. Inasmuch as this technique assumes that arousal of motivation and reinforcement will occur without any specific planning by the teacher and that the student will adequately assess his readiness—assumptions which many psychologists would not be willing to grant—further research is imperative.[1]

PRINCIPLE 5: If a pupil has had training in imitation, then he is capable of learning by observing demonstrations of the skills to be acquired. . . .

Utilization of the Principle by Different Teaching Methods. Few teaching methods have been clear in the application of this principle. Despite general agreement that many attributes of character are learned by an imitative process, there is little agreement that intellectual skills are learned by a similar process. Indeed, the concept that has found its way more and more into education during the last half-century has been that learning is most effective when the learner performs directly the response to be learned. One claim of progressive education was that traditional education involved learning by vicarious experience and that greater activity on the part of the learner was desirable. In the new education, learning by imitation was not to be a central method of intellectual development. A similar emphasis is seen in many "plans" such as the Winnetka Plan and the Mor-

[1] Since the writing of this chapter, *Summerhill,* by A. S. Neill, has appeared and requires comment. Although not a research report, this description of the techniques and results of 40 years of experience with self-selective procedures in a small residential school is a persuasive argument for their effectiveness. It is to be hoped that further work meeting the more rigorous definition of research advocated here will be done and reported.

rison Plan. Such approaches to education and the teaching methods which they imply leave little place for the application of the principle under consideration. Perhaps the "learning by doing" concept of education has had an undue influence on educational planning. Certainly other methods of learning have value, and these include learning by imitation and learning by being shown, as when the teacher takes the hand of a child and guides it in the writing of his name. The latter process, studied in a variety of situations, has been shown to produce learning, sometimes of a kind that is hard to produce by other means.

PRINCIPLE 6: The learner will learn more efficiently if he makes the responses to be learned than if he learns by observing another make the response or makes some related response. . . .

Utilization of the Principle by Different Teaching Methods. Many traditional forms of teaching relied heavily on learning occurring through the learner's observing the response of another. In the lecture method, as it has been used in teaching mathematics and the physical sciences, the teacher often solves a problem in front of the class and expects the pupils to learn thereby the problem-solving technique. Doubts concerning the efficiency of this approach were highly influential in bringing about educational change during the first half of the present century. Another common approach to education has been for the pupil to make, not the response to be learned, but some substitute or related response. Thus the student may discuss how he would behave in certain situations involving moral issues and indicate the moral stand he might take. For years, Sunday schools relied upon this method of teaching moral values. The assumption was that verbal behavior which reflected high moral values would be followed by other forms of behavior which reflected the same values. The classic research of Hartshorne and May (1930) demonstrated that this assumption was not sound. The project method of Kilpatrick was an attempt to abandon the method of learning by indirect experience or by substitute verbal responses. Some educators trained in group dynamics have also suggested teaching methods where the learner practices responses or aspects of responses to be learned rather than practicing verbal responses. The danger of designing a teaching method around single principles is seen in many of these efforts to apply a "learning by doing" concept of education, to the neglect of other approaches to learning or other variables.

BEFORE YOU GO BACK TO YOUR CLASSROOM—
REMEMBER THIS

George V. Sheviakov, Fritz Redl, and
Sybil K. Richardson

We do not believe the tremendous issue of "discipline" can be taught in a few sententious words. However, an occasional guidepost is often a help to the hurried practitioner on the job.

1. Routine tricks aren't the whole show. You can't sew discipline together out of rags. Often, especially when we get jittery or when non-understanding superiors or colleagues put the thumbscrews upon us for the wrong things, we develop undue admiration for the organizational "gadget." We develop the illusion that the gadget could do the trick for us, would save us thinking, planning, loving, and understanding. Well, it won't. If you overload your group atmosphere with the rattle of organizational machinery—try to have a "rule" for everything under the sun and another principle of revenge, if that rule is broken, for everything under the moon—you are just going to thwart your best efforts in the long run. Don't think you have to run

---

SOURCE: George V. Sheviakov, Fritz Redl and Sybil K. Richardson, *Discipline for Today's Children and Youth* (rev. ed.) (Washington, D.C.: Association for Supervision and Curriculum Development, NEA, 1956), pp. 62–64. Reprinted by permission.

around with your belt stuck full of guns and lollipops all the time, either. Rely a little more on yourself, your "person," and your sense of humor. It saves you lots of headaches and leads to disciplinary poise.

2. *The "mystery of personality" is good, when it works. But it is a poor excuse for failure.* This second statement is to keep you from falling into the opposite extreme after reading the first. While our personality—and the way we get it across to children —establishes most of what·we call "respect" and "leadership," there is also the 'everyday trifle' that is more easily settled through a rule or common agreement than by your magic gaze. Children have, although sometimes they are unconscious of it, considerable need for regularity and predictability in what is expected. If their *whole* life is dependent on the whims of your genius, little frictions begin to increase. So, don't extend your contempt for using routine tricks instead of personality into mistaken contempt for *any* planning and organization.

3. *Don't try to wash all your laundry with the same cake of soap.* Sometimes we discover two or three nice little tricks that work. Then we develop the delusion that, if we just keep on sticking to these tricks, the rest of the problems of life will dissolve. Well, it won't wash. Don't expect tricks to work under all circumstances, and don't blame yourself or the children. Blame those tricks or, better, blame the way you translated them without enough planning.

Watch out, when you begin to tell "anecdotes" of how this or that "always works," for these are the moments when mental petrification begins.

4. *Children are at least as complicated as a piece of wood.* So you had better find out about their texture, elasticity and grain fiber before you apply your various tools and machinery upon them. Sometimes we want to get places fast, and then we spoil the whole show by using too coarse an instrument. If you do that, don't blame it on the instrument but upon your incomplete analysis of your material.

5. *If you make a fool of yourself, why not be the first one to find out and have a good laugh about it?* The worst superstition about discipline is that "respect" and "leadership" melt as easily

as a chocolate bar. It is not true. If they do, they never were "real" respect and leadership to begin with.

So don't be jittery for fear that you will "jeopardize" your dignity in the eyes of your youngsters if they find out you aren't the Archangel Michael after all. The fear of exposure to ridicule has caused more intangible discipline problems than anything else. There is a difference between the laughter you start and ridicule. Real, especially self-directed humor, is the most disarming thing in the work with children that you could find.

6. *Don't develop suicidal fantasies, just because you aren't almighty after all.* There are limits to the power of the biggest magician among us as well as to the omnipotence of the most conscientious scientist. Every once in a while we run up against those discoveries. If you do so, don't blame your youngsters because they can't be cured by you, nor blame yourself. The biggest hurdle in our work is time. It takes at least as many months of planful work to undo a wrong trait in a child as it took years of planful mishandling to build the wrong trait. But don't forget, many things can be started on the right track through long-range planning, though those same things can't be followed through to their final development. Don't be afraid of making mistakes. It isn't one particular mistake that produces distorted children—it is the wrong way of reacting to the mistakes after we make them. And that is entirely in your power.

7. *What do you want to be, anyway, an educator, or an "angel with the flaming sword"?* It is upon your answer to this question that your decisions about discipline techniques will finally depend. For it requires one type of person to be the proud avenger of infantile wrongs and sins against defied "rules and regulations," and another to be the guide of human beings through the turmoil of growth. You have to make up your mind.

8. *Remember you're human, too.* Many of the understandings required of you as a teacher today come into conflict with values learned before you can remember. In our earliest years, we accept certain behaviors of adults toward children and of children toward adults as "right" and natural. These convictions were learned in close emotional relationship with our own parents and teachers and are painful to change. It is hard to be objective

about the child who still exists within each of us. Perhaps you have already realized that not all parents are like yours and that each child must be helped to grow wholesomely in his world as it is. Then you are well on your way to the emotional maturity, the sense of perspective and the freedom from threat, needed by leaders of today's children and youth.

Trends

~~~~~~

The major underlying theme that marked the development of secondary education in the United States prior to the twentieth century was that from the outset some form of extended education beyond a basic one was recognized as essential to the advancement of the democratic concept.

From the Latin Grammar schools of Europe the seed of secondary education was transplanted to the shores of Colonial America. The Academy, sponsored by the ubiquitous Benjamin Franklin, appealed to a growing middle class. The public English High School, in turn, challenged the Academy and succeeded in winning the support of a country that took pride in the fact that the children of all men, from every walk of life, were entitled to maximum educational opportunities. The capping of this well of ambition was the momentous Kalamazoo Decision, which gave legal tax support to the idea of universal education through the high school. No other nation at this time committed itself to the point of view that free public education should be mandatory for its children through the high school years.

By mid-century 87 percent of the youth of America were

enrolled in the secondary schools. Having achieved this goal, educators began to reflect about the kind of secondary education that would best serve these young people. Sputnik helped to sharpen their focus in this regard. A major reconsideration of the approach to teaching the gifted and the place of science and mathematics were consequences of this sober reflection. Most compelling was the desire that quality education be the characteristic of this decade.

Quality, however, is ephemeral. What is quality education? Is quality synonymous with academic excellence? Does quality in education imply that only the academically talented can benefit from the curriculum of a comprehensive high school? Is it possible that those students not so intellectually endowed can benefit from this type of curriculum as well? All Americans want the best education for their youngsters regardless of their ability, but exactly how shall this be achieved?

The intent of this section of readings is to highlight some of the more recent developments of secondary education which portend to resolve some of the problems suggested above. There is every indication that the next decade of educational history will be one of serious experimentation and progress. Not only have prominent educators become concerned with the future trend of secondary education, but subject matter specialists in universities and colleges have joined the battle to revitalize curricula and instructional practices. Educational reforms have been encouraged by governmental efforts in the form of legislation and funds to provide programs for the gifted and culturally deprived youths, improved guidance services, and new curricula and methods in the sciences, foreign languages, and mathematics. Programs with the intriguing titles of Project English and Project Social Studies are already in operation. In the field of mathematics at least four systems developed by specialists have found their way into high school programs. Colleges, universities, and school districts have sponsored institutes, workshops, and seminars to acquaint experienced teachers with new developments. Textbook publishers have upgraded their books by making them more functional as well as extending the breadth and depth of their coverage.

Recent reports on automated devices for learning predict the role that the electronic age will play in the education of the future. Experiments in educational television and auto-instructional devices have been conducted in many school districts with varying results. Some critics maintain that the human quality of teacher-student relationship must remain paramount when such devices are introduced into the school.

Recognition of the need to explore more efficient methods of individualizing the school programs has resulted in the adoption of approaches such as team teaching, which utilizes the specialized talents of individual teachers and provides for independent study time for the students. This same concern for capitalizing on the special capabilities of students is described in the work experience programs in Santa Barbara County. The most dramatic of these experimental programs for improving learning conditions for the culturally disadvantaged, which has attracted national attention and imitation, is the Higher Horizons program which was first initiated in New York City and has now spread to several other major urban areas.

One of the most impressive trends in secondary education has been the upward extension of the high school into the thirteenth and fourteenth years, whereby institutions commonly known as Junior or Community Colleges have been established. This movement has had its greatest success in California, where more than seventy such institutions are tax supported. The objectives of the junior colleges have been modified considerably since the first one was established in Joliet, Illinois, in 1902, and it is likely that further modifications will take place in the very near future. For example, rather than an extension of the high school upward, these institutions may become the downward extension of the universities and four-year colleges. In either case, what is particularly significant is that the trend indicates that free public education for all American youth might well be extended into the 13th and 14th year.

Trends such as those mentioned above promise much for the secondary school of today and tomorrow. However, major questions are raised by their introduction into the school life of America. Can school districts afford to invest in constructing or renovating buildings to adapt them to flexible scheduling or team teaching? Will the emphasis on homogeneous ability groupings enhance or retard the democratic process? Will the education of teachers be able to keep pace with the newer trends in the curriculum and methodology, or will there be a repetition of our historical past, which indicated that experimentation was often far in advance of the teachers' interests or their ability to adapt? Is our concept of the gifted challenged by the investigation of Torrance, Getzels and Jackson, and others? Will the high school of the future be radically different from the one Kvaraceus contends exists today?

Some other problems are suggested by the emphasis on quality education. Must care be taken that quality education not be misinterpreted to mean merely longer hours in school, longer homework assignments, and increased teacher domination? Will those aspects of the curriculum that have previously emphasized social living, citizenship training, aesthetic values, and physical fitness now be neglected? Does the increased attention to the extremes of our school population suggest that the middle ability group will now go unrecognized? Finally, will the pressures of the labor market insist that all students attend college? How large a percentage of our school population are capable of benefiting from a college education?

These and many more questions need consideration by educators. One trend is evident; education everywhere is in ferment. The teacher of today can be encouraged by the fact that he is part of a profession that has a continuing concern for answers to questions that have a long history. Quick solutions will probably not be forthcoming. Experimentation, research, and study by all those involved in the educative process is imperative if the American secondary school is to continue to be a vital force in our democratic society.

As we move into the sixties, it will be interesting for the reader to compare the trends as reported by Romine in 1954 with the practices of today. By the same measure let the reader project himself ten years into the future to assess how accurately the trends described in this section have been realized.

TRENDS IN THE SECONDARY–SCHOOL CURRICULUM

Stephen Romine

〰〰〰〰〰〰〰〰〰〰〰〰〰〰〰〰〰〰〰〰〰〰〰〰〰〰

One of the fundamental trends in curriculum building today is that of moving toward a broader concept of the job which the high school is called upon to do and a more functional concept of how this job can be done. The two-by-four curriculum, as someone has aptly called it, with its restriction to the two covers of a book and the four walls of the school, is becoming a thing of the past. It is obvious today that the school alone cannot accomplish the challenging and complicated task of educating our youth for productive citizenship. This is a job calling for the effort of the entire American community. Only to the

SOURCE: Stephen Romine, "Trends in The Secondary-School Curriculum." From the *Proceedings* of the Northwest Association of Secondary and Higher Schools, Annual Convention, 38th Year, held at Salt Lake City, Utah, November 28–December 1, 1954, pp. 43–47. Reprinted by permission.

315

degree that we can secure such effort will American education be able to retain its forward thrust.

This broader and more functional viewpoint is growing in general acceptance and is reflected in at least four less inclusive but related trends, each of which merits consideration.

First, there is a trend for the high school curriculum to be more concerned with important, present-day life problems than was true in the past. Courses which have been in the curriculum for years—in English, mathematics, science, social studies, and other fields—are being given a more practical slant and a more truly cultural focus in the broad sense of the term. Problem-centered courses are more prevalent today, and out-of-school experiences are given more consideration than in years past.

The use of a wider range of resources also fits into this broader and more functional concept of the curriculum. Many books instead of one, audio-visual aids of many types, and the use of out-of-school personnel and places illustrate this trend. School libraries are becoming communications centers and laboratories of learning, instead of merely serving as repositories of books. School librarians are spending less time with the technical details of "minding the library" and more in working with teachers and students in learning situations.

Work experience and camping also reflect the broadened concept of curriculum. More and more effort is going into the development of a high school curriculum which really makes a difference in the way people live and behave. This effort is carrying the school beyond its four walls and bringing the student body in contact with the ongoing turmoil of the world in transition. Distributive occupations courses and school-work programs are enlarging and enriching educational opportunities in a realistic manner.

In the future we shall likely see the emergence of what may be called a K–13 program involving closer cooperation between secondary schools and colleges and universities. Next week in Colorado, for example, we are holding the third in a series of conferences aimed at coordinating more closely the curriculum in English in the Denver high schools and in the University of Colorado and pointed also at helping students to bridge the gap between English instruction on these two levels. If we are successful, and the approach thus far has real promise, the plan is to expand the effort to include other subject fields. This is a cooperative project in which neither level is attempting to dominate the other. The focus has been on common problems and what we can do together for the welfare of our common student body.

As a third major trend, newer types of curriculum organization are also becoming more common than in the past. Broad-fields courses which combine elements of courses formerly taught as separate entities are helping to bring some sense and unity out of the hundreds of courses accumulated over the years through a process of addition. As you know, all roads have led into the curriculum, and once a course has become established it has tended to enjoy permanent tenure. Curriculum surveys have revealed much unnecessary overlapping among such courses, as well as important gaps in the total education program.

The core curriculum also continues to become more popular, especially on the junior high school level. More commonly this now develops slowly through the unification of language arts and social studies, and group approaches to guidance are also associated with the core program. Many schools are avoiding a mistake all too common in years past—that of identifying such courses with a special label.

Another major trend consists of increased activity in the revision of courses within the existing framework of organization. . . .

For example, just as the K–12 idea promotes better vertical articulation, more effort is now going into establishing better correlation and articulation among courses taught on the same grade level. Teachers of English and social studies, as an illustration, are doing much to relate and reinforce their instruction. In many fields common goals, themes, or experiences are serving as bases which promote a more effective total curriculum and a more efficient learning process.

There is also a shift within courses from emphasis on subject matter *per se* to content and experiences justified on the basis of making a genuine contribution to important educational goals. Increasingly the curriculum is coming to be viewed as a means instead of an end. Pupil-teacher planning is finding a place in the scheme of things, and courses are being broadened to include a richer variety of activities pertinent to a broader range of outcomes beyond academic information and skills.

Growing attention to individual differences marks another major trend in curriculum and instructional procedures. In furtherance of this, an increasing number of schools are considering ability grouping or some other plan of reducing the heterogeneity of instructional groups. Temporary grouping within heterogeneous classes is also employed, and various schemes of assignment are being utilized to provide greater opportunity and challenge to students of varying abilities, backgrounds, interests, and needs.

Along with and as part of these trends is another which is perhaps more administrative than curricular. For a long time study halls have posed a very real problem. Many students use them badly, if at all, and teachers have been unhappy with them also. Particularly because of this, and recognizing that students might more profitably be occupied in classes, activities, and study under supervision, many schools are moving toward a schedule of fewer and longer periods in the school day. Students are also carrying heavier loads, which permit them to pursue basic courses fundamental to the education of all youth and still elect other courses and activities in accordance with their particular interests and needs. We have come to realize that the elective system, carried to unreasonable extremes, has contributed to the multiplicity of overlapping courses found in some schools and has permitted students to avoid experiences which they should have. Often it has been easier to add courses than to appraise critically and revise those which we have in order that they might serve more effectively. The new trends seem to be giving students a richer experience in high school, as well as yielding greater educational returns on the tax dollar.

Related to these changes, and pertinent to meeting individual needs and interests, there is a trend toward greater flexibility in time requirements for high school credit. The Carnegie Unit, as old and revered as it is, has serious weaknesses. Consequently more attention is being given today to the qualitative aspects of learning and to the growth and development which students attain, rather than to the time they spend in studying a given subject. On this point accrediting agencies may be a great help or a serious handicap.

In one of our high schools last year, a selected group of students met their advanced algebra class only three times per week, the other two days being spent on another project. A standardized achievement test administered at the end of the year clearly indicated the superiority of this group in algebra over two other classes meeting five times per week, even though the two latter classes compared favorably to national norms. With unselected groups in other schools we have found that careful planning permits wiser use of time than is customarily made, the net result of which is a richer course of instruction and more efficient learning. . . .

In speaking of these trends I have also attempted to think of both theory and practice. We all realize, I am sure, that practice lags behind theory. Growing enrollments and the concentration of attention and resources on housing our students also pose problems to be solved in moving ahead toward a better curriculum. So also do rising costs of education. The teacher supply bears directly on all of this, and in some quarters unwarranted criticism of the schools and a call to return to the fundamentals are to be reckoned with. Progress—real, substantial, and lasting progress—does not come without sustained and intelligent effort, even in the face of discouragement. I am confident that our secondary-school principals can and will give the leadership necessary that our curriculum may become increasingly potent in educating our American youth. Upon this trend—greater and wiser educational leadership—rest not only the other trends which have been mentioned, but the future of American education.

EXCELLENCE IN A DEMOCRACY

John Gardner

‹‹

It is now widely recognized that our society has given too little attention to the individual of unusual talent or potentialities. To make such an assumption is not to deplore the unprecedented time and money we have devoted to raising the general level of achievement. It would serve no purpose to replace our neglect of the gifted by neglect of everyone else. We are all too prone to such wild swings of the pendulum in our national life. We must learn to view these matters in a perspective which will permit us to repair one omission without creating others.

It has not always been easy for Americans to think clearly about excellence. At the heart of the matter is a seeming paradox in democracy as we know it. On the one hand, ours is the form of society which says most convincingly "Let the best man win" and rewards winners regardless of origin. On the other, it is the form of society which gives those who do not come out on top the widest latitude in rewriting the rules of the contest. It is crucial to understand this tug of war between equality and excellence in a democracy. When the rewriting of the rules is prompted by the standards of fair play, by elementary considerations of justice, by basic value judgments as to what sort of a "best man" the society wants, democracy can have no quarrel with it. Indeed it is the core process of a democracy. But when the rewriting of the rules is designed to banish excellence, to rule out distinguished attainment, to inhibit spirited individuals,

SOURCE: From *The Pursuit of Excellence: Education and the Future of America,* by Rockefeller Brothers Fund, Inc., Copyright © 1958 by Rockefeller Brothers Fund, Inc. (as it appears in *Prospect for America,* copyright © 1961). Reprinted by permission of Doubleday & Company, Inc.

then all who have a stake in the continued vitality of democracy must protest.

Every democracy must encourage high individual performance. If it does not, it closes itself off from the main springs of its dynamism and talent and imagination, and the traditional democratic invitation to the individual to realize his full potentialities becomes meaningless. More, perhaps, than any other form of government, a democracy must maintain what Ralph Barton Perry has called "an express insistence upon quality and distinction."

The eighteenth-century philosophers who made equality a central term in our political vocabulary never meant to imply that men are equal in all respects. Nor do Americans today take such a view. It is possible to state in fairly simple terms the views concerning equality which would receive most widespread endorsement in our country today. The fundamental view is that in the final matters of human existence all men are equally worthy of our care and concern. Further, we believe that men should be equal in enjoyment of certain familiar legal, civil and political rights. They should, as the phrase goes, be equal before the law.

But men are unequal in their native capacities and their motivations, and therefore in their attainments. In elaborating our national views of equality, the most widely accepted means of dealing with this problem has been to emphasize *equality of opportunity*. The great advantage of the conception of equality of opportunity is that it candidly recognizes differences in achievement. By allowing free play to these differences, it preserves the freedom to excel, which counts for so much in terms of individual aspirations, and has produced so much of mankind's greatness.

Having committed ourselves to equality of opportunity, we must strive incessantly to make it a reality in our society. This is a task which will concern us at many points in the present report.

With respect to the pursuit of excellence there are several considerations that we must keep firmly in mind.

First, we must not make the mistake of adopting a narrow or constricting view of excellence. *Our conception of excellence must embrace many kinds of achievement at many levels.* There is no single scale or simple set of categories in terms of which to measure excellence. There is excellence in abstract intellectual activity, in art, in music, in managerial activities, in craftsmanship, in human relations, in technical work.

Second, we must not assume that native capacity is the sole ingredient in superior performance. Excellence, as we shall later have occasion to note, is a product of ability and motivation and character. And the more one observes high performance in the dust and heat of daily life, the more one is likely to be impressed with the contribution made by the latter two ingredients.

Finally, we must recognize that judgments of differences in talent are not judgments of differences in human worth.

To sum up, it is possible for us to cultivate the ideal of excellence while retaining the moral values of equality. Whether we shall succeed in doing so is perhaps the fundamental issue in the development of our human resources. A challenge must be recognized before it can be met. Our society will have passed an important milestone of maturity when those who are the most enthusiastic proponents of a democratic way of life are also the most vigorous proponents of excellence.

THE MEANING OF GIFTEDNESS

J. W. Getzels and P. W. Jackson

When a concept becomes the focus of critical concern it is almost inevitable that its original meaning will simultaneously be expanded and differentiated. The concept of *giftedness* is, of course, of critical concern at this time, and the purpose of this paper is to examine the transformations this concept is presently

SOURCE: J. W. Getzels and P. W. Jackson, *Phi Delta Kappan*, November, 1958. Reprinted by permission.

undergoing and to suggest some additional modifications in its application.

Giftedness as related to children has most frequently been defined as a score on an intelligence test, and typically the study of the so-called gifted child has been equated with the study of the single I.Q. variable. Involved in this unidimensional definition of giftedness are several types of confusion, if not outright error. First, there is the limitation of the single metric itself, which not only restricts our perspective of the more general phenomenon, but places on the one concept a greater theoretical and predictive burden than it was intended to carry. For all practical school purposes, the term *gifted child* has become synonymous with the expression *child with a high I.Q.*, thus blinding us to other forms of excellence. Second, within the universe of intellectual functions themselves, we have behaved as if the intelligence test represented an adequate sampling of *all* these functions. For example, despite the growing body of literature concerning intellectual processes which seem closely allied to the general concept of "creativity," we tend to treat the latter concept as applicable only to performance in one or more of the *arts*. In effect, the term *creative child* has become synonymous with the expression *child with artistic talents*, thus limiting our attempts to identify and foster cognitive abilities related to creative functioning in areas other than the arts. Third, there has been a failure to attend sufficiently to the difference between the *definition* of giftedness as given by the I.Q. and the variations in the *value* placed upon giftedness as so defined. It is often taken for granted, for example, that the gifted child is equally valued by teachers and by parents, in the classroom and at home; that he is held an equally good prospect by teachers and by parents to succeed as an adult; and that children themselves *want* to be gifted. It can be demonstrated that none of these assumptions regarding the value of the gifted child can be held without question. Empirical data related to these assumptions indicate that the gifted child is *not* equally valued by teachers and by parents, in the classroom and at home; he is *not* held to be an equally good prospect by teachers and parents to succeed as an adult; and children themselves do *not* necessarily want to be gifted, at least not in the traditional sense of the word.

Despite its longevity, there is nothing inevitable about the use of the I.Q. in defining giftedness. Indeed, it may be argued that in many ways this definition is only an historical happenstance—a consequence of the fact that early inquiries in this field had as their context the classroom and its attendant concern with academic progress. If we moved the focus of our inquiry from the classroom setting, we might identify qualities defining giftedness for other situations just as the I.Q. did for the classroom. Indeed, *without* shifting our focus of inquiry, if we only changed the original criteria of learning, we might change the qualities defining giftedness even in the classroom. For example, if we recognize that learning involves the production of novelty as well as the remembrance of course content, then measures of creativity as well as the I.Q. might become appropriate in defining characteristics of giftedness.

A research project, under the direction of the authors, is now being conducted at the University of Chicago in order to provide empirical data related to the considerations outlined above.[1] As subjects of our research we have used a group of approximately 500 adolescents attending a Midwestern private school. The grade range covered by our group extends from the end of the sixth grade to the end of the senior year in high school. Because of the broad purpose of the research, we have inaugurated an extensive testing program involving the assessment of traditional qualities, such as intelligence and psychological health, and including attempts to assess less conventional dimensions such as creativity, morality, and the like. The study to be discussed here is but one small aspect of the larger investigation and concerns specifically a description of two of our experimental groups: one which we shall label the "highly intelligent" group, and the other the "highly creative" group.

TWO GROUPS MUTUALLY EXCLUSIVE

Our "highly intelligent" subjects were defined as those who were in the top 20 percent of the sample population on conventional I.Q. measures, but who were *not* in the top 20 percent on

[1] This project is supported by a grant from the U.S. Office of Education.

measures of creativity. Our "highly creative" subjects were defined as those who were in the top 20 percent of our sample population on measures of creativity, but who were *not* in the top 20 percent in I.Q. The groups comprised twenty-eight and twenty-four subjects respectively, with approximately an equal proportion of boys and girls in each.

Limitation of space does not permit a complete description of the instruments included in the creativity battery. However, an adequate understanding of the way in which the term *creative* is used in the material to follow requires at least passing comment concerning these tests.[2] Most briefly, all of the tests in the creative battery involved facility in dealing with verbal and numerical symbol systems, and object-space relationships. Some instruments called for rapid verbal associations to stimulus words; others called for the ability to structure quickly an incomplete or distorted perceptual stimulus; still others required remote, or clever, or original responses to complex verbal situations (e.g., supplying last lines to a fable). In one test the subject was to respond to a complex paragraph involving numerical values by suggesting all of the mathematical problems which could be solved with the information in the paragraph.

It should be noted that we did not include in our experimental groups those children who were high in *both* creativity and intelligence, and there were many such individuals. Our attempt was to isolate the two qualities under study from each other as much as possible in order to examine the relative contribution of each to the functioning of the child. Those individuals who excelled in both areas are the objects of further investigation still in progress.

Having identified our two experimental groups, we compared them to each other and to the population from which they were drawn on a number of relevant variables, including: school per-

[2] Some of these instruments were adapted from the more inclusive test batteries of J. P. Guilford, professor of psychology at the University of Southern California, and R. B. Cattell, professor of psychology at the University of Illinois. Others were developed by the staff of the research project. A more complete description of these instruments is given in J. W. Getzels and P. W. Jackson, "The Highly Creative and the Highly Intelligent Adolescent: An Attempt at Differentiation," paper read at the American Psychological Association Meetings, Washington, D.C., August, 1958.

formance as measured by standardized verbal and numerical achievement tests appropriate to each grade level; teacher preferences as measured by teacher ratings of the pupils on how much they "liked to have them in class"; the preferences of the children themselves for personal qualities they would like to possess; the children's perception of the personal qualities they believed would lead to success in adult life and those they felt teachers would most prefer in children. In addition, the children were asked to write four-minute stories in response to six pictures flashed on a screen for twenty seconds each. An examination was made of the differences in the writing "style" of the two groups.

EXPERIMENT SUBJECTS EQUAL IN ACHIEVEMENT

The results of these comparisons may be summarized as follows:

First, with respect to school achievement, despite a difference of twenty-three points between the *mean* I.Q.'s of the two groups, they were *equally* superior in school achievement to the student population as a whole.

Second, when asked to rate the children on the degree to which they would like to have them in class, the teachers exhibited a clear-cut preference for the high I.Q. child. The ratings given the high I.Q. group were significantly higher than those of the total student body; the ratings given the high creativity group did not differ significantly from those of the total student body. This occurred despite the fact, as we have seen, that *both* the high I.Q. and the high creative group were *equally superior* to the other students in school achievement.

Third, comparing the personal aspirations of the children as reflected in the personal qualities they would like to possess, we find that the creative child himself rates high marks, I.Q., pep and energy, character, and goal-directedness *lower* than do members of the highly intelligent group, and that he rates wide range of interests, emotional stability, and sense of humor *higher* than do members of the highly intelligent group. The last item, sense of humor, is particularly noteworthy since the value which the creative child puts upon this quality so far exceeds the ranking it receives from high I.Q. children as to make it one of the outstanding differences between the two groups, and indeed sets the creativity group apart most sharply from *all* our other groups.

Fourth, the groups show distinct differences in the degree to which they aspire for "success" in adult life. The high I.Q. child desires to possess those qualities *now* which he believes will lead to success in adult life; the creative child does not seem to use this remote goal as criterion in the selection of his present aspirations.

Fifth, the relationship between the child's own personal aspirations and those qualities which he believes teachers prefer is quite different for the two groups. The high I.Q. child holds to a self-ideal which is consonant with the one he believes teachers will most readily approve; the self-ideal of the creative child is not only *not* consonant with what he believes to be the teacher approved model but shows a slight *negative* correlation with such model.

Sixth and finally, in their written responses to our six stimulus pictures, the creative students exhibited a degree of imagination and originality (not by any means the same as correct grammatical construction) unmatched by the high I.Q. students. Compared to the latter group, the creative students produced stories which seemed to "spring from" the stimulus rather than appeared to be "tied down" by it. Their stories made abundant use of humor, novel situations, and unexpected endings. They seemed to "play with" the picture stimulus for the pleasure of invention rather than "labor" the stimulus in order to find the "correct" theme.

SOME IMPORTANT IMPLICATIONS

There is, it seems to us, a consistency and unity even in these preliminary findings which may have important implications for defining and identifying so-called gifted children in the educational setting. We believe the high academic performance of our creative children coupled with the related lack of recognition which they may receive from teachers points to the core of the problem of expanding the present conception of *giftedness,* and of breaking the bonds that the I.Q. has on this concept in the school situation. The personal qualities of such presently neglected groups as our creatives which tend to estrange teachers from them may very well derive from the very neglect which these children suffer in the educational setting. With respect to our creative students, for example, the quality of "disillusionment" which appears to be reflected in the discrepancies between their personal aspirations and the aspirations they believe to be valued by teachers and by society in general may be a function of just the neglect to which we have been pointing. Despite their exceptional talents, they may miss identification by the usual I.Q. instrument; and despite their superior achievement, they may fail to gain the same personal preference from teachers that the high I.Q. children seem to have. We venture to suggest that a consideration of these discrepancies may deepen our appreciation at once of the need for expanding the concept of giftedness in the school setting and of the very real difficulties involved in such expansion.

A CHALLENGE FOR EDUCATORS, RESEARCHERS

Once we set a precedent by allowing an exception to the practice of labeling only high I.Q. children as "gifted," the possibility of expanding the concept to include other potentially productive groups becomes a genuine challenge to both educators and research workers. The not inconsiderable dangers inherent in the possibility of expanding the concept to a point where it becomes meaningless seem to us to be compensated by the possibility of increasing the effectiveness of our education for *all* children.

THE BEHAVIORAL DEVIATE IN THE CULTURE

OF THE SECONDARY SCHOOL

William C. Kvaraceus

~~~~~~

LEARNING BY CLOCK AND CALENDAR

The tempo and rhythm of learning in the high schools is fast, brief, and staccato. The student studies by clock and calendar. Learning stops for frequent holiday and vacation periods. Entrance to school and withdrawal from school are based on birth certificates rather than on any measure of ability or achievement. Learning is always shorttimed and truncated and operates in fifty-minute periods in which teacher and pupil study to beat the clock. All of this is alien to a studentship and a scholarship which is continuous and permeating, and which must race in the long arduous marathon rather than the fifty-minute dash in a five-period day. Much of the pseudo-intellectualism of our day can be traced to the "quickie" nature of the school's learning-teaching process.

Organizationally the high-school program sorts out classes (not individuals) among teachers about every fifty minutes. The frequently-shifted youngster belongs to no one. Even with a "homeroom period" he suffers a feeling of rootlessness and impersonality. As a member of a class he may achieve the status of a pupil but seldom that of a person. When the adolescent calls attention to himself as a person through misbehavior, help may be extended to him but through the impersonal bureaucracy of the guidance department.

Secondary schools have shown a complete lack of imagination

SOURCE: William C. Kvaraceus, *Frontiers of Secondary Education,* Proceedings and Conferences on Secondary Education (Syracuse: Syracuse University Press, 1958). Reprinted by permission.

and ingenuity in developing programs that would insure the establishment of strong and extended teacher-pupil and pupil-teacher relationships on which instruction and learning can be anchored. Attention should be given to the possibilities inherent in arranging programs in much longer time patterns by spending a half day or full day within each area of instruction, or even a week with the science teacher followed by a full week each in the round of other teachers in other areas. High-school programming will make learning and scholarship pervasive only when schooling itself is pervasive. Obviously this means that the calendar year must become the school year and that there can be no long holidays from learning.

GROUPING ON THE AGE–GRADE PRINCIPLE

High-school classes are very tightly grouped on the age-grade principle, with subdivisions according to interests in different curricula which reflect, in turn, educational and occupational levels of aspiration. Grouping tightly on the age-grade basis can affect behavior and misbehavior two ways:

First, by implying to both teacher and pupils an equality and homogeneity that actually does not exist and in consequence of which instruction is undifferentiated through the slavish use of the single text and the identical lesson assignment. This invites the problem of the bored learner at the upper levels and the frustrated learner within the lower ranges of ability and achievement. Only by individuating instruction within the classroom can the great educational superstition that all children of the same age who come to school can learn the same things, at the same time, at the same pace, and to the same degree, be broken. High-school students taught under this American superstition of equality are bound to suffer the trauma of a bad hangover once they leave school and meet the competitive climate in the world of work.

Second, grouping in tight age brackets tends to reinforce the already overly strong youth culture which is so often irresponsible to anyone but itself. The teen-ager notoriously would rather be wrong with his peers than right with his family or other adult authority. When this happens, as Margaret Mead has pointed out, American youth tend to surrender some moral autonomy for the comforts of the irresponsible crowd. This is the inherent nature of the delinquent act, particularly of the "group-intoxicated" and "socialized" types.

How much leeway is possible in grouping more broadly but within the chronological age span of the secondary school presents a real problem. Surely more could be done in the six-year secondary school by overlapping membership in some classes such as music and art, and by adhering more closely to an ability-achievement criteria in others, thereby breaking the solid age-grouping that now prevails. At the same time, the pressure to differentiate instruction for extremes will be lessened.

Contrary to some fears and even some evidence that pre-adolescents, adolescents, and post-adolescents cannot be effectively grouped for instruction, careful observations of the social and emotional situations on the ski slope, or in the swimming pool, or on the stage (where instruction is frequently imparted to groups having very wide age ranges but in accordance with a continuous growth principle), will reveal many positive outcomes, particularly in terms of a reciprocal respect and a camaraderie rare even in closely knit pressure groups.

THE CULTURAL SURROGATES OF THE SCHOOL

When Kahlil Gibran speaks on teaching in *The Prophet* he describes the teacher walking in the shadow of the temple among his followers, giving "not of his wisdom but rather of his faith and his lovingness." I suppose the emphasis here is not so much on subject matter as it is on the kind of warm personality who could relate easily to others through trust and affection. But let us not dispense entirely with wisdom or even subject matter, especially at the high school level!

Teen-age behavior can be strongly influenced by any glamorous figure with whom adolescents so easily identify. But who wants to identify with the teacher? Who wants to be like you? This is the painful "mirror, mirror on the wall" self-inquiry that every teacher should undergo in searching out his own self-concept. If the general public and the teacher himself are disenchanted with the teacher's status and role, the high school will not be highly populated by influential or glamorous imitative examples. Is it true that we are, as Phyllis McGinley portrays us in her cruel sonnet on the P.T.A. "listless mentors of the young" and are we who are hired to teach others all too often uninspired and uninspiring? Yet teaching conceived as changing the behavior of others can be an exciting, glamorous, even dangerous occupation as we work on the critical frontier of human influence.

In this periodic self-inquiry the teacher should also raise one other allied question: "Why am I in the teaching profession?" The high-school learning situation cannot be very hopeful if teaching is elected only as a secondary or tertiary choice. In these and the coming days of spiraling high-school enrollments, will we be luring and pressing into service large numbers of workers whose basic motivations are extraneous to living, working, liking and especially abiding as well as enjoying adolescents—workers who see themselves only as harassed and temporary hired hands in this vineyard? Some of these same teachers, who may render a higher quality of service strictly in the line of duty, may still fail to influence the behavior of others for the better so long as duty remains duty without love.

One last question on the school parent surrogate. What effect have debates on public education of the past few years had on the classroom teacher in the high school? If the teacher is frightened, insecure, and jittery, you can be sure that the pupils in his classes will also reflect some measure of this insecurity. If the teachers are not sure of themselves, their training, and their community roles, the result will again be seen in jittery pupils. I believe that evidence can be found in the high rates of truancy, expulsion, withdrawal, and delinquency (particularly in the large city high schools where relationships are apt to be impersonal and anonymous), that the level of frustration tolerance of the school staff has been significantly lowered. Unless the teacher emerges from this exciting and promising period of debate and criticism as a stronger and more secure person, irreparable harm will have been done to large segments of the youth population. It is platitudinous to preach, but nonetheless true, that the high school cannot be any better than its teachers. Whatever role and status the high-school teacher now enjoys or suffers is partly attained and partly attributed. But the limits of what can be attained are set only by the teacher's own self-concept.

THE UNDETERMINED AND UNSPECIFIED GOALS

While there is much learning activity visible in every American high school, not every teacher and student is always aware of the goals toward which the activity is directed. Rarely does the high-school staff explore and examine with the rest of the community, including the students, just what they want the secondary school to perpetuate beyond the simple and comfortable vagary of "the healthy and good citizen of a democracy." The result is that students, through their daily activities and assignments, aim only to please teacher or, stated negatively, to avoid the displeasure of the teacher, rather than to achieve some worthwhile objective *per se*. The extrinsic rewards of the mentor's smile, the marks on the report forms, and the honor roll can be unhealthy substitutes for real goals.

School personnel and the lay community need to arrive at some consensus on those issues basic to our American way of life that will help describe the kinds of persons we want and will need in our fast-changing world. In arriving at some statement of desirable school outcomes we will need to know more about the kind of society we want now and in the future. How nationalistic or internationalistic should the future citizen of the United States and of the world be? How religious or non-religious? How competitive and how cooperative? How leisure- and how work-oriented? How individualistic and how socialistic? Unless the school and community can look ahead with some clarity of goals in what is a rapidly changing and perhaps unpredictable world, secondary schools—goal-less and directionless—can become educationally anachronistic. In transmitting the culture and heritage of the past the high school may stand rooted in the past, but the high school must also face up to its full responsibility for improving the way of life of the future.

SUCCESS IN ACADEMIC ACHIEVEMENT

Status in school is always linked to successful achievement in the classroom. For the adolescent, one source (often the only source) of teacher-parent approval can be found in academic achievement via the report card route. Unless the student shows a satisfactory level of attainment, he is not apt to find himself surrounded by smiling and approving adult faces.

School failure is frequently a concomitant and forerunner of deviant behavior. Studies of delinquents and nondelinquents indicate a wide split between the educationally bankrupt and the educationally affluent. Delinquents frequently make a success of failure by using this means to thumb their noses at the home and school.

It is easy to understand how failure can be used to strike back at the teaching authority, or to demolish the school, by students whose neighborhood or peer group value system is contrary to that of the school or of the dominant society; it may not be so easy to understand how the upper middle-class child can use failure as a powerful weapon to cut down his parents. When school success becomes a paramount issue to the parent who draws selfishly his own brand of personal satisfactions from the achievement of his youngsters, academic failure can prove a subtle and satisfactory boomerang for any youngster. In fact, this is one of the few ways that many high-school adolescents have of getting back at their own offensive parents.

How to insure success for the less academic or "non-academic" pupil in the high school presents a difficult curriculum problem. Until this issue is met by the secondary school of the future, many of the students who must enter high school will run the risk of breaking their backs as they reach for unattainable goals. When satisfactions that can come only through achievement, success, and approval are not attainable, the youngster may well resort to other means to achieve some measure of these satisfactions. These means may frequently follow the antisocial route of misbehavior.

EXTERNAL AND FORMAL DISCIPLINE

The future high school, if it is to diminish deviate behavior, must aim to develop inner behavioral controls that will make its graduates less dependent on the supervising, monitoring, and policing authority. Self-discipline as contrasted with external-control dependency has been the aim of the secondary school, but this aim can hardly be attained so long as the school culture continues to dominate with adult controls and continues to tell the student what to do, when to do it, how to do it, and whether it is right when done. Such heavy dependence upon forces of external and formal discipline tends to deepen misunderstanding and resentment that exist between youth and adult and to intensify the hate and hostility now manifest in much of the deviate behavior in youth culture. Both the sociologist and the psychiatrist have independently come to the conclusion that the culture of formal and external controls, when it succeeds, frequently creates a reluctant and recalcitrant conformist living close to the letter of the law. When it fails, it creates "the outlaw" best exemplified by the overt, aggressive delinquent who is a member of an "outlaw gang" in the depths of the big city.

SUMMARY STATEMENT

These and other cultural determinants found operating in most public secondary schools will continuously precipitate crises, tensions, and frustrations for the high-school student. David Segel has pointed out three kinds of behavior solutions that can follow on frustration in the high school: (1) regression as exemplified by school leaving; (2) aggression as seen in disorderly conduct, overt attack, and vandalism; (3) fixation as found in the sitting out of the school activities or going through the motions.

Of all these behavior solutions to inimical school situations, perhaps the most wholesome or promising will be found in the overt-aggression pattern in which the delinquent is doing something about it. He is putting up a fight. He is adjusting the best

and usually the only way he knows how. He is calling our attention to himself and to his problem situation. He is not retreating,
nor is he giving up, nor is he resorting to fantasy in solving his
terrible problem. There is much that is positive—even wholesome
—in the delinquency phenomenon. Needless to say, this is not
well understood generally and can be readily misunderstood.

Knowledge of these cultural contingencies of behavior and
misbehavior in the high school will enable the professional youth
worker in school and community, together with the parent and
the pupil, to plan cultural change. By changing the behavior of
large masses of young people, the great American secondary
school of the future may even be able to change and influence
the culture of the community. If the secondary school fails to
have any widespread effect on the behavior of the masses of
youth, it will suffer the awful tragedy of the most expensive
irrelevancy of the mid-twentieth century.

THE SANTA BARBARA COUNTY HIGH SCHOOLS

WORK EDUCATION PROGRAM

Myron S. Olson

If your 1954 graduating class was typical, there were many
graduates who were hoping to enter the professions; far more
than will be accepted by the professional schools. There were also
many "hoping to be" radio announcers, newspaper editors, busi-

SOURCE: Myron S. Olson, "The Santa Barbara County High Schools
Work Education Program," *Journal of Secondary Education*, Vol. 35,
October, 1960, pp. 330–336. Reprinted by permission.

ness managers, movie actors, disc jockeys, salesmen, ranchers, doctors, lawyers and dentists; many of these ambitions will never mature.

We have had these boys and girls for twelve years and yet many of their ambitions are unrealistic. Why? One city school official recently stated that one half of that city's graduates would be misfits on their jobs. Why?

Youth of today have many doors closed to them which were open to our generation. Most urban youth do not even have the opportunity to watch their own fathers at work. They have little opportunity to see what a professional, business, or skilled adult worker actually does. Many have no actual work experience before entering the armed services. When they are released from service they often take the first job available to enable them to marry or become a wage earner. Here they many times remain as misfits and discontents.

We have tests, literature, "career days" and other short-lived experiences to aid us in counseling and guiding these youth, but these alone have evidently not been sufficiently effective. Do not these youth need day by day realistic experiences in adult society during their last year in high school? Have we really made use of our available community resources?

Realistic planning and choices cannot be based only on classroom experiences. In fact, very few of the teachers of those classes have had recent prolonged experiences in business, industry, or a profession other than teaching. Are these teachers able to direct the student's understanding of modern free enterprise, labor-management relationships, our country's tax burden, governmental red tape, and employer-employee relationships? Yet, these students must make a choice of a vocation or profession soon after graduation.

Some schools and communities are in the process of doing more about this. They are opening almost as many exploratory possibilities for youth as there are good adults in the community.

Many schools in the United States have found "work experiences" for a small proportion of students in the distributive occupations or in diversified fields for those who may not go on to college. Now high schools in Santa Barbara County are also providing opportunities for youth to work side by side for a sizable portion of the school day throughout the senior year with teachers, doctors, lawyers, furriers, architects, bankers, attorneys, law enforcement officials, clergymen, butchers, jewelers, tailors, mechanics, laboratory technicians, electronic experts, and the like.

These students are closely supervised by school co-ordinators and are jointly rated by the employer and co-ordinator in all of the areas of general education.

Lay citizens who were dubious of the Santa Barbara County Program at first are now praising it. They are complimenting the schools on "meaningful," "realistic" and "worthwhile" education. Labor union officials and management have listened and co-operated.

THE SANTA BARBARA COUNTY
WORK EDUCATION PROGRAM

On February 1, 1953 a five-year study began in the five high schools of Santa Barbara County, California; Carpinteria, Lompoc, Santa Barbara, Santa Maria, and Santa Ynez. A lay-citizen committee was formed in each high school district and a county-wide lay-citizen-school personnel committee agreed to co-ordinate and direct the county-wide program. A professor of secondary education from nearby University of Southern California was secured as Consulting Director for the study. Two full-time Co-ordinators were also added to the Program staff. Under this arrangement, masters' and doctoral students in the University were encouraged to choose their thesis and dissertation problems from within this County study and contribute to the research in the areas of administration, curriculum, and guidance.

Three objectives were uppermost in the minds of all those in the five-year study:

1. How may we aid youth in exploring their own interests, aptitudes, and abilities in business and professional fields of their choosing while they are yet under the direction of the school?

2. How may we aid youth in realistically experiencing status in his community—which each needs; the importance of reliability, initiative, good appearance, accuracy, promptness, confidence of

adults, and the importance of adjusting to young adulthood without violent results?

3. How may we provide application for the courses which we teach in such ways that our curriculum will have new meaning for our students?

In the beginning the child labor and minimum wage laws were interpreted in such a manner that each student was paid a minimum of seventy-five cents per hour (some qualified for sixty) but under this plan the work was repetitive and the jobs limited.

In the fall of 1954 a new interpretation was issued by the appropriate officials which classified these youth as "students" and not "employees" if they entered a business or profession on school time for exploratory and participatory purposes. This allowed them to observe and participate without pay on school time. Now the doors of exploratory opportunity were opened in every direction for every senior student for the school morning or afternoon throughout the school year.

Working side-by-side with a nurse, lawyer, banker, labor leader, doctor, architect, etc., now became a reality. Lay citizens, who were partially skeptical of the capabilities of the modern school's students, soon began to sing their praises. In a few cases, students did not come up to expectations and were counseled on the basis of employer-school co-ordinator evaluations. Some of these latter were moved to areas of vocational or professional choices, which were more in keeping with their abilities and aptitudes.

Students entered community service work—serving with public libraries, community agencies, and with elementary school teachers. In these, too, they explored the vocational possibilities at the same time that they rendered service. These youth gained the confidence of adult leaders in the community who in turn recommended these youth to paid positions or encouraged them to secure further educational or vocational training.

Some visitors ask, "Will youth work day after day without pay?" The youth often reply, "I could work for pay in some job in which I am not interested as a future career, but where could I receive more long-term remuneration than to be able to explore side-by-side with a professional worker in the field of my choice?" The answer is best given through such evidence as students remaining on these non-paid jobs throughout vacations, or remaining at home in the evenings away from the gang reading books which their building contractor, doctor, or lawyer "bosses" have suggested that they read.

This fall some 65 percent of one of the high schools' senior classes requested work education on school time and four out of every five of these chose the "non-pay" type. They will enter the local hospitals to explore the fields of medicine, nursing, X-ray technicians and laboratory technicians. One will work with a local pharmacist, another in a legal office, garage or department store, etc. To be sure, some may work at other paid jobs on Saturdays to obtain spending money but even if paid jobs were available on school time during the week, many students prefer the non-pay work education because of its wider possibilities of exploration and more personal guidance from the co-operating lay citizen.

People in this county who are close to the Program already know what happens to a community using this type of education. The employer or lay citizen begins to better understand the school program and its problems and he serves as a co-educator with the teacher. Weaknesses in formal training of students can lead to changed curriculum emphasis. Community resources and person-nel are made available to a school which no school could provide even with an unlimited budget. Adult citizens work cooperatively. For example, the printer's son is spending his day in the large garage while the son of the mechanic is working side-by-side with a lawyer. All these experiences, which parents could not alone provide are available under the direction of the local high schools which saw the need to bridge the gap between school and community life, between youth and adult activities, between a theoretical and a practical, meaningful education.

The guiding force of this entire study is the county-wide com-mittee composed of outstanding business and labor leaders and the co-operating school administrators and co-ordinators.

There are legal problems such as liability and compensation which are in the process of being solved in co-operation with the State Department of Education, other State Divisions and legal authorities. No school should begin this non-pay activity at the present time without a detailed understanding of the possible involvements and a full approval of its local enforcement officials.

HE THAT HATH A TRADE

Time Magazine

~~~~~~

Posted throughout Dunbar Vocational High School are cards bearing a Ben Franklin motto: "He that hath a trade hath an estate." The exhortation is hardly needed at the rambling tan brick school on Chicago's squalid South Side. To its 2,300 youngsters, 99 percent of them Negro, Dunbar is a life raft in a sea of poverty. It is perhaps the most effective vocational school in the U.S.

Dunbar's importance lies in harsh statistics: 30 percent of U.S. high school students never graduate; the rate hits 50 percent in some blighted urban areas. As automation invades new fields, as unions make old fields tougher to enter, the unskilled dropouts are almost unemployable. Unwanted, they wallow in anger and sometimes crime. The U.S. can ill afford such "social dynamite," wrote James B. Conant recently in *Slums and Suburbs*. At Chicago's Dunbar,[1] Conant was delighted to find just about "the ideal in vocational education."

Dunbar's students get a crack at 28 skills, from welding to aviation electronics. And they get the backing of a school administration, largely Negro, that is fiercely dedicated to upgrading Negroes on the economic scale—first by the best possible training, second by fighting for job opportunities. Assistant Principal Victor D. Lewis recalls, for example, "a big decorating firm downtown that wouldn't hire a Negro, even to clean a brush. Now one of our

[1] Named for Paul Laurence Dunbar, the nineteenth-century Negro poet who wrote:
But it's easy 'nough to titter w'en de stew is smokin' hot,
But hit's mighty ha'd to giggle w'en dey's nuffin' in de pot.

SOURCE: The following article is reprinted by permission from *Time,* The Weekly Newsmagazine; copyright Time, Inc., 1962. *Time* magazine, June 26, 1962.

341

people is a foreman there. We simply produced a good decorator and challenged them to hire him."

TOO BUSY FOR TROUBLE. Dunbar keeps in close touch with the job market, constantly seeks to raise its high level of basic training. The school's 37 shop teachers all have at least ten years outside experience, stay well up on new techniques. Stressing meat-and-potatoes training that will pay off on payday, they talk up the benefits of belonging to a union (many do themselves).

To produce "employable" graduates, Dunbar insists on promptness and tidiness. The students work harder and longer (and drop out less often—the rate is only 7½ percent) than those at many academic high schools. Discipline is well in hand. Future aircraft mechanics are too busy peering into a jet engine, or revving up a mounted piston engine, to get into much trouble. In the auto shop, young tinkerers stay out of trouble with "outside jobs." At Dunbar, a price-wise Chicagoan can get a Cadillac engine overhauled for $160, *v.* $350 at the factory.

Academic work is not skimped: Dunbar requires four years of English, three years of science and social studies, two years of mathematics. The problem is how to make this palatable for future beauticians and bricklayers. Dunbar has a handy solution: it puts all machinist students in the same math class, for example, so the teacher can deal not only with abstractions but also with applications of math to machine tools. Dunbar's graduates also acquire enough academic work to enter college if they wish to (10 percent to 15 percent do). Says Principal Joseph J. Dixon: "We never want to close the door on further education."

PROUD PAY STUBS. Dunbar keeps the door open for dropouts from other Chicago schools, holds afternoon classes for unemployed youngsters in everything from job hunting to repairing electric toasters and preparing for civil service exams. In the evening, it teaches new skills to 3,100 adult students. Moreover, some of Dunbar's teachers have their own outside businesses and hire graduates. "Our problem is not placement," says Dunbar's Assistant Principal Everett M. Renfroe. "It's training more people." Nor do Renfroe and his colleagues fear automation. "We don't think of it as wiping out jobs," says Renfroe, "but as creating new ones."

Dunbar's bulletin boards are full of its graduates' most satisfying diplomas: their first paycheck stubs. Last week one teacher proudly pointed to two more $176 (weekly) stubs, brought in by new bricklayers. "They get dirty after a few weeks," said the teacher. "But I always know there'll be fresh ones."

IMAGES OF THE FUTURE—A NEW APPROACH TO THE SECONDARY SCHOOL

J. Lloyd Trump

ALTERNATIVES IN IMPROVING QUALITY

Some of the proposals made by critics of education are inconsistent and contradictory. Those who would improve the *quality* of education must consider the consequences as well as the alternatives to their suggestions. Here are some criticisms of today's education and some alternative plans:

"STUDENTS NEED TO TAKE MORE ACADEMIC SUBJECTS." This usually refers to the more capable students. The suggestion would cause students either to drop such subjects as music, art, physicial education, practical arts, and some elective courses, or to take six or seven subjects instead of the usual four or five. This latter proposal calls for the addition of two periods to the school day, assuming that classes would con-

---

SOURCE: Trump, J. Lloyd, "Images of the Future—A New Approach to the Secondary School," Commission on the Experimental Study of the Utilization of the Staff in the Secondary School, Ford Foundation, 1959. Reprinted by permission.

tinue to meet five days a week. This would, of course, add considerably to the cost of education and increase the demand for already scarce teachers. Moreover, increasing the number of courses may carry the risk of superficiality.

Alternative: The proposals for the school of the future call for a reduction of time students spend in group instruction. Classes do not meet five days weekly. This flexibility would permit broader study in a variety of fields, or deeper in a few. This would hold true not only for talented youth, but also for slower-learning students. Those students able and interested in doing so could elect more academic subjects. Vocational education programs would also be easier to schedule. The increase in length of the school day and week—when appropriate for selected students—would be carried out in the area of *individual study.*

* * *

"PAY MORE ATTENTION TO GIFTED YOUTH." Suggestions include grouping students more rigorously, organizing curricula on various levels of difficulty, establishing separate schools, and reducing emphasis on extraclass activities. The critics would toughen up on students and institute externally given examinations. Students with lower ability would receive less attention and probably leave school at earlier ages.

Alternative: The organization of instruction proposed in *Images* provides for individual differences more effectively. Talented students will spend at least 40 percent of their time—as much as 12 or more hours a week—in *study* activities with emphasis on creativity, depth, and development of independent learning abilities and habits. This might be better than merely adding content or being tough. At the same time, the less able would not be forced out of school or placed in undesirable situations. Grouping of students to provide more effective instruction also would be possible on a more flexible basis. Above all, providing better for individual students thus provides better for the talented.

* * *

"MEET THE NEEDS OF THE SPACE AGE." Mathematics, science, and foreign language are singled out for special emphasis. The humanities are also mentioned occasionally. Schools are urged to enlarge requirements in these subjects. Relatively little—sometimes nothing—is said about how the subjects are to be taught or how elementary and secondary school programs are to be coordinated.

Alternative: Foreign languages could be more effectively taught with even less time spent in class when students have language laboratory facilities available. Mathematics and science materials, both in general education and at elective levels, will be presented more effectively and efficiently with material aids when teachers have more time to plan, prepare, and evaluate. Fostering interest and developing creativity will be natural outcomes of more emphasis on *individual study* and *small-group discussion*. Making educational facilities available more hours also will help.

❋   ❋   ❋

"IMPROVE THE QUALITY OF TEACHING." Reducing the size of classes is frequently suggested even though research has produced little convincing evidence that a class of 20 is better than one of 25 or 30 students. Other suggestions call for more attention to problem solving, more projects, and more work with individual students. Critics also request improvements in both content and methods of teaching. Following these suggestions would require more time and energy of teachers who already work an average 48 hours a week.

Alternative: Redeploy students and teachers. . . . Students then are grouped according to the purposes and content of instruction. Teachers have time to work on improved teaching because they are with students fewer hours during the week and have help with tasks not requiring the services of a professional teacher.

❋   ❋   ❋

"RAISE PROFESSIONAL STANDARDS OF TEACHERS." Increasing salaries for all teachers largely or completely on the basis of training and experience and insisting on higher certification standards for all persons employed in schools are two suggestions usually made.

Alternative: Provide substantially higher salaries for career teachers and use professional persons only for professional duties. Use other lower salaried personnel, such as clerks and general aides, for work not requiring the services of a teacher. The community can then see that there are differences between professional and nonprofessional services, and that professional services merit considerably higher pay.

* * *

"SOLVE TEACHER SHORTAGE PROBLEMS." Some proposed or implied measures are to recruit and retain more teachers, increase standard class size, lower standards, and eliminate or curtail services.

Alternative: Recognize there are never enough top quality teachers, so it is imperative that professional abilities be used as effectively and efficiently as possible. Experienced career teachers can reach more students. Improve staff recruiting and training as suggested here.

* * *

"LIGHTEN TEACHING LOADS." Critics usually define *load* as the number of students, the number of classes, and the total of school duties. Proposals would reduce the number of students per class rather than reduce the number of classes. Not taken into account are numerous time-consuming, nonprofessional tasks.

Alternative: Although an excessive number of students in *all* classes is undesirable, real relief will come when teachers are with students fewer hours per week as suggested here. Individual differences among teachers also must be recognized when assignments are made. Both material and personal assistance will help free teachers for professional tasks. Frustration from doing subprofessional work can be reduced.

* * *

"IMPROVE SCHOOLS BY ELIMINATING THE INEFFICIENT." Consolidation of schools is recommended so there will be at least 100 or 150 students in each grade. Sometimes little is said about fundamental improvement, even though it is entirely possible to combine several small poor schools into a larger *poor* school.

Alternative: When consolidation is educationally and financially desirable, use the opportunity to improve the consolidated schools by trying new approaches. Avoid mere duplication of the *status quo.* The idea put forth here also can be applied to small schools.

❋ ❋ ❋

"BUILD NEW BUILDINGS OR ADD TO EXISTING ONES." An examination of new construction reveals more standard-sized rooms with the principal changes being more glass, better lights, improved acoustics, and colored walls.

Alternative: Further experimentation is needed to develop flexible, functional, pleasant, and utilitarian facilities. The school building should contribute or adapt to, rather than inhibit, reorganization of classes and methods of instruction.

❋ ❋ ❋

"INCREASE FINANCIAL SUPPORT." Suggestions basically call for spending more funds for the same kind of organization and staffing that exist today in order to serve greatly increased numbers of students. The principal change suggested is to give all teachers an across-the-board pay raise, based solely on training and experience.

Alternative: Further experimentation is needed to discover more effective and efficient ways of spending money to improve the quality of instruction and teacher satisfaction. A number of such suggestions are included in this pamphlet.

CURRICULUM AND CLASS SCHEDULES

Much more emphasis will be placed on training students to check their own progress. Students will be able to make more immediate self-appraisals, using a variety of machines and self-marking tests, instead of waiting for teachers to grade their work. Obviously, there also will be independent evaluation by the faculty, but this will occupy a less important position than it

ORGANIZATION OF INSTRUCTION

Teaching-Learning Experiences:

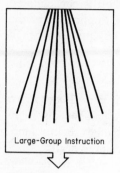

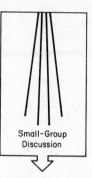

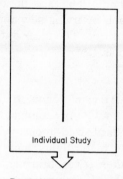

Introduction
Motivation
Explanation
Planning
Group Study
Enrichment
Generalization
Evaluation

PLACE

Auditorium, little theater,
cafeteria, study hall, classrooms joined via television
or remodeling, other large
room

about 40 percent

Group examination of
terms and concepts
and solution of
problems

Reach areas of
agreement and
disagreement

Improve inter-
personal relations

PLACE

Conference room,
classroom

about 20 percent

Read

Listen to records and tapes

View, Question, Analyze,
Think

Experiment, Examine,
Investigate, Consider
Evidence

Write, Create, Memorize,
Record, Make

Visit

Self-appraise

PLACE

Library, laboratories, workshops, project and materials
centers, museums — inside
or outside the school plant

about 40 percent

does now. Teachers will have more time to plan and conduct
evaluations that will be helpful to students in showing progress
toward achieving *all* the purposes of instruction rather than
merely the possession of facts, the principal area of evaluation
at present.

The school will do less scheduling of students in 40- to 55-minute class periods. A student absorbed in work on a project will more frequently not have to stop when a bell rings at the end of a relatively short period. He will be able to continue his work instead of going on to something perhaps quite unrelated which often seems less interesting and less important. Possibly no bells will ring in the school of the future.

Today's school schedules students tightly so that they go from one class or study hall to another, six or more periods a day, with the same periods repeated five days a week. Students now spend about six hours a week on each of five subjects. These six hours per subject usually involve attending a daily 50- to 55-minute class session, plus approximately 20 minutes of work daily in study hall or at home. In the case of 40-minute class sessions, students are expected to do about 30 to 35 minutes of outside preparation. This means that students spend some 30 hours a week in school, not including time at extraclass activities, or in the homeroom.

The school of the future will schedule students in class groups an average of only 18 hours a week, instead of the present 30 hours. Twelve of the 18 hours will be spent in *large-group instruction* (100 or more students) and six will be spent in *small-group discussions* (12 to 15 students). In addition to these 18 hours, the average student will be scheduled for about 12 hours a week in *individual study*. Most students will continue to spend about 30 hours a week on their regular subjects, as they do now, but it also will be possible for them to spend more.

Students who do not have out-of-school jobs or heavy activity schedules often will spend as much as 20 or 24 hours weekly, instead of the average 12 hours, in *individual study*. The number of hours and locations of independent study will vary with the needs and the capacities of individual students. Using recommendations of teachers and counselors, individual schedules will be worked out by electronic devices. Although there will be flexibility in scheduling, the school will continue to know where its students are and what they are doing. Students will have adult supervision as needed.

The 12 hours a week spent in *large-group instruction* will be divided among the subject areas as seems desirable. Experience and judgment will determine how many hours yearly are desirable in such fields as mathematics, science, foreign language, history, English, physical education, music, practical arts, or general education. Similarly, experience will determine the optimum length of time, the frequency, and in what portion of the school day these large groups should be scheduled. The same policies will apply to scheduling the six hours a week of small *discussion* groups. Some of these periods will be 20 to 30 minutes, others will be longer.

An underlying purpose of the school will be to develop ability to study, think, and solve problems, in contrast to today's emphasis on memorizing facts. In large groups, small-group discussions, and individual study, the emphasis will be put on the goal of helping the student develop the ability to solve problems on his own.

PROMISING PRACTICES IN EDUCATION

Robert S. Gilchrist

Two years ago last fall I was asked to discuss "promising innovations in secondary education" for the University of Chicago conference on the American high school.[1] . . .

But how did I determine what constitutes a "promising practice"? Well, I decided to ask four questions which have to do with the larger problems I have hinted at. These questions are:

[1] Reported in *The High School in a New Era* (Chicago: University of Chicago Press, 1959).

SOURCE: Robert S. Gilchrist, "Promising Practices in Education," *Phi Delta Kappan*, February, 1960. Reprinted by permission.

1. What are life's demands upon children now and what will they be in the foreseeable future?

2. What are the values that America holds dear and which our society expects the schools to perpetuate and strengthen?

3. In the light of the vast amount of research already performed in the area of developmental needs, what can the school do to promote the best development of children and youth?

4. What practices measure up in terms of what we know about the learning process?

I applied these four questions in five areas about which I want to talk.

The first of these areas is curriculum content. As one illustration, in the field of science and math the National Science Foundation and other groups are stimulating the schools in our country to take a new look at these subjects. Max Beberman at the University of Illinois and Jerrold Zacharias at M.I.T., to mention only two people, are assuming leadership in changing our science and math curricula. One of the significant things they are doing, in terms of the above four questions, is to allow youngsters to discover principles for themselves. Thus science and mathematics cease to be dead, cut-and-dried subjects, as they too often are now, especially at the senior high level, where youngsters merely learn in a somewhat repetitive way what scientists have discovered in earlier years. . . .

Harry C. Kelly of the National Science Foundation says science should be an integrated kind of course in our secondary schools, with individual laboratory work and discovery more pronounced than now. At the University of Illinois Laboratory School, for instance, each youngster in the eleventh and twelfth grades has a little cubicle of his own in the science suite. He is a budding scientist, himself, while he is learning. . . .

Since Sputnik, we have had pressures to teach people more and more, faster and faster. We have had more and more emphasis on testing programs. The easiest kinds of tests to make are facts and skills tests, as you well know. I think there is a dangerous possibility that we are shifting into a superficial kind of education where facts and skills learned in a rote, repetitive way may be too much a part of our educational program. I hope that this is *not* the case. I hope that we are recognizing that there are different levels of outcomes. Facts and skills are tremendously important. But facts and skills, related to each other in such a way that people understand concepts and generalizations and in order that they master a problem-solving approach, are more important. We must always remember that our democratic way of life calls on each one of us to think for himself rather than that we permit someone to tell us what to believe.

Now let me shift into another area, the language arts, foreign language, and social studies. In the language arts, the National Council of Teachers of English is taking definite positions that we give youngsters much more practice in communicating with each other in correct and acceptable and meaningful ways; that we delay the teaching of grammar until a time when youngsters can utilize formal study of the subject in a functional way. . . .

There is great emphasis upon the theme that individuals will never learn to write and express themselves effectively unless they have practice, and that you can't have practice that leads anywhere unless someone helps you understand where and how what you are doing is bad and where it is good. This means that some understanding person has to read what you write; therefore, the emphasis is upon a written composition once a week or once every two weeks, with the insistence that it be read by a mature adult who knows how to advise the writer.

Perhaps the most dramatic revolution that is taking place is in foreign language instruction. I am nearly dizzy with trying to keep up with what is happening. It seems that the oral-aural approach to the teaching of language is actually being accepted as sound, even by the old-line academic high-school foreign language teachers. It further seems that colleges are dropping their formal grammar tests for entrance and will increasingly test whether a person actually has command of a second language. . . .

NO "GROWING EDGE" FOUND IN SOCIAL STUDIES

I feel that we have not as yet discovered a very good growing edge in social studies. . . .

Somehow, I am afraid, we have not related social studies

teaching too concretely to citizenship in this country. Frankly, I have not discovered too many promising practices in social studies, except that in certain pupil participation programs I am sure that many of our schools are doing a very good job.

For the last four or five years, the students at Scottsbluff have earned enough money to send five youngsters to different countries of Europe and spend a year there. They have had eight students from abroad spend a year in their high school as well. It seems to me that Scottsbluff believes that international understanding, as an objective of social studies, cannot be obtained from textbooks alone. I know of some programs where students are going abroad in the summer with the help of their high schools. . . .

Out in San Francisco at the Polytechnic High School there is an electronics lab that industry helps support. Youngsters work on science there after school, and they go in on Saturday and in the summer. At Cranbrook School, a private school near Detroit, arts and industrial arts labs are kept open after school hours. Doubtless some other schools have similar programs.

These developments illustrate the fact that an old concept is giving way, and I am glad it is. I refer to the notion that what you learn has to be something in a fixed, rigid curriculum, and that you do your living outside of the places where you do your learning.

Summer sessions are developing rapidly, too. This means we can no longer think of educating all youngsters in so many neat nine-month packages. If a student goes to a few summer school sessions, he may graduate a year early unless parents and school people decide that he isn't mature enough and help him understand that he ought to enrich his program instead of accelerating.

I would say in summary that both at the elementary level and at the secondary level there is a pronounced trend toward individualization of education. . . .

I want to mention a danger, though. Grouping plans are widely adopted, as you know. . . .

The emphasis on education for the gifted has given impetus to the movement. I think that the Evanston, Illinois, Elementary School District #65 has a good answer for the advocates of grouping. Research conducted in the Evanston system shows that grouping may increase achievement, but it also indicates that if you group only part of the day, three periods for an hour-and-a-half a week, achievement also increases; or if you just leave children heterogeneously grouped and work at treating the students as individuals the achievement will still increase! At the secondary level there is even more team teaching experimentation. Evanston is doing quite a bit of it. For instance, in biology the Evanston High School has ninety-six youngsters divided into A and B groups. Once a week, at least, all ninety-six are together. About twice a week half of them are in a lecture section. There are then two other sections with about twenty-two people each in lab groups. There is some time when still smaller groups are with individual teachers. Again, the goal of the experiment is to discover whether, with the same amount of outlay, you can do a better job with team teaching.

Actually, three goals are being tested in team teaching. One is to see whether there are some things that can be taught just as well in a large group.

The second goal is to see if there are special skills of teachers which can be used better than we traditionally use them. Maybe there are some teachers who are especially good at remedial work—English teachers, for instance, gifted in helping youngsters with speech difficulties.

The third goal is to see whether children with different achievement and ability levels in different aspects of a course can be regrouped in terms of different phases of the activities of the course.

ELECTRONIC AIDS

There is a third area in methods that I can discuss only briefly; this is the use of electronic aids. We are all aware of the stratovision experiment, in which an airplane over Lafayette, Indiana, will send out televised programs which can be received in the schools of six Midwest states. This has broad possibilities, but we must always judge every TV program to see that it is more valuable than the experience it replaces. In another example, out in Nebraska, there is a less spectacular project which seems to be a good thing. Television carries high-school subjects to little hamlets in Nebraska from the University of Nebraska, where the project is sponsored. A youngster can in this way take an advanced science course with a teacher who may not be thoroughly competent in science.

Without discussing all the different aspects of television and radio instruction, and without enumerating the many real uses and advantages of the new learning machines and language laboratories, I would like to echo something said recently by William Alexander of Peabody, president of the Association for Supervision and Curriculum Development. He suggested that if we are smart enough to utilize automation and electronic equipment where it is appropriate in large groups, and where it helps in providing a variety of experiences for different individuals, if we capitalize on these new developments for good ends, then we can free ourselves to work with children and provide genuinely individualized education. But if we somehow forget about the human element, the need in teaching for a warm, friendly child-adult relationship, then these new developments will not be good for education.

It is a little harder to choose a single outstanding development in methods at the secondary level, but if anything there is a bigger ferment there. First, of course, is the guidance area. Dr. Conant has convinced the American people of the need for more guidance in our secondary schools. He emphasizes the need for the technically trained guidance person. I would like to stress the importance of having teachers who know children intimately and who know the parents. A few educators are insisting that a child has a right to be known by some faculty member. Some schools are striving for this goal.

A "HOME BASE" FOR SECONDARY STUDENT

A development in methods to implement this concept would give the child a "home base" in school and a home base teacher. The idea is propounded by two Californians, Charles W. Bursch of the State Department of Public Instruction and John Lyon

Reid, a San Francisco architect, in *High Schools—Today and Tomorrow*.[2]

These men find they must deal with curriculum as they discuss school buildings. What they say is consistent with what Kim Wiles and Franklin Patterson propose in an ASCD booklet, *The High School We Need*.[3] I predict that the high school of the future will have basic rooms in it with basic teachers. . . .

They say each youngster deserves an office just as much as ·his dad does. Going to school is business to him. It should be serious business. So they give him a little partition-type office.

About fifty of these offices constitute a suite, and the students' basic teacher works in that suite with them. If it is a three-year senior high school, the basic teacher and those fifty children go through high school together for three years. The teacher will probably teach these children in some areas of their general education. He will know the parents of all these children. He will help the students plan summer trips or help them get summer jobs. He will be their guidance officer, the person who keeps them on the track, a central and continuing influence in the establishment of individual values and goals.

You see, this illustrates what Will French once said to me, "We need a revolution in secondary education. . . ."

This concept of secondary education is a radical shift. In it you build a secondary program around the goals and aims of an individual arrived at by each pupil in cooperation with his parents and his basic teacher. The youngster goes out to the laboratories over the school and learns. The difference is that when he goes to science he knows why he is there. He doesn't simply have a kind of a blind faith, along with his parents, that if he takes physics for a year he is going to have a year of physics education.

Another development is the "little school" movement. Many of you live near some district that is divided into little schools. There are examples in Azusa, California; Fairfield, Connecticut;

[2] Charles W. Bursch and John Lyon Reid, *High Schools—Today and Tomorrow*. New York: Reinhold Publishing Co., 1957.

[3] ASCD Commission on the Education of Adolescents, Kimball Wiles and Franklin Patterson, *The High School We Need*. Washington: Association for Supervision and Curriculum Development, 1959.

Syosset, New York. This concept is a recognition that we should not lose secondary school children in a great mass of humanity.

There are many new and different specific programs related to or affecting methodology. The advanced placement program, for example, recognizes that there is nothing sacred about the typical high-school curriculum. Some students ought to be having experiences beyond it. As another example, some schools now offer algebra in the eighth grade to some of their youngsters, and others are considering the "unified math" which is proving successful at the university level. In this approach students learn elements of algebra, geometry, and advanced mathematics as they solve increasingly difficult problems which require several types of math in their solution. Developments like this are breaking down the stereotype of secondary education.

Another development is the science seminars.

CURRICULUM DEVELOPMENT

In closing, I want to discuss two related areas. I have talked about curriculum. I am convinced that unless we have really dynamic programs of curriculum development under way in our school systems, education cannot move forward as fast as these times demand. I am convinced that the classroom teacher has to be involved in curriculum development. True, he has to work with the people in the school system who do not teach classes, and with the college professors, the state department leaders, and others. But we can't get along without teachers in planning the curriculum—not if we want to plan it in terms of children's growth and development, and have it tailor-made for the needs of individuals. Therefore I believe that each teacher has to be engaged in an appraisal program.

Each teacher each year needs to have his goals pretty clearly in mind. He has to propose what to do during the year in order to achieve those goals, and then he has to carry on an evaluation program by which he finds out how well he has been achieving them. The principal and the supervisor and the superintendent and the rest of us should help the teacher expedite this process of appraisal. Sometimes a weakness discovered in this process can be corrected by development of a new sequence in social studies; sometimes an in-service education course in mathematics will fill a gap. Whatever it is, this is a sound procedure for determining our curriculum development and instructional improvement programs. . . .

COMMUNICATION

We must be more articulate, as educators, if we are going to give leadership to education. We must be able to talk with our citizen friends, helping them clarify their thinking about the kind of schools they want for their children. . . .

A SCHOOL OF THE FUTURE IN OPERATION

Dorsey Baynham

Ridgewood High School, Norridge, Illinois, is a working model of the complete school blueprint developed by the NASSP-established, Ford-financed Commission on the Utilization of the Staff in the Secondary School. Other schools from Massachusetts to California have adapted segments of the commission's recommendations, but Ridgewood was planned, built, and now functions in accordance with ideas which grew out of the commission's four-year research project. A summary report of the project *Focus on Change*, was published last month.

SOURCE: Dorsey Baynham, "A School of the Future in Operation," *Phi Delta Kappan*, February, 1960. Reprinted by permission.

The new school opened its doors last fall to 425 freshman and sophomore students from three suburban communities located about fifteen miles northwest of Chicago. Designed to hold 1,000 students, it will expand to include grade eleven in 1961–62 and grade twelve in 1962–63.

Other statistics include the fact that the school cost $2 million, including equipment. The basic contract was $13.50 per square foot, without equipment, a low figure for high schools in this area. The budgeted per pupil cost for 1960–61 was about the same as that for other nearby schools.

A first step in any new secondary school, apparently, is the building up of student morale. For Ridgewood, this was doubly necessary. Not only would its students be pulled from the security of well-known schools and established routines; they would also be thrust into a strange, new building with stranger still classes and schedules, one period listening to a lecture with more than 100 other students, the next period joining a discussion group of only ten or twelve.

The staff also outlined five beliefs basic to Ridgewood's curriculum planning and their implications for the school's teaching and learning. . . .

Here are the five beliefs:

1. The unique purpose of education is development of intellectual powers.

2. Basic skills, knowledge, and appreciations should be attained by each person to the highest level possible.

3. An important aim of the school is to develop each individual's capacity to assume more and more responsibility for his own education. Intellectual development must not cease when the student leaves school.

4. Every area of human knowledge has significant contributions to make to each student's intellectual growth. Thus, students should *continuously* participate in learning activities in the humanities, mathematics, science, practical and creative arts, and health and physical education.

5. The rate of progress through the school should be determined by the readiness of the individual to move from one stage to the next. The stages do not necessarily synchronize with pupil age.

To translate these beliefs into action, Ridgewood's master schedule calls for pupils spending, on the average, 35 percent of their time in large-group instruction, 30 percent in seminars and laboratories, and 35 percent in individual study. (It is sometimes a source of wonderment to commission members that the project recommendations today are known primarily as "large-class" recommendations. Small classes and individual study are equally important commission recommendations, with the latter being perhaps the single most important characteristic of projected "schools of the future," especially for academically talented or highly creative students.)

Ridgewood was built with special facilities for the three types of learning—large classrooms for large, so-called lecture groups; small classrooms for small discussion groups; and individual study areas, some of which contain individual study booths. Ridgewood offers the sharpest contrast to older schools in its study areas. There are ten: the foreign language, homemaking, and reading laboratories; the science and humanities resource centers; the art rooms; the typing room; the music area; the mathematics study groups; and the library. Each study area is located next door to or right across the hall from the staff office for its particular study subject. At least one staff member is always available for student consultation or guidance. Also, each study area is furnished with its own specific equipment, books, and study resources. This allows the science student to proceed on science projects, the home economics student to design her own clothes, and the art student (and also those who seek merely an appreciation of the arts) to hear taped music and to explore the cultures of the world.

Ridgewood's study arrangements allow a one-to-one pupil-teacher ratio. Certainly they bear little similarity to most study halls, where a teacher, instead of teaching, stands guard at the head of a long line of desks. . . .

Study booths are used to great advantage by the more self-directed students, but teachers are wary of permitting their use by gregarious pupils.

The school's large classrooms, big enough to hold about 125 students, are equipped with rows of auditorium seats with arm rests. Overhead screens, microphones, tape recorders, and curtains to eliminate light are regular equipment. Installations are ready for closed circuit television but this is a project for the future.

Small discussion classrooms are only large enough to seat fifteen students and a teacher around a big discussion table.

Ridgewood's staff is made up of twenty-one professional teachers, six instruction assistants, three clerical assistants, and three part-time general aides for such non-professional tasks as mimeographing, record keeping, and cafeteria supervision. For the purpose of curriculum planning, the school's professional teachers have been divided into two divisions, humanities and sciences, with two teaching teams in each division. The humanities division plans courses of study for English, history, art, music, and foreign languages; the sciences division for science, mathematics, practical arts, physical education and business education.

SCHOOL ORGANIZATION PLAN

The school's organizational plan for instruction is a pyramid in shape, with the four teaching teams at its base. Directly above the teams are an administrative assistant who is responsible for attendance and business management; and a director of guidance, who acts as testing consultant to all teams and whose responsibilities includes personal, vocational, and educational counseling. The next three levels of the pyramid are, respectively, the assistant superintendent for instruction, the superintendent, and the seven-member school board.

The school's outlined plan for organization at instruction states: "The organization plan at Ridgewood High School encourages teacher cooperation across subject-matter lines, so the students may achieve a depth of understanding not usually possible." And, "The management portion of the principal's job has to a large extent been delegated to an administrative assistant, thus freeing the assistant superintendent and the director of guidance to work directly with the teaching teams in improving instruction." . . .

Most members of the teaching staff are quite young, or perhaps they just seem that way because of their zeal for what they're doing. Each one went through an extended two-way interview with Superintendent Howard, lasting several days, before there was mutual agreement that the applicant would fit into the new school staff. Science teachers came straight from the National Science Foundation. . . .

Last summer Ridgewood's teaching teams made extensive plans during a month-long workshop. They emphasized a unified approach to subject matter in the respective areas, but they also spent a great deal of time and deliberation on plans for crossing subject matter lines wherever possible.

At the high school today most teachers are scheduled for class instructional activities for slightly more than half the time that school is in session. The remainder of their time, divided into blocks of one hundred minutes or more, permits other professional activities, uninterrupted time for preparation and study, and time for consulting with individual students. While there are comparatively few meetings of the staff as a whole, there are division meetings almost daily. The science staff, also, meets daily. . . . How do the students feel about this strange new school? As far as they're concerned, by now it is neither strange nor new.

The Saturday Review of Literature

~~~~~~

A SUMMARY OF NEA RECOMMENDATIONS

√ Local school boards are the legal instruments through which the state fulfills its responsibility for education. The distinction between lay control of school policies determined by the board of education and implementation of these policies by the professional staff, with the leadership of the local superintendent, should be delineated, understood, and respected.

√ Local school faculties should have the freedom and the authority to make decisions about what to teach—within state and local requirements—and how to teach. Final instructional decisions should be made by the teacher, taking into consideration recommendations from appropriate local, state, and national groups representing the teaching profession, academic scholars, and the public.

√ State legislatures should set forth general goals for the schools, provide adequate financial support, and delegate broad powers of implementation to the state and local educational authorities. The state legislature should *not* prescribe curriculum content or legislate specific courses.

√ School systems should allocate an appropriate proportion of their annual operating budgets—not less than 1 percent—for the support of research, experimentation, and innovation. Adequate time should be provided for each staff member to participate in curriculum planning, research, evaluation, and other activities designed to improve the instructional program.

SOURCE: "NEA Project on Instruction," *The Saturday Review of Literature,* October 19, 1963. Reprinted by permission.

√ Priorities for the school are the teaching of skills in reading, composition, listening, speaking (both native and foreign languages), and computation . . . ways of creative and disciplined thinking, including methods of inquiry and application of knowledge . . . competence in self-instruction and independent learnings . . . fundamental understanding of the humanities and the arts, the social and natural sciences, and mathematics . . . appreciation of and discriminating taste in literature, music, and the visual arts . . . instruction in health and physical education.

√ Rational discussion of controversial issues should be an important part of the school program. The teacher should help students identify relevant information, learn techniques of critical analysis, make independent judgments, and be prepared to present and support them. The teacher should also help students become sensitive to the continuing need for objective re-examination of issues in the light of new information and changing conditions in society.

√ The school curriculum should include a study of political and social ideologies focusing upon Communism. The methods of rational inquiry should be stressed. The study should be set in the perspective of the modern world and be incorporated into the instructional program at appropriate points. If a special unit on Communism is deemed desirable in the secondary school, it should supplement and complement earlier study of these topics. As with other areas of the curriculum, decisions about *what to teach* and *how to teach* about these topics should be based upon policies developed by school administrators and teachers of the local school system. In the formulation and implementation of such policies, school personnel should utilize the resources of scholarship and be supported in their decisions by the school board and by an informed community opinion.

√ The objectives of the school, with a clear statement of priorities, should give direction to all curriculum planning. This applies to adding content, eliminating content, or changing the emphases on various topics and fields of study.

√ The public, through the local school board, is responsible for determining the broad aim of education. The professional staff is responsible for translating the broad aims into specific objectives that indicate priorities and define clearly the behaviors intended for the learners. The local board of education has responsibility for seeing that an acceptable statement of objectives and priorities is prepared and for endorsing such a statement.

√ The fact that very young children *can* learn relatively difficult aspects of science, mathematics, and other subjects is at best an incomplete answer to the question of whether they *should* learn them at this particular stage of their development. Decisions about *when to teach what* should be based on both the learner's ability to understand and the relative importance of alternative ways of using the learner's time at any given point in his school experience.

√ The vertical organization of the school should provide for the continuous, unbroken, upward progression of all learners, with due recognition of the wide variability among learners in every aspect of their development. The school organization should, therefore, provide for differentiated rates and means of progression toward achievement of educational goals. Nongrading and multi-grading are promising alternatives to the traditional graded school and should be given careful consideration in seeking to provide flexible progress plans geared to human variability.

√ Well-planned cooperative efforts among teachers—efforts such as team teaching, for example—should be encouraged and tested.

√ The use of educational television (ETV) and radio, to broaden and deepen learnings, should be encouraged. Such use should be accompanied by a vigorous program of research and experimentation.

√ Schools should make use, with proper supervision, of self-instructional materials and devices (programed instruction) that facilitate varied learning opportunities and continuous progress for learners of widely divergent abilities. The use of programed instruction should be accompanied by a vigorous program of research and experimentation.

√ New concepts of space should permit and encourage: (1) varying sized groups ranging from small seminars to multiple-

class; (2) independent study with visual and/or acoustic privacy
as required; (3) access to a variety of instructional media; (4)
multiple use.

A DEMONSTRATION GUIDANCE PROJECT

Henry T. Hillson

The Board of Education of the City of New York adopted a
program four years ago to increase educational opportunity in
the public schools of the city. The program followed from a
recommendation of a subcommittee of the Board's Commission
on Integration, and was known as the Demonstration Guidance
Project.

The primary purpose of the project was to identify and up-
grade potential college students coming from a background of
limited cultural experiences. The program was formulated and
counseled by the Bureau of Educational and Vocational Guidance of the New York City School System. The College Entrance
Examination Board sponsored and helped finance the program
from its inception.

The first three years of the Demonstration Guidance Project
at George Washington High School have been completed with
the graduation of the first project class in June 1960. This has
been one of the most intensive experimental programs ever undertaken by the Board of Education of New York City. It has
enlisted the cooperative assistance of many groups and agencies;

SOURCE: Henry T. Hillson, "A Demonstration Guidance Project," from
Proceedings of the National Association for Secondary-School Principals, 45th Annual Convention, 1961. Reprinted by permission.

it has been followed with keen interest by educators throughout this country and abroad. It has been of particular concern to all those who are grappling with the many-sided problem of improving the educational achievement of pupils with backgrounds that have not been conducive to full educational development.

THE NATURE OF THE CLASS

The first group of students selected for the experiment entered the George Washington High School in September 1957, and graduated in June 1960. Two other classes in the experiment still remain in the school; one will graduate in June 1961, and one in June 1962. This report deals with the records and achievements of the first project class that graduated.

In order to appreciate the progress that the students in this first graduating class made during their three years in George Washington High School, it is necessary to keep in mind certain facts concerning them when they were admitted in September 1957 from the junior high school. The group consisted of 148 boys and girls. Its ethnic composition was as follows: 87 Negroes, 36 Puerto Ricans, 1 Oriental, and 24 others. Since the project was experimental in nature, many students were included although their records indicated that they had little or no chance of succeeding in academic work. The group was thus thoroughly heterogeneous.

The nature of the group can be seen from their junior high-school test data—their intelligence quotients measured by verbal tests, ranged from 70–141; 70 percent had IQs below 100; 89 percent were below grade level in reading, and 88 percent below grade level in arithmetic. The *Iowa Tests of Educational Development,* given at George Washington High School in January 1958, showed 72 percent below the 50th percentile in social studies background; 70 percent below that level in correctness in writing; 63 percent below in general vocabulary; and 80 percent below in quantitative thinking. At the other end of the scale, 6 percent of the group had an IQ of 120 and above; 5 percent was one year or more above grade level in reading; and 3 percent was one year and above grade level in arithmetic.

In the *Iowa Tests,* in the four categories indicated above, the group was 12 percent, 15 percent, 16 percent, and 10 percent, respectively, above the 70th percentile.

Many of the students in the project came from homes with serious family problems. Almost half the pupils had lost one or both parents. Poverty was a common denominator in the group.

In view of this situation, it is not surprising that many of them were badly handicapped by emotional problems that required careful diagnosis and treatment. Many of the students in the class were deficient in the basic skills of reading, writing, and computing, and were unaccustomed to meeting the normal requirements of academic work—the doing of homework, the completion of long-range assignments, the budgeting of time, *etc.*

THE SPECIAL PROGRAM

If any expectations of the experiment were to be realized, it was apparent from the beginning that a tremendous amount of individual attention would have to be given to the pupils to compensate for their deficiencies. Both in their subject classes and in their guidance program, the needs of the individual students would have to receive paramount consideration. We were given practically a free hand to devise the necessary program along with the personnel with which to carry it out. For the 148 pupils, 5 teaching positions beyond the normal quota were allotted, plus a full-time counselor and clerical assistant. Subsequently, a psychologist and social worker were added on a two-day a week basis. The additional cost, including the expenses of a rich cultural program, was approximately $250 per pupil per year.

Since all the project students were, theoretically at least, aiming toward college, they were placed in the academic course, and every effort was made to meet their needs within that framework. In order to provide learning conditions that would be as favorable as possible, the students were grouped homogeneously in each subject class on the basis of test data and school records. Ten separate classes, for example, were formed in English. In art appreciation, music, and health education, the grouping was heterogeneous. To afford the students intensive training in the basic skills of reading and writing, they were programmed for a double period of English every day. The registers of all the subject classes were well below normal. In English and science, the registers were 25 to 28, and in language and mathematics, only 10 to 15. To enable the project students to extend their social contacts, their classes in English, science, and the home room included an equal number of students from other schools with approximately the same potential as that of the boys and girls in the experiment. Most of these classes were kept together for a year with the same teachers, but considerable flexibility was permitted and pupils were changed from one group to another depending on their progress. Those who needed more help were tutored after school in small groups, and occasionally individually. The selection of teachers for the project classes was purposely kept representative of the entire staff, and included relatively new as well as thoroughly experienced teachers.

The guidance counselor worked very closely with the students and teachers.

The counselor spent a tremendous amount of time interviewing individual students. More than two thirds of the students were interviewed four or more times a term—some were seen as many as twenty times. Students were counseled about their programs, their educational progress, their vocational plans, and such perennial problems as financial need, discord at home, and boy-girl relationships. The principal and the guidance coordinator also met with the students, individually and in groups.

CLINICAL SERVICE

From December 1957 on, the project students had the help of a psychologist and social worker, each serving one day a week for the balance of the first year, and subsequently two days a week. Approximately 25 percent of the class was serviced by the clinical team. The problems handled by the specialist involved acute emotional disturbances, severe social pathology, and some minor emotional difficulties. About half of the group referred to the clinicians benefited considerably. The others presented such severe personal and family problems as to require treatment over a long period of time. Help was afforded in many instances not only by the specialists, but also by the psychiatric facilities of the Bureau of Child Guidance and other community agencies.

But for the intensive clinical help these and other young people received, in all probability, they would not have remained in school. The report of the clinicians states that "for a great many students, contact with the clinical services brought about a change in attitude toward their personal problems, their school work, and their home situations. They were given support and a measure of self-confidence. In the very attention they received, the students and their parents gained a sense of dignity and importance."

GROUP GUIDANCE

Group guidance was conducted by the counselor one period a week. In the students' first year in the high school, the group guidance focused on orientation to school, the importance of good citizenship, how to develop good study habits, how to prepare for tests and self-evaluation. In the next year, there was a shift in emphasis to the world of work and planning for college entrance requirements. The last year was concerned with the transition from high school to college and work.

In their senior year, provision was made for the students who were not going to continue their education, but who were going to work. Classes for them were established under the direction of the school placement counselor. In these classes, the pupils learned about employment opportunities, and received training for civil service examinations and in applying for jobs. Thirty students had jobs waiting for them on graduation.

THE OUTCOME OF OUR COLLEGE PROGRAM

What was the specific outcome of our college training and advisory program? Sixty students in the first project class are continuing their education beyond high school. Nineteen are in four-year colleges, fourteen in two-year colleges, and fifteen are attending colleges in the evening. One is in a school of nursing, six in a business school, one in a school of aeronautics, one in a technical institute, one in the Air Force Technical School, and two have been admitted to a special program in the Bronx Community College to help prepare for admission to college as fully matriculated students. Eighty-five percent of those who completed the academic course went on to further education.

Some of the colleges and institutes to which the students were admitted are: Amherst, Columbia, University of Michigan, Howard University, Franklin and Marshall, Union, New York University, the University of Portland, the municipal colleges, the New York City and Bronx Community Colleges, the Fashion Institute of Technology, and the Farmingdale Agricultural and Technical Institute.

COMPARISON WITH PAST RESULTS

It is difficult to make any truly valid comparison between results obtained by the project group and other students. However, we have used four previous classes coming from the same junior high school and graduating from George Washington High School as the most meaningful basis of comparison. The project group was somewhat superior to those with which it is being compared and the results should be better. However, even after taking this into consideration, the differences are impressive.

The median IQ for the project group was 92. For the four previous classes the median IQs were 85, 87, 90, and 90. Forty-one percent of the project group went on to further education compared to an average of 12 percent for three of the four previous groups for whom we have these data. Forty-two pupils, or 28 percent of the project group completed the academic course of study, compared to an average of 11 percent for the four previous classes. Sixty-four percent of the group graduated compared to an average of 47 percent for the four previous classes.

The graduation of this group takes on far more meaning when we examine their qualifications upon entering George Washington

High School. Of those who graduated with academic diplomas, 59 percent were retarded one year or more as shown by the *Nelson Reading Test* given after they entered the high school. Twelve of this group had been retarded two to four years. Fifty-one percent of them had been retarded one year or more in arithmetic. Fifty percent had IQs below 100 before entering George Washington High School. Four of the group came to us with IQs of 74, 83, 85, and 72; and reading scores, respectively, of 6.3, 6.5, 7.6, and 5.7. They had been handicapped by foreign language difficulties or personality problems. In the first eight months with us, they gained 3.2, 2.1, 1.3, and 2.9 years, respectively, in reading. In three years, their IQs went up to 106, 118, 98, and 96, respectively.

REACHING AND INFLUENCING THE PROJECT PARENTS

The school recognized that the parents had an important role to play in the project. Every effort was made, therefore, to acquaint the parents with the objectives of the program and the benefits that would accrue to their children from it, and secure their cooperation in making the program effective.

Contacts were often difficult to make, but every effort was made to reach the parents through telephone calls, letters, visits by the counselor and social worker, and individual and group meetings at the school. Offers of assistance were made to solve such problems as medical needs, unemployment, and poor housing.

Where there was a poor response from the parents, efforts were made to reach older brothers and sisters, grandparents, aunts, and even neighbors. Parents who were recent arrivals from Puerto Rico and the South had to be re-educated in the folkways and *mores* of a different culture. They lacked an understanding of the social, emotional, and material needs of adolescents. They were not aware, and many were not interested, in the educational and cultural opportunities available to their children. Some felt that a girl should not have more than elementary schooling.

When a parent refused to accept our point of view, we would try to work with other relatives who could reach the parent.

Where the parent was inflexible, we tried to build the child's inner strength to adjust to the situation.

CULTURAL ACTIVITIES

An extensive program of cultural activities was carried on for all the project students. The program included trips to museums, libraries, colleges, industrial plants, motion pictures, concerts, the ballet, and the theatre. Money was made available for all students who could not afford the expenses involved, although in most cases, however, the pupils insisted on paying a share of the cost. The trips that the pupils particularly enjoyed were those to the United States Military Academy at West Point, the Brookhaven Atomic Laboratory, and the Shakespeare Festival Theatre in Stratford, Connecticut, where they saw *A Midsummer Night's Dream*. Briefing sessions took place at school before each trip or event.

INDIVIDUAL CHANGES IN IQ

The *Pintner Test of General Ability* (Verbal Series, Advanced Form B) was given to the project class in May 1959. Intermediate Form B of that test had been given to the same class in February 1956. One hundred and five (105) pupils took both tests.

It is interesting to note that seventy-eight pupils showed an increase in IQ; twenty-five showed a drop; two were identical. There was a range from a gain of 40 points to a loss of 31 points. Forty students gained more than 10 points; 6 students lost more than 10 points; 59 students had IQs within 10 points of the earlier results (38 higher, 19 lower, 2 identical).

In 1956 the median IQ in the *Pintner Intermediate Test, Form B* was 92.9; in the 1959 *Pintner Advanced Test, Form B*, the median IQ was 102.2. The changes in IQ in the project pupils are more significant, perhaps, in view of previous findings that the IQ of students with a community background of educational limitations goes down as the students grow older.

BRIEFING THE FACULTY

One of the factors essential for the success of a project of this kind is the necessity of having the entire faculty of the school understand the purpose and objectives of the program. Therefore, discussions relating to the project were held with the entire staff from time to time, and, at regular intervals, meetings were held with the project chairmen, teachers, and counselors. These meetings made possible an exchange of views and recommendations concerning the project. At these conferences the teachers were also briefed on the significance of their observations and the preparation of evaluative reports.

CONCLUSIONS

What have the results been? Thirty-nine more pupils finished high school than before; 2½ times as many completed the academic course of study; 3½ times as many went on to some form of higher education. Many developed interests in the theatre, concert, and the ballet. Many who had never shown any concern for books developed an interest in reading fine literature.

There were also many intangible results that were directly due to the project. Most important of all their attributes was this new image of themselves, which enabled them to achieve in many areas and face the future with hope and confidence. By far the most costly part of the program resulted from the additional teacher time used for subject matter accomplishment, but this was imperative to the program.

We have found that a thorough and solid educational and guidance program can succeed in discovering and developing abilities which otherwise may be lost to the nation, but we learned no easy way of accomplishing this.

The most important thing we have learned from three years of living with the project is that there can be the promise of a good life for an untold number of boys and girls for whom, heretofore, there has been little promise.

WHAT IS THE MOST CONSTRUCTIVE ROLE
OF THE JUNIOR COLLEGE?

Leland L. Medsker

~~~~~~

Determining the role of an educational institution is difficult and particularly so in the case of the junior college.

The Open Door College (a case study of the San Jose City College). Clark comments on the outside forces which shape the character of the junior college, particularly its unselected clientele. Of this he says:

> In its lack of autonomy, the open-door college has the definition of character taken away from planning and professional control and diffused to external sources. Thus we find a type of formal organization determined to a large degree by context and hence to be explained largely in terms of sociological determinism. Institutional leadership is minimized, and direction by context, maximized. Along a continuum of organizational power in environmental relations, ranging from the organization that dominates its environmental relations to one completely dominated by its environment, the public junior college tends strongly toward the latter extreme.

All this we have observed. As the 1960's loom ahead, there seem to be no signs of deviation from such trends.

It is within this picture that we must project the junior college. . . .

It is designated as an institution which:

1. Affords many people the opportunity to attend college who otherwise would not be able to do so.

SOURCE: Leland L. Medsker, *The Junior College, A Powerful Motivating Force for Educational Advancement* (Washington, D.C.: American Association of Junior Colleges, 1961), pp. 7–8. Reprinted by permission.

2. Offers appropriate educational programs for the great diversity of its regular students.

3. Renders special services to its community, especially through its program in adult education.

But although the junior college is acclaimed for these worthy purposes, it also is often the subject of criticisms. Some relate to the fact that many of the claimed functions of the junior college are not fulfilled. The lack of emphasis on the terminal function as compared with the number of students who never transfer is cited as an example, as is also the fact that student personnel services and the emphasis on general education are frequently not commensurate with the avowed objectives of most junior colleges. Frequently, the criticism pertains to the basic idea of the junior college and its position in the local community. A well-known sociologist has commented on more than one occasion about the desirability of students attending college away from home. Other critics contend that public junior colleges are associated too closely with the secondary schools. Some people denounce the open-door policy which admits high school graduates with all levels of ability to the junior college. . . .

Still other critics express the belief that no one institution can discharge both the transfer and the terminal functions adequately. They suggest dividing these functions between two types of two-year colleges—one for terminal and one for transfer students.

These criticisms and suggestions must be considered as we attempt to delineate the role of this kind of college.

Despite some agitation to the contrary, the social setting in the next several years would seem to dictate that the junior college continue to serve all high school graduates as economically and as realistically as possible.

That there must be some institution to perform a distributing role and to give an increasing percent of high school graduates an opportunity for education beyond high school is made evident by several factors. In the first place, a paradoxical situation is arising. At the very time that society is demanding more education after high school for more people, higher education is, in some ways, becoming more difficult to obtain. Costs to the student are increasing, and admission to many colleges, both public and private, is becoming more difficult.

Yet in the long run, it is doubtful that higher education *as a whole* will be permitted to become more selective or unobtainable. Social forces all point to the fact that the nation's welfare depends upon the upgrading of talent to the greatest extent possible. Furthermore, the parents of high school graduates place an intrinsic value on advanced education and are prone to demand opportunity for it. Continuation of the current trend toward greater selectivity on the part of most four-year colleges and universities at an accelerated pace without other opportunities becoming available, would mean our moving toward a system such as has operated in many European countries—a system which, incidentally, appears now to be under question in these countries. . . .

There is every reason to believe that an increasing percent of the nation's four-year institutions will continue the move toward differential selectivity. Furthermore, the pressure of numbers may necessitate that the larger state institutions restrict the size of their lower division and increase the proportionate size of their upper division. Just recently the Master Plan Committee for Higher Education in California recommended that this be done by the California state colleges and the University of California.

This paradox of demand on one side and restricted opportunity on the other side suggests that the people will insist on some type of collegiate institution which will constitute the middle arena in which students have the opportunity to prove themselves and find their avenues to an appropriate place beyond. In many parts of the country citizens have observed the extent to which the junior college can provide both economic and academic democratization of post-high school education. . . .

What happens in society when the last open door is closed to many students who for various reasons may not have been awakened in high school or who, though they may not be of the calibre who would normally pursue a baccalaureate degree, find themselves in a world for which they are unprepared either personally or vocationally? Those who argue that a junior college cannot serve a student body with a wide range in ability assume the burden of proving that this is true. If they contend that the more able student is handicapped in the junior college, they forget two facts: (1) the generally good record made in four-year colleges by junior college transfers speaks well of the preparation in the junior college, and (2) there is the possibility in the junior college of differential treatment of the more able students, particularly those who plan to transfer.

Those who believe that terminal students should go to one type of junior colleges and transfer students to another forget a host of considerations. For one thing, students do not divide themselves into two discrete groups. Many do not make a firm decision about their educational and vocational plans while in high school and there is evidence that this decision on the part of young people is coming at an increasingly later age. Even the students who feel sure about their future often change their plans during and after junior college. We have found that about two-thirds of the students entering junior colleges plan to go on for a baccalaureate degree, but that only about a third do go on. Students cannot be divided on the basis of ability alone since many vocational-technical programs require ability as high as that required for transfer work. By serving all students in the same institution provision can be made for changes or modification of vocational goals in an orderly way that is neither wasteful nor embarrassing. Moreover, it is doubtless true that the general educational phase of the program for terminal students will be better conceived and taught if it is a part of a comprehensive junior college program than if it is regarded as "related work" in a specialized technical school.

In the final analysis, therefore, it simply does not seem logical that the junior college can be anything other than an open-door, comprehensive institution. If it is not such, what agency will provide the exploratory and distributing functions which the people are almost sure to demand? . . .

It seems to me that the function of the junior college involves more than screening—that *distributing* is a better term. It may be true, however, that insofar as transfer students are concerned, the junior colleges will really have to screen. . . .

The junior college has to serve everybody as economically and as realistically as possible. The concept of realism gives rise to the question of academic standards. We in higher education must admit that the recent emphasis on academic performance has much to commend it. The junior college can ill afford to gain the reputation of educational shoddiness. In fact, it must insist on high standards if its students are to compete successfully in either the world of work or as transfers in colleges or universities where they will be compared with "native" students who were a highly select group as freshmen. There is, however, a danger that administrators and teachers in junior colleges may become so imbued with the idea of high standards that they will cause the institution to lose sight of its fundamental goal. They cannot measure excellence by what the upper 10 percent—or even the upper 25 percent—in ability can achieve. For a junior college to be concerned about how well its transfers will perform at a major university is most desirable—for the group will go to that university, but not necessarily for the group that will not go there.

If junior colleges do not practice selective admission, the question is how "tough" they should be after admission. . . . I am developing a fear that in our drive for "standards" we are in danger of becoming unrealistic. Worse still, we are in danger of overlooking the individual student as a person, forgetting that he is an entity who, with the dignity and personality that characterize him, must take his place in a society that each year becomes more complex. . . .

It is obvious that the terminal, transfer, general education, and guidance functions must be maintained if the college is to serve its diverse population. . . .

It could be that the lack of attention, money, and time devoted to the terminal program could result in its being even more neglected than it has been. . . .

There are tremendous difficulties to overcome and . . . not all the problems lie with the junior colleges themselves. Our very culture has not been too helpful in popularizing any type of vocational training at the junior college level, nor has industry been articulate about its needs in the area of technical occupations. In fact, good questions arise as to what education is really of the most worth in preparing junior college students for immediate employment or for other pursuits which do not require further college work. . . .

Since the very nature of the occupational structure is undergoing vast change as a result of technology, the needs of people as well as the needs of the nation will demand attention to the problem of training, at the vocational-technical or semiprofessional level. . . .

The preparation of workers will likely be more costly than the preparation of transfer students. . . .

A volume could be written about the importance of guidance and other student personnel services in junior colleges. How can this institution perform its central mission—its distributing function—unless it emphasizes these services to the utmost? . . . But such services cost money and the necessity for more of them is coming at a time when the educational dollar must be stretched. Junior college administrators will not find it easy to get sufficient funds to keep these services commensurate with the increase in students and with the complexity of the distributing task. But if they fail in this effort, they will undermine the central mission of the institution. . . .